IMAGES
of America

Miami's Richmond Heights

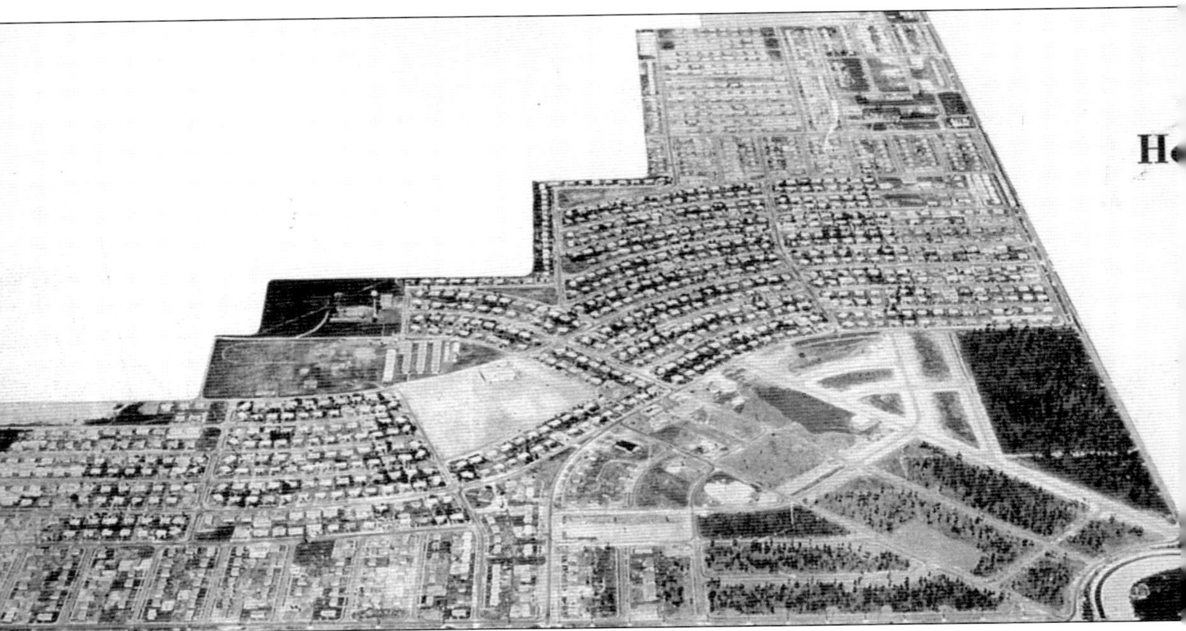

This 1955 aerial map shows the first phase of development for the Richmond Heights community, which was bordered to the north by SW 136th Street, to the south by SW 152nd Street, to the west by SW 117th Avenue, and to the east by SW 107th Avenue. Many areas were yet to be developed and are shown with trees still covering the land. (Courtesy of Richmond Heights Homeowners Association.)

On the Cover: These are the American Federation of Labor and Congress of Industrial Organizations (AFL-CIO) Transportation Coalition members who worked as skycaps for Miami International Airport. These gentlemen were very instrumental in urging Capt. Frank C. Martin to develop the community of Richmond Heights. In this photograph, the union members are at Dinner Key Auditorium in Coconut Grove at the AFL-CIO union's annual dance. Dinner Key Auditorium was located in one of Pan American World Airways' original four hangars for seaplanes. (Courtesy of Mona Jackson.)

IMAGES
of America

MIAMI'S RICHMOND HEIGHTS

Patricia Harper Garrett
and Jessica Garrett Modkins

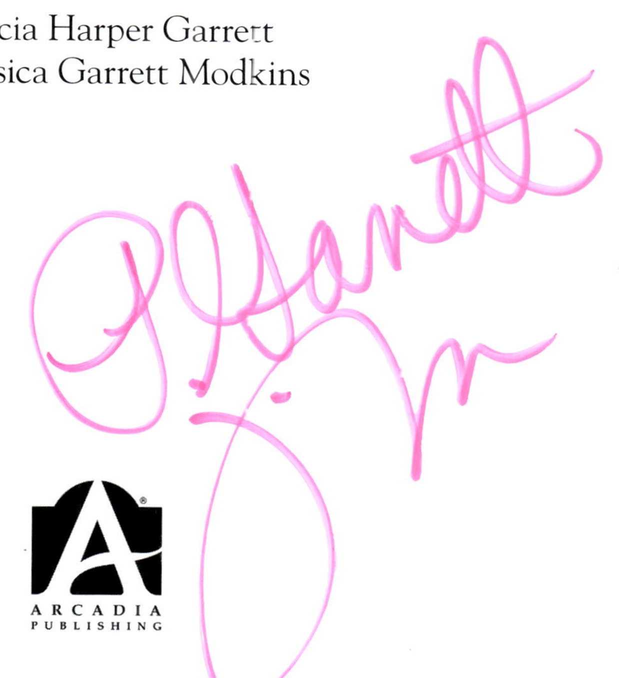

ARCADIA
PUBLISHING

ISBN 978-1-4671-1102-7

Published by Arcadia Publishing
Charleston, South Carolina

Printed in the United States of America

Library of Congress Control Number: 2013938515

For all general information, please contact Arcadia Publishing:
Telephone 843-853-2070
Fax 843-853-0044
E-mail sales@arcadiapublishing.com
For customer service and orders:
Toll-Free 1-888-313-2665

Visit us on the Internet at www.arcadiapublishing.com

To Charlie Harper, whose dedication in World War II for the United States of America made this book possible.

Contents

Acknowledgments

The spirit and pride of Richmond Heights are illustrated throughout this book. It was our attempt to preserve the essence of Richmond Heights that was created by its residents, and we hope that the love that went into making this book is with you once you read it. We would not have been able to achieve this without the resources and support from the following: Rev. Alphonso Jackson Sr., pastor of Second Baptist Church, for the use of the conference room for interviews; Miami-Dade County Public Schools for the direct access of information; Miami-Dade County Planning and Zoning Department for the countless documents; the University of Miami Libraries for its special collection on Richmond Heights; Willie Garrett Jr. for his patience in turning our house into our headquarters during the Christmas holiday; and Shelby Turner, a budding photographer.

Special thanks go out to the following people for their time, willingness to share their stories, and for going above the call of duty: Queen Armstrong, Mary Cambridge, Jacqueline Cambridge-Porter, Dr. Herbert Greene, Cecilia Gaines Williams, Kristal Hickmon, Bessie Holloway, Mona Jackson, Wanda Dorsey Jenkins, Felicia Joseph, Capt. Frank Carroll Martin, Sadie Miller, Rev. Twila Payne, Archibald Pinder, Warren Raulerson, Eddie Redding, Rev. Ron Smith, Ruth Taylor, and Lt. Col. Eldridge Williams.

These pages by no means will ever be able to capture the full scope of our beloved neighborhood, but hopefully, it will spark memories and conversations as well as provide insight into the vision of Frank Crawford Martin's goal for Richmond Heights. Unless otherwise noted, all images appear courtesy of the authors.

Introduction

I, Jessica Garrett Modkins, thank my parents, Willie and Patricia Garrett, for raising me in such a nurturing environment and community as Richmond Heights. In the 1970s, I grew up with the Fields, Hinsons, Moores, Mathises, and Paramores. These families had kids who were my neighborhood friends and also my classmates. We lived next door to each other and walked, and later drove, to school together. We were playmates for kickball, foursquare, hide-and-go seek, and track. We basically engaged in anything we could do outside in the front of our homes in Richmond Heights.

When it came to food, we climbed the trees at Carlton and Colette Moore's house to get the ripe Chinese plumbs. We ate cherries off the hedges on the perimeter of homes. We cut up nearly ripe mangoes and put them into vinegar with salt and pepper. We would soak the mango until we could not stand to wait anymore to eat it. We bought cookies from Mrs. Edwards's Drugstore. From Pablo, the ice cream man, we got our usual. Melissa Mathis would get pickled eggs and Hot Fries, and I would get a hot sausage and salt-and-vinegar chips. To this day, I still buy those Tom's chips. Those were our things—food and games.

In my naiveté, I thought everyone grew up with the same warmth in his or her community, but I learned this was not the case. I thought that everyone played games smack-dab in the middle of the street as a child and that everyone had a neighborhood drugstore and a five-mile-per-hour ice cream truck, waiting on kids to yell, "Hold!" I thought that all families went to church and Sunday school because it was fun. I thought that they ate dinner together as a family every night and that they danced to the music of 8-tracks, 45s, and albums on their disco-illuminated stereo system. This was my Middle America.

Who knew that my love for Richmond Heights would lead to me writing a book on the vision, history, families, and businesses that this community has birthed? My childhood was so endearing that I wanted to share it. So, I dusted off my degree in communications to put my journalistic skills back to work. I had not done any investigative news reporting since waking everyone up on the radio in Miami with those catchy words of "Good Morning, South Florida" as the news director for WEDR 99 Jamz.

That was almost 20 years ago, but I quickly realized that discovery and truth were instinctive to me and that writing and fact finding were closer to my heart than I knew. In my research for this book, I dug deep into the lives of our ancestors and the kids of Richmond Heights. Those kids are all adults now with their own families, but I saw the childish smiles come to their faces as they reminisced about growing up in "the Heights," as this community is affectionately known.

We gathered information with the help of technology. In 2011, we set up a Facebook fan page. For years, current and former residents have expressed their affection for Richmond Heights by writing updates on the Richmond Heights Legacy.. The Children of the Heights Facebook fan page. With over 450 members, fans have talked about Harry's Sweet Shoppe, Tot's Town, Ms. Aranha, "The Front," and Frank C. Martin Elementary. Everyone wanted to share his or her memories.

The influences of Richmond Heights' original residents spread across the United States; many residents were World War II veterans, Tuskegee Airmen, politicians, musicians, Fortune 500 presidents, doctors, dentists, lawyers, teachers, professional athletes, television executives, and industrial and professional leaders. I was well aware of these accomplishments prior to writing the book, but I certainly did not know that this vetting process would lead me to the US Oval Office and to Pres. Harry Truman.

In 1949, Capt. Frank Crawford Martin was a trailblazer. He envisioned and developed Richmond Heights as a self-sufficient little town that would have all of the amenities that a family could desire. Captain Martin was white, and to build a community specifically for black veterans was a bit of a leap for 1949. He did this as a good sound business decision. He did not have a desire to be the creator of social change, but he created one anyway. He orchestrated many firsts for blacks. He paved the way for the first black postmaster in Florida. He created the first pool in Miami for blacks in a community. He also created the first form of public transportation for blacks in southwest Miami-Dade.

His vision for Richmond Heights would be designed with curved intersecting streets so that drivers would intentionally have to cruise at slow speeds. It would be fashioned in a way to encourage cohesiveness among neighbors. The avenues in the neighborhood would be named after presidents of the United States. The streets in the neighborhood would be named after black community leaders. Richmond Heights would become home to various church denominations, creating an inclusive spirit for many beliefs. A shopping center with a meat market, convenience store, several doctors of internal medicine, a dentist, a service station, a dry cleaner, two gasoline stations, a barbershop, a beauty salon, an ice cream parlor, and a pharmacist would have a home in the community. And last but not least, the community would provide schooling from infancy through high school graduation.

My candid interviews with the family of Capt. Frank Crawford Martin revealed many hidden truths behind his ultimate goal in building Richmond Heights as well the financial, structural, and political challenges he faced. I was privileged to have countless interviews and correspondence with Capt. Frank Crawford Martin's only child, Frank Carroll Martin, who was also a pilot, and granddaughter Allyson to get these answers and many more nuggets of truths. These findings led to research with the University of Miami, Miami-Dade County Public Schools, the Miami-Dade County Department of Planning and Zoning, and the US Veterans Administration.

Capt. Frank Crawford Martin, known to friends as "Skipper," deliberately created this self-sufficient and self-reliant little town. Captain Martin did not live to see the completion of Richmond Heights, but the vision he had for this community and its people is vested in them today. Because of this, his vision will never die—it lives in the residents, and it lives in the children, their children, and their children's children. The self-reliance that we see in the residents today was set it in motion because of him. None of this was happenstance.

One

THE VISION

The community of Richmond Heights was founded on strong morals, invaluable ethics, and unyielding love. The founder and developer, Capt. Frank Crawford Martin, a white man, determined that this community was going to be built for black World War II veterans in spite of any racial or financial hurdle he faced. He sought out the strictest building codes to guide the building standards. The construction would mirror the building codes for the community of Coral Gables, Florida. It would be built with quality materials and impeccable workmanship. This included CBS (concrete block stucco) construction and awnings to shield each home from the elements of the weather. This spirit of excellence permeated into the mind-set of each resident, creating a culture unlike any for blacks.

It was all thanks to the black skycaps that worked at Pan American Airlines in 1949. These men were also World War II veterans and were in search of homes for their family. At the time, they were disturbed with the overpriced shabby projects being built for blacks in North Miami and were reluctant to make a home there. They knew that Pan American Airlines coworker Captain Martin was the owner of acreage in an undeveloped area of South Dade County. They urged him to build homes for them.

Captain Martin did not have fortune with his papaya groves on section No. 19 of his acreage after the 1945 hurricane, so he gave the idea some consideration as a possibility for his land. After thought, he agreed to move forward with the idea. He ventured to the University of Miami to get a blueprint of his vision for a little town. This vision is what is known now as Richmond Heights. In addition to the University of Miami, he formed a counsel of black community leaders, including David Douglas, Rev. Edward T. Graham, and Rev. Theodore R. Gibson, to advise him. All three men have streets named in their honor in the community. Captain Martin retired from Pan American Airlines in 1949 in order to devote all of his time to the development of the community.

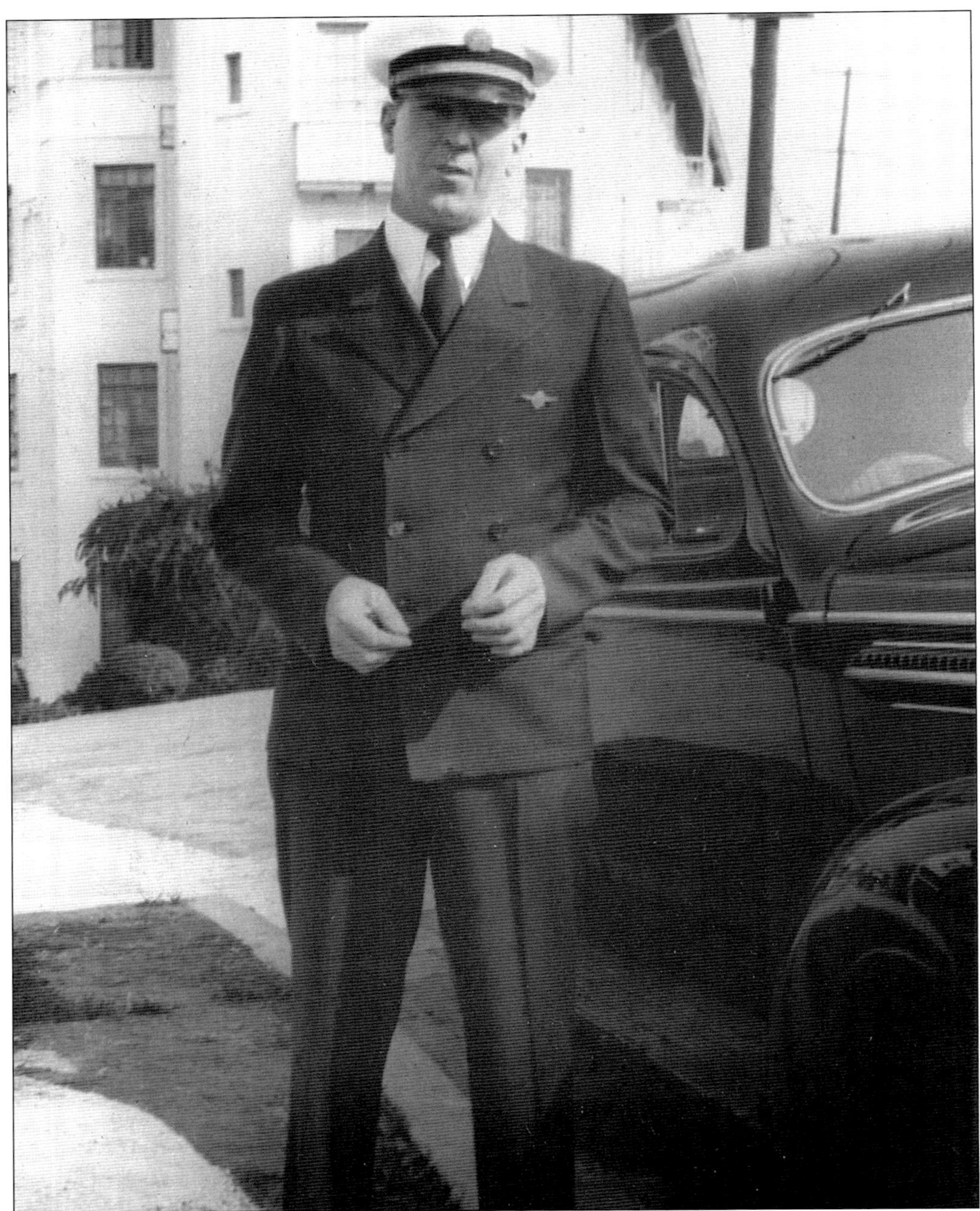

Capt. Frank C. Martin was the founder of Richmond Heights. He was born on October 22, 1907, in Maryville, Missouri, and was brought up in Wyoming. He was raised as a cowboy and had odd jobs as a theater usher and sold newspapers. He later went on, during high school, to be a commanding officer in the Reserve Officers' Training Corps (ROTC) during his junior and senior years. As an adult, he served in World War II and became a pilot and traffic manager for Pan American Airlines. It was during his time flying for Pan American that he discovered the property and purchased 3,000 acres of pineland from Richmond Timber Company in the early 1940s. (Courtesy of Miami-Dade County Public Schools.)

RESOLUTION No. 3461

The following Resolution was offered by Commissioner Jesse H. Yarborough, seconded by Commissioner I. D. MacVicar, and upon vote duly adopted:

Reso. approving plat of "Richmond Heights".

WHEREAS FRANK CRAWFORD MARTIN and MARY CARROLL MARTIN, husband and wife, have this day presented to this Board a plat of certain platted lands lying in Dade County, Florida, said plat to be known as RICHMOND HEIGHTS; and

WHEREAS FRANK CRAWFORD MARTIN and MARY CARROLL MARTIN, husband and wife, the owners of the land shown on said plat, have submitted to this Board their proposed personal bond for the construction of all streets, alleys and other rights of way shown on said plat, and secured by a mortgage covering a portion of the lands shown on said plat, in lieu of the customary agreement and surety bond, which personal bond and mortgage, in the opinion of this Board, constitutes sufficient guaranties for the construction of such streets, alleys and other rights of way; and

WHEREAS it appears that all requirements of law concerning said plat, insofar as the authority of this Board is concerned, other than certain technical engineering requirements, have been complied with;

NOW THEREFORE, BE IT RESOLVED BY THE BOARD OF COUNTY COMMISSIONERS OF DADE COUNTY, FLORIDA, that said plat is hereby approved, subject to the compliance with certain technical engineering requirements, the same to be evidenced by the written approval of the County Engineer on said plat, and that the dedication of the streets, alleys and other rights of way, however designated, depicted on said plat, is hereby accepted.

PASSED AND ADOPTED this 22nd day of November, 1949.

- - - - - - - - - - - - - - - - - -

There being no further business to come before them, upon motion duly seconded and carried, the Board adjourned.

Hugh Peters
Chairman

ATTEST: E. B. Leatherman
Clerk.

* *

Captain Martin and wife, Mary, had to file a resolution to begin the community of Richmond Heights with the county engineer, who served as the chairman of the board for Dade County. The paperwork, Resolution No. 3461, was approved to be built on November 22, 1949. (Courtesy of the City of Miami.)

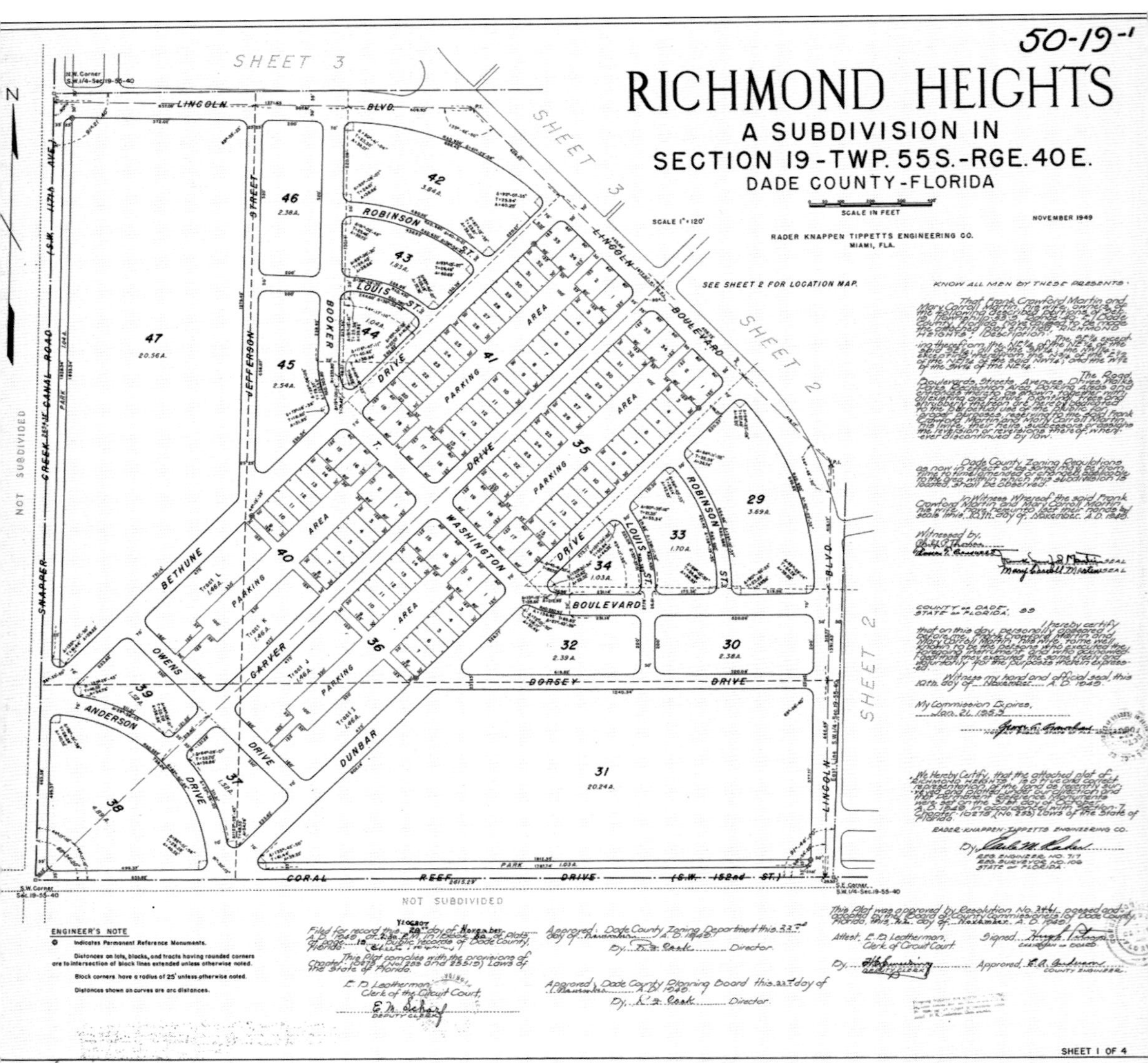

This is Plot Sheet No. 1 of the southwest corner of Richmond Heights. Zoning for this area, as shown, has intersecting avenues all named in homage to former US presidents. Several streets are also named in honor of black activists who made a difference. Two community residents with street names are Olivia Edwards and Herbert Ammons. All of the winding streets are measured at 50 feet wide or 75 feet wide while Harrison Street is measured at 100 feet wide. The Dade County Planning Board certified this plot on November 22, 1949. (Courtesy of the City of Miami.)

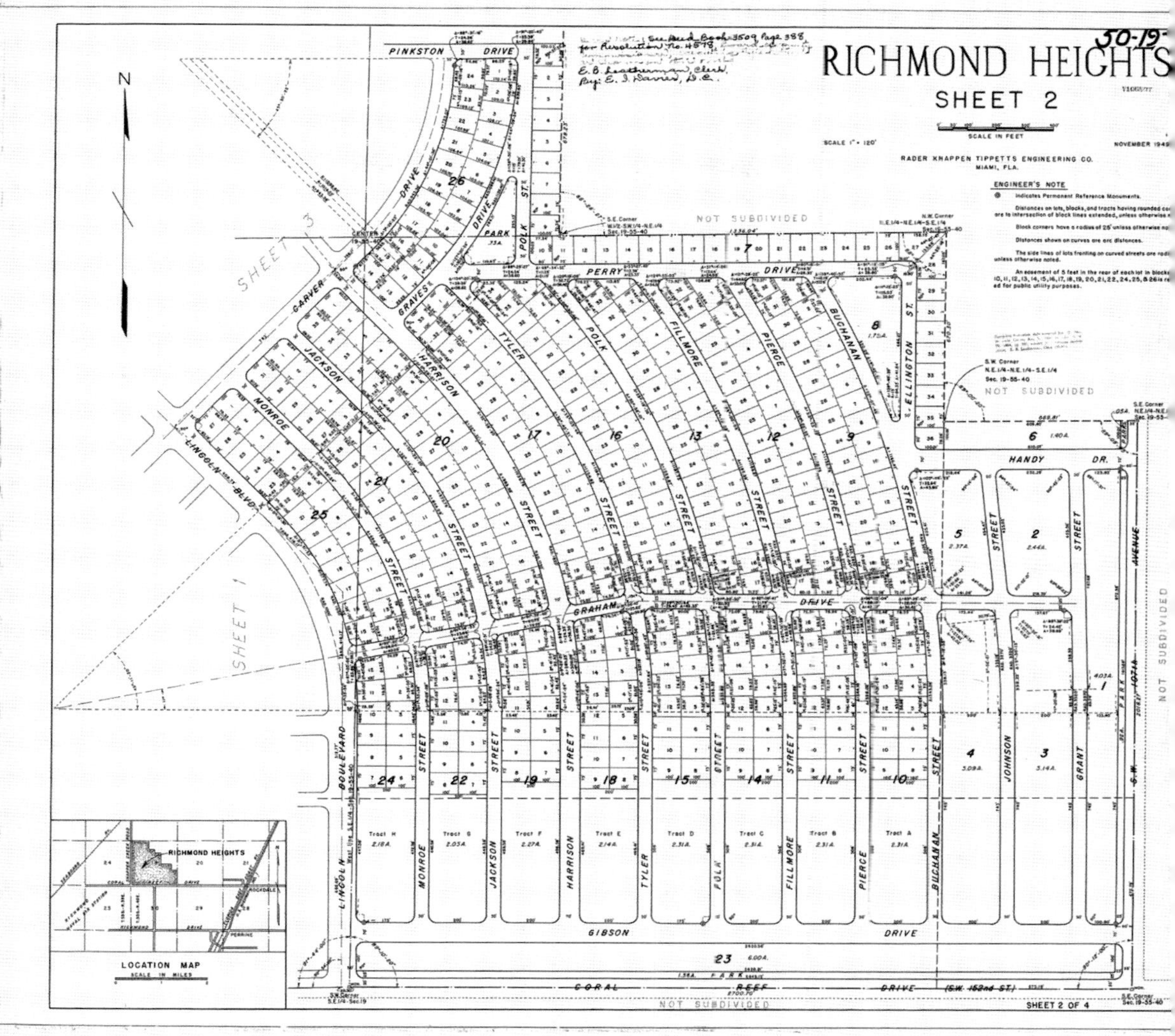

This is Plot Sheet No. 2 of the southeast corner of Richmond Heights. This sheet shows intersecting streets and a park. It also shows the original planned single-family homes that all have addresses that begin with the No. 14. Out of these original 457 homes, less than 100 of these are two-bedroom homes while the majority of these homes have three bedrooms. All homes have an easement of five feet in the rear of each lot for public utility purposes. A few months into construction, developer Captain Martin paved all streets and sidewalks as well as had the water mains installed to avoid any future county assessments for improvement if the residents so desired to become incorporated with its own municipal government. (Courtesy of the City of Miami.)

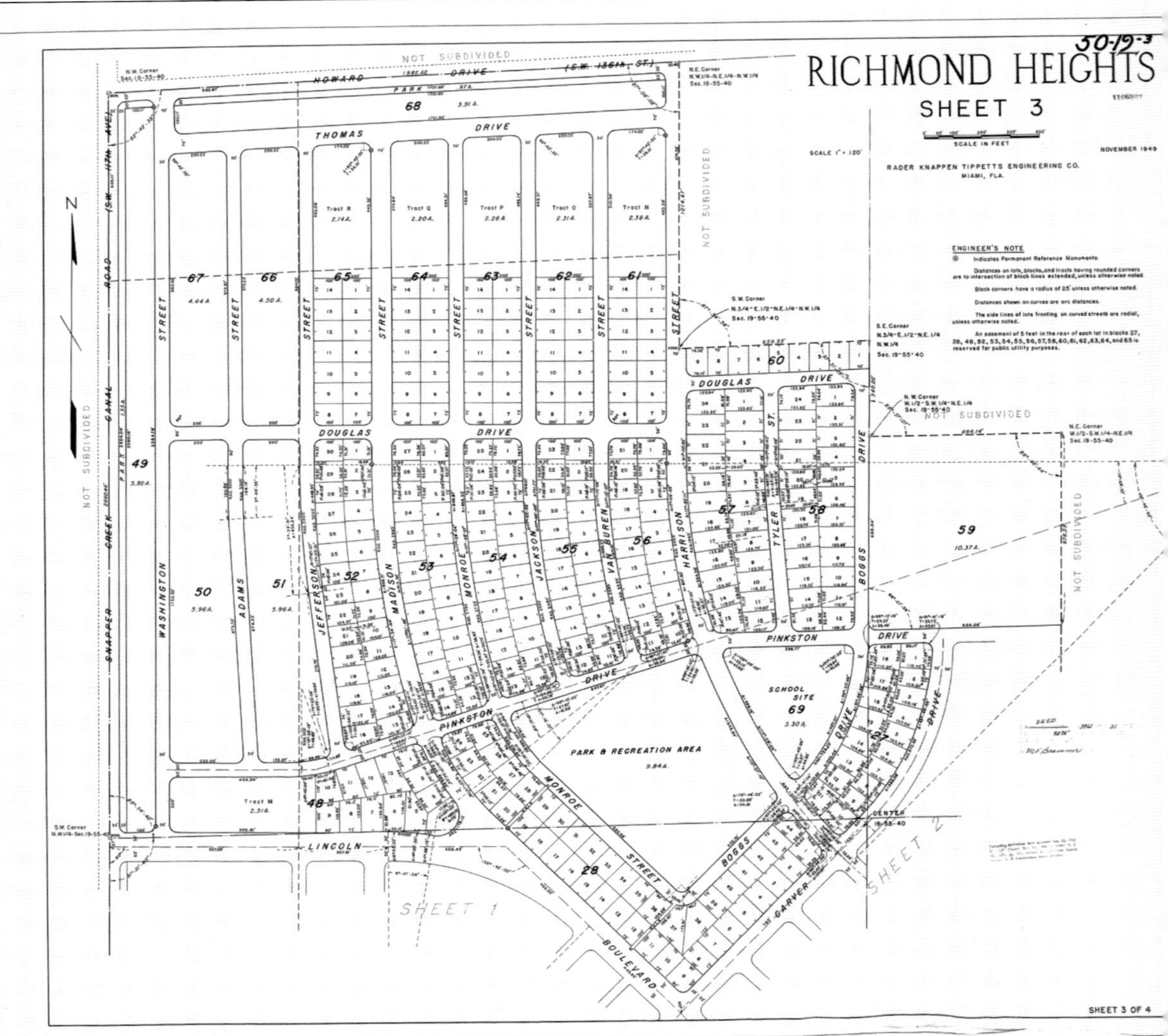

Captain Martin received many road blocks in getting Federal Housing Administration (FHA) approval for the community, so he reached out to a classmate from West Point who was an aid for Pres. Harry Truman. This classmate informed the president of Captain Martin's plight. President Truman played a pivotal role in the evolution of civil rights. For example, in 1948, President Truman desegregated and required equal opportunity in the US Armed Forces. So this situation with Captain Martin was no different for his administration. He faced many foes in his quest for equality. President Truman instructed the FHA officials to move swiftly in approving the community for FHA financing. This is Plot Sheet No. 3 of the northwest corner of Richmond Heights. (Courtesy of the City of Miami.)

Richmond Heights — 336 — PAGE 3

BLOCKS 1 TO 69 inc. · 90 to 91 inc. 60 21

LOTS a TO R inc. (sheets 1 to 4 inc.)

SEC. 19 TWP. 55 RG. 40 PLAT BOOK 50 PAGE 19

Book	Page	Grantor	Grantee	Ins't	Date	Record	Lot	Block
3216	133	Frank C. Martin	Johnnie Henderson + wf.		121249	121349	8	22
3216	135	do	Earnest White Sr. +	"	121249	121349	12	25
3216	137	do	Livingston James	"	121249	121349	7	25
3216	139	do	Warrie R. Ferguson		121249	121349	14	22
3216	141	do	George E. Swain	"	121249	121349	4	25
3216	143	do	Buchie McCray	"	121249	121349	4	24
3216	145	do	Willie H. Johnson +	"	121249	121349	8	25
3216	147	do	Barfield Birch	"	121249	121349	10	22
3216	149	do	James C. Holmes +	"	121249	121349	5	24
3216	151	do	Dewey E. Kelse +	"	121249	121349	11	22
3216	153	do	John E. Byrd	"	121249	121349	13	22
3216	155	do	Richard G. Bullard +		121249	121349	3	25
3216	157	do	Spencer N. Murray + wf.		121249	121349	11	25
3216	159	do	Willie L. Pearson +	"	121249	121349	2	24
3216	161	do	Lee M. Burton +	"	121249	121349	5	25
3216	163	do	William R. Phillips Jr. +		121249	121349	6	24
3216	165	do	Grady Holloway + W.S.		121249	121349	12	22
3216	167	do	Henry Prince +	"	121249	121349	10	25
3216	169	do	Luther H. Wallace	"	121249	121349	2	25
3216	171	do	Samuel E. Hutchinson		121249	121349	6	25
3216	173	do	James Wanza + wf.		121249	121349	14	25
3216	585	do	Albert D. Sample +	"	121249	121449	9	25
3216	587	do	Walter Bethel +	"	121249	121449	13	25
3217	287	do	Gladstone L. Taylor		121449	121549	3	24
3217	289	do	Stephen Worthy	"	121449	121549	9	22
3217	291	do	Oliver A. Page +	"	121449	121549	1	24
3248	473	Do	Brooker T. Jordan +	"	3 3 50	3 6 50	12	25
3252	336	Do	James C. Rowely +	"	3 8 50	3 13 50	21	21
3252	338	Do	Leroy Wilson +	"	3 8 50	3 13 50	26	21
3252	340	Do	George B. Cambridge	"	3 8 50	3 13 50	24	21
3252	342	Do	Julius C. Boyd +	"	3 8 50	3 13 50	20	21
3252	344	Do	Norman L. Davis +	"	3 8 50	3 13 50	22	21
3252	346	Do	Carter L. Hartley +	"	3 8 50	3 13 50	25	21
3252	348	Do	Jack W. Smith +	"	3 8 50	3 13 50	29	21
3252	350	Do	James Almond +	"	3 8 50	3 13 50	23	21
3253	291	Do	Wilbert Grant +	"	3 8 50	3 14 50	28	21
3253	293	Do	Willie J. Neal +	"	3 8 50	3 14 50	19	21
3253	295	Do	Algerial Farrington	"	3 8 50	3 14 50	18	21
3253	297	Do	Willie L. Stark +	"	3 8 50	3 14 50	27	[illegible]
3253	299	Do	Ezekiel Bermal +	"	3 8 50	3 14 50	30	[illegible]
3254	211	do	Board of Public Instruction	"	3 15 50	3 16 50	37	[illegible]
3256	203	Livingston James	Willie Gaines +	"	3 20 50	3 21 50	7	[illegible]
3257	133	Earnest White Sr. +	Frank C. Martin +	"	3 3 50	3 22 50	12	[illegible]
3257	549	Frank C. Martin	David Delaney	"	3 10 50	3 23 50	8	[illegible]

A Mr. Zimmerman, bookkeeper, kept a ledger to record the sale of each lot. This ledger would detail the block number, lot number, guarantee, and date. This historic ledger chronicles all of the details of home sales from the first home sold on December 12, 1949, through November 8, 1951. (Courtesy of Eddie Redding.)

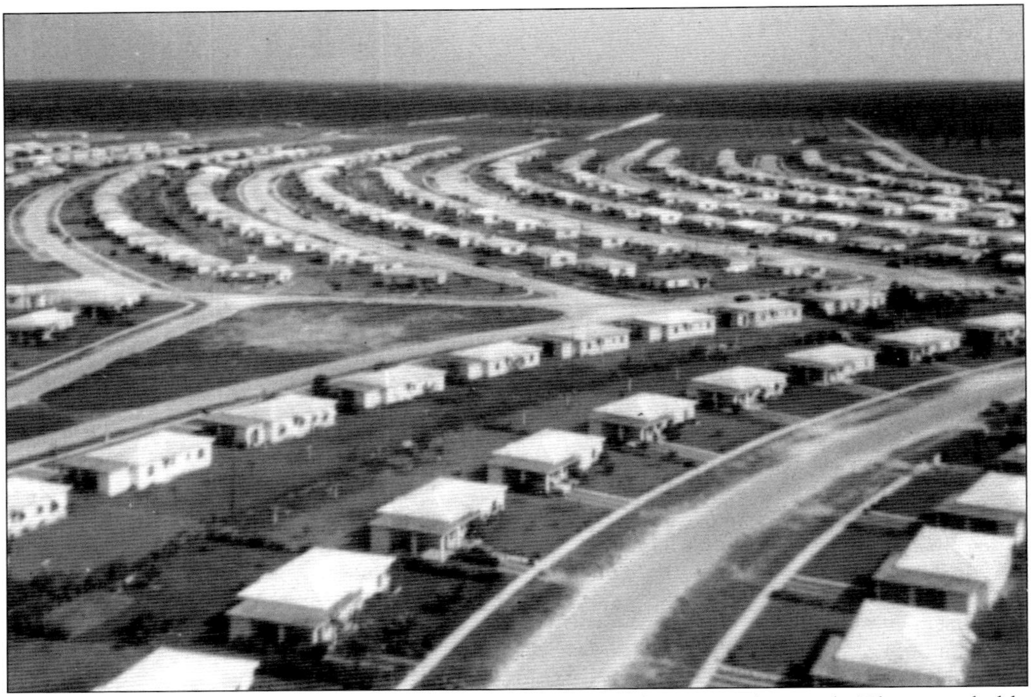

Taken from the water tower, this 1952 aerial view shows the homes to the south. This is probably a similar view of what Captain Martin saw while flying over Hong Kong prior to World War II—a small town built by Catholic priests. This is said to have been the inspiration to the design of Richmond Heights. (Courtesy of the Martin family.)

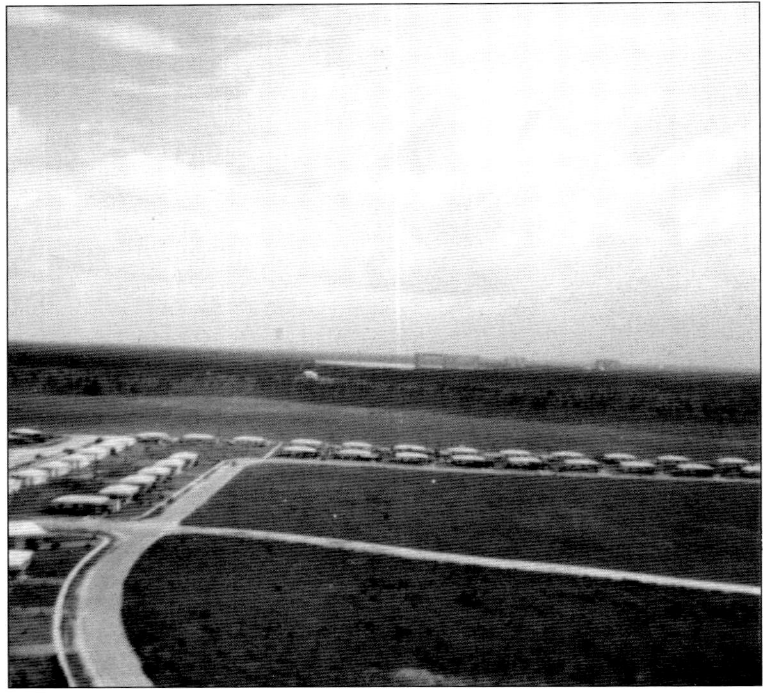

In an effort to ensure that construction workers were doing the job correctly, Captain Martin's son, Frank, would watch over workers from the water tower. This 1952 aerial view shows 35 open acres to the west; Richmond Heights Elementary School and Richmond Heights Park would later be erected there. (Courtesy of the Martin family.)

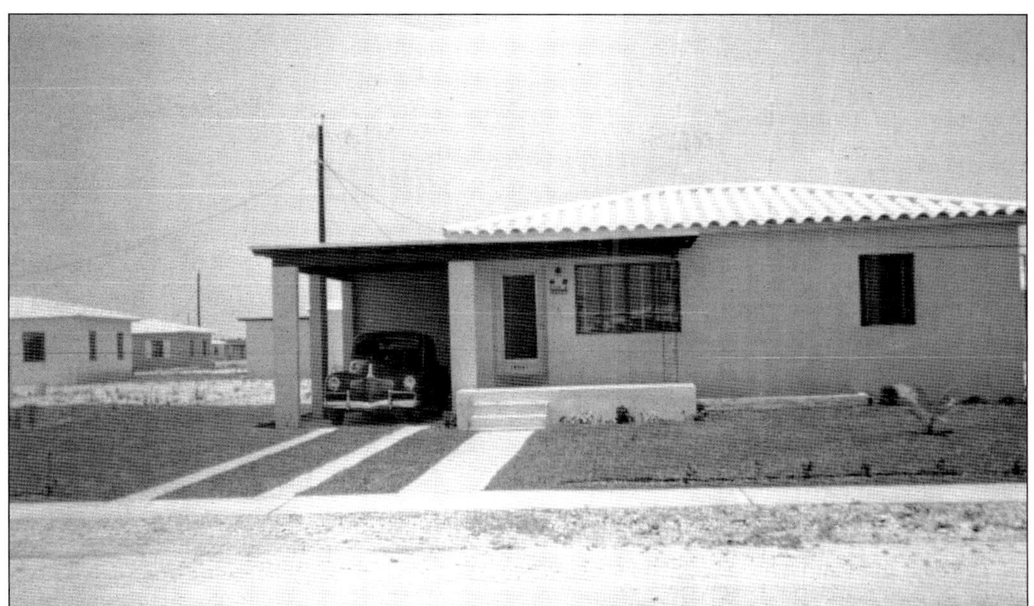

The first 40 homes were constructed by Babcock of Babcock and Lamont in Miami, and the homes were not built to the standards Captain Martin had requested. He fired the construction company and established Richmond Development Corporation. Moving forward, he served as the contractor, building four homes to an acre. They had flat hipped-barrel roofs, which were unique, as all the other comparable homes built for blacks had graveled roofs. (Courtesy of Doran Porter.)

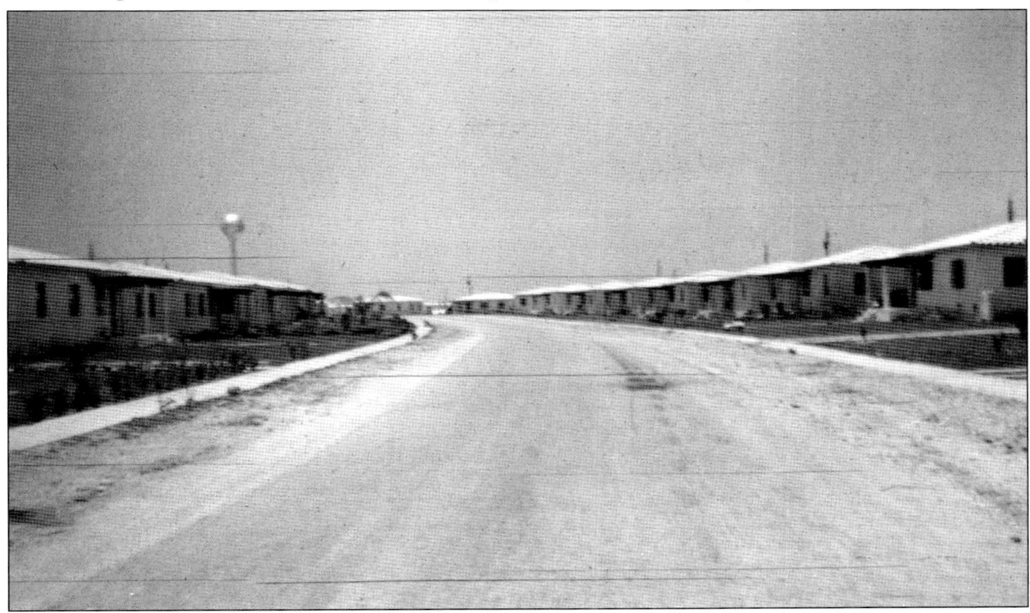

Many residents remember the water tower in Richmond Heights. It served as a landmark and was located off Pinkston Drive. It also served as the water filtration center and reservoir for the community. It also had office space. There was an early learning center inside of this water tower. This is a photograph of Fillmore Street. The water tower, shown in the background, was demolished in 1984. (Courtesy of Doran Porter.)

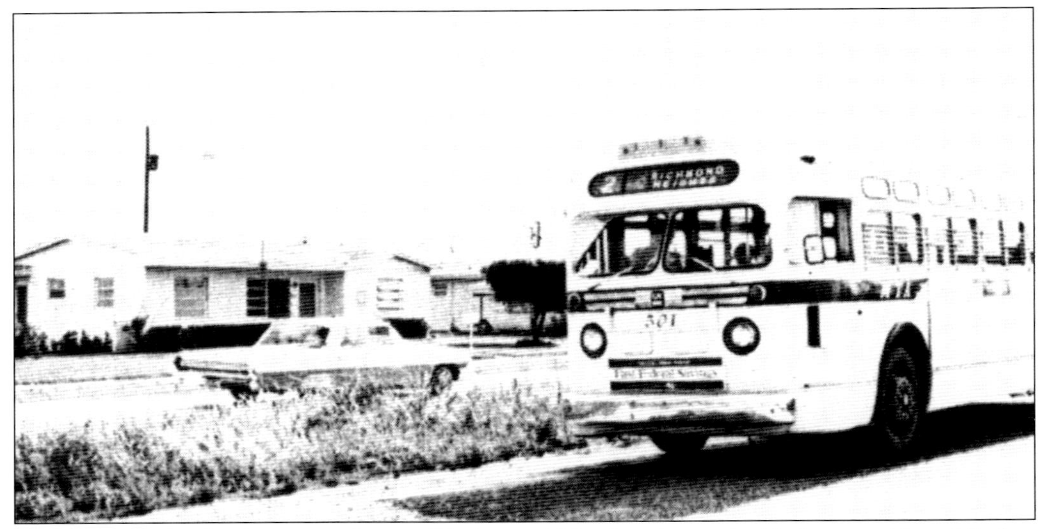

In order to serve the future residents of Richmond Heights, it was decided to provide public bus transportation. Captain Martin met with politicians in Tallahassee, Florida, as well as Congressman Claude Pepper to get approval to run a bus line over the Greyhound bus route. The area was not developed and was so far south that this proposal was met with great opposition, but eventually, it was approved. He then purchased buses from Eastern Georgia and had them refurbished by Marion League, the former chief executive officer for South Miami Coach. (Courtesy of the Richmond Heights Homeowners Association.)

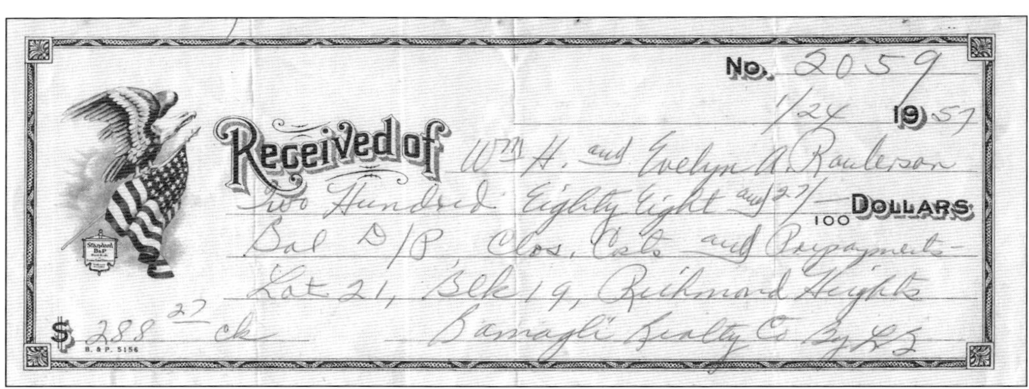
No. 2059
1/24 1957
Received of Wm H. and Evelyn A. Raulerson
Two Hundred Eighty Eight and 27/100 DOLLARS
Bal D/P, Clos. Costs and Prepayments
Lot 21, Blk 19, Richmond Heights
$ 288 27 ck
Bamagli Realty Co By L.Z.
B. & P. 5156

All buyers had to provide proof of employment and go through a process to prove that their way of life would not be hindered by obtaining a monthly mortgage payment. Captain Martin did this to insure that the monthly mortgage payment would not be a burden for the lifestyle of future residents. Homes in 1949 cost on average $7,050, and this receipt shows a down payment and closing cost on a home. (Courtesy of the Raulerson family.)

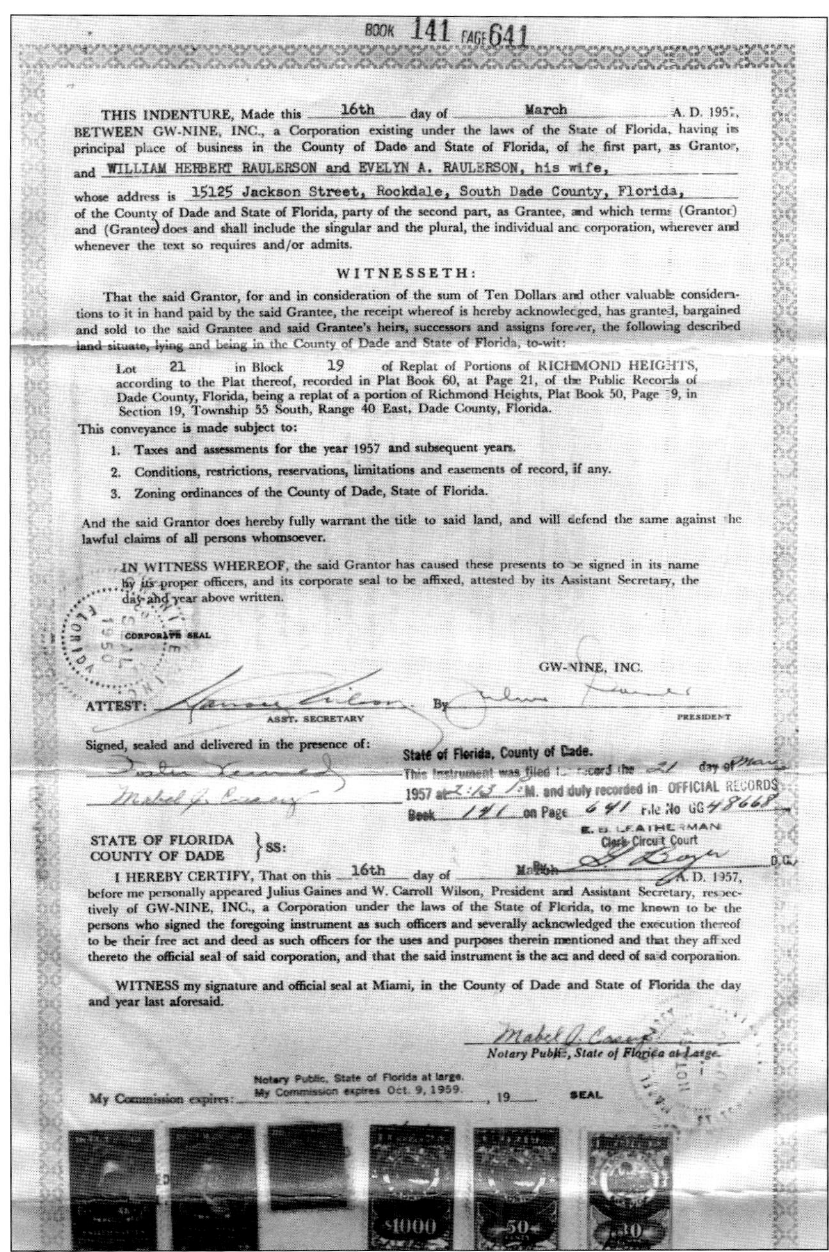

BOOK 141 PAGE 641

THIS INDENTURE, Made this 16th day of March A. D. 1957, BETWEEN GW-NINE, INC., a Corporation existing under the laws of the State of Florida, having its principal place of business in the County of Dade and State of Florida, of the first part, as Grantor, and WILLIAM HERBERT RAULERSON and EVELYN A. RAULERSON, his wife, whose address is 15125 Jackson Street, Rockdale, South Dade County, Florida, of the County of Dade and State of Florida, party of the second part, as Grantee, and which terms (Grantor) and (Grantee) does and shall include the singular and the plural, the individual and corporation, wherever and whenever the text so requires and/or admits.

WITNESSETH:

That the said Grantor, for and in consideration of the sum of Ten Dollars and other valuable considerations to it in hand paid by the said Grantee, the receipt whereof is hereby acknowledged, has granted, bargained and sold to the said Grantee and said Grantee's heirs, successors and assigns forever, the following described land situate, lying and being in the County of Dade and State of Florida, to-wit:

Lot 21 in Block 19 of Replat of Portions of RICHMOND HEIGHTS, according to the Plat thereof, recorded in Plat Book 60, at Page 21, of the Public Records of Dade County, Florida, being a replat of a portion of Richmond Heights, Plat Book 50, Page 9, in Section 19, Township 55 South, Range 40 East, Dade County, Florida.

This conveyance is made subject to:

1. Taxes and assessments for the year 1957 and subsequent years.
2. Conditions, restrictions, reservations, limitations and easements of record, if any.
3. Zoning ordinances of the County of Dade, State of Florida.

And the said Grantor does hereby fully warrant the title to said land, and will defend the same against the lawful claims of all persons whomsoever.

IN WITNESS WHEREOF, the said Grantor has caused these presents to be signed in its name by its proper officers, and its corporate seal to be affixed, attested by its Assistant Secretary, the day and year above written.

CORPORATE SEAL

GW-NINE, INC.

ATTEST: [signature] ASST. SECRETARY By [signature] PRESIDENT

Signed, sealed and delivered in the presence of:

State of Florida, County of Dade.
This instrument was filed for record the 21 day of Mar 1957 at 2:13 P.M. and duly recorded in OFFICIAL RECORDS Book 141 on Page 641 File No GC48668
E. B. LEATHERMAN
Clerk Circuit Court
By [signature] D.C.

STATE OF FLORIDA
COUNTY OF DADE } SS:

I HEREBY CERTIFY, That on this 16th day of March A.D. 1957, before me personally appeared Julius Gaines and W. Carroll Wilson, President and Assistant Secretary, respectively of GW-NINE, INC., a Corporation under the laws of the State of Florida, to me known to be the persons who signed the foregoing instrument as such officers and severally acknowledged the execution thereof to be their free act and deed as such officers for the uses and purposes therein mentioned and that they affixed thereto the official seal of said corporation, and that the said instrument is the act and deed of said corporation.

WITNESS my signature and official seal at Miami, in the County of Dade and State of Florida the day and year last aforesaid.

Mabel J. Casey
Notary Public, State of Florida at Large.

My Commission expires: Notary Public, State of Florida at large. My Commission expires Oct. 9, 1959. , 19 SEAL

Louis S. Edwards had the unconstrained task of being the only sales person for Richmond Heights in 1949. There were no high-pressured tactics; in fact, hopeful future residents had to wait at least a year on the home prospect waiting list before buying a home. Captain Martin set out to exclude any possible troublemakers from moving into his community. Even if a veteran had a stellar credit report, the most important determining factor for future residents was their character, and Martin met with each applicant for a screening process. Of the original land owned by Capt. Frank Martin, 615 acres was taken by Miami-Dade County. They later developed the land, and it became the home of the Metro Zoo. This is the deed for lot No. 21, block No. 19. (Courtesy of the Raulerson family.)

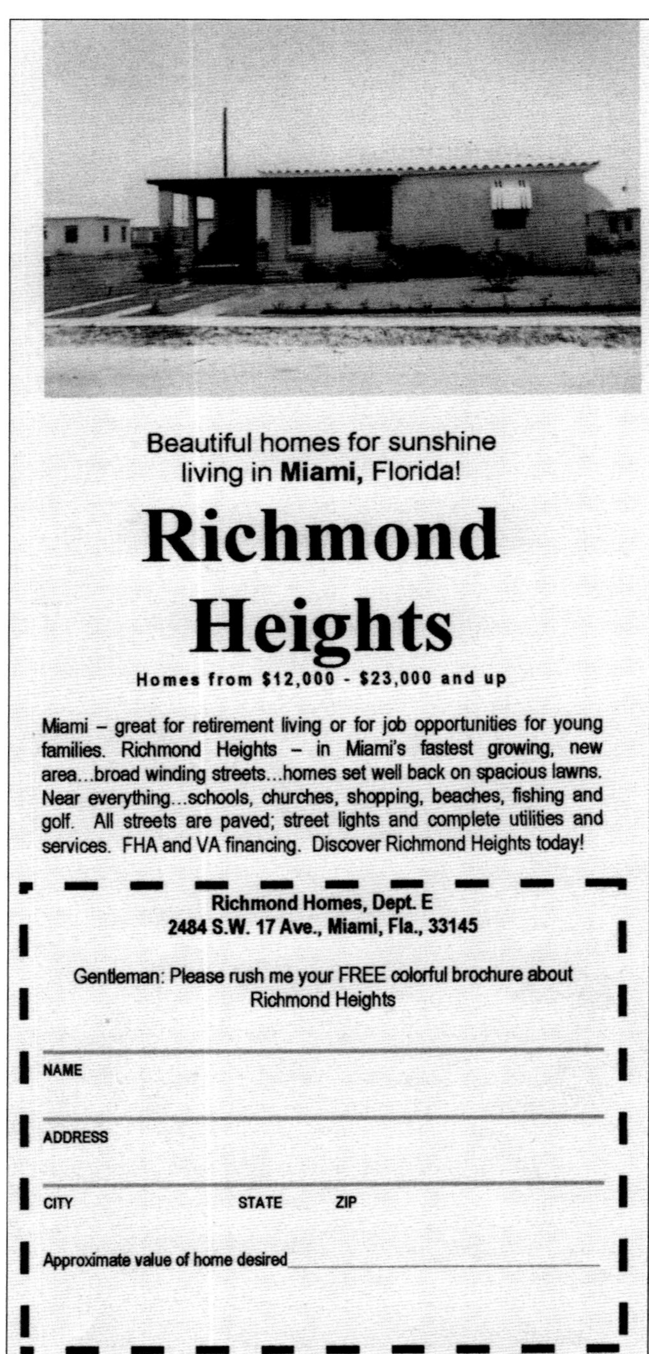

Advertisements for the community of Richmond Heights were put in national magazines and newspapers, such as the one shown above for *Ebony* in 1967. This advertisement informed potential residents of the benefits of moving into the community. Construction for the neighborhood went on for years. While under construction, security guards would ride down each street to insure the security of homes.

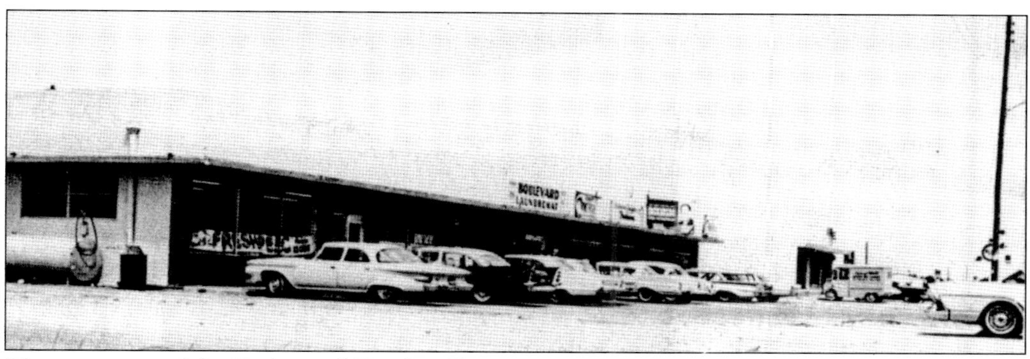

This picture is of the Richmond Heights Shopping Center in the 1960s. It offered Dorsey's Pure Oil gas station, Harry's Sweet Shoppe, a meat market, a Laundromat, a doctor's office, a dentist office, and Stylecraft Cleaners. It also served as a meeting place for residents. To the neighborhood, it was known as "The Front." (Courtesy of the Richmond Heights Homeowners Association.)

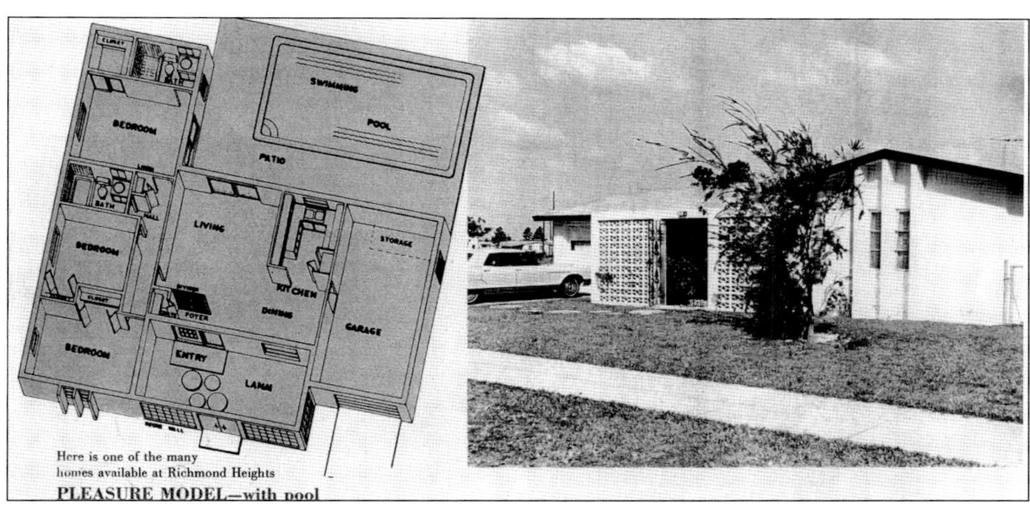

In 1968, the sale of homes in the community continued to be advertised. Sales person Leon Earles worked to show and sell homes for Arthur Shandolff. Shandolff took over building the community after the untimely death of Capt. Frank Martin in 1951. Shandolff built homes under the company name of Richmond Homes. The prices ranged from $18,000 to $35,000 for three-bedroom, two-bath homes. Shown above is an excerpt from a brochure. This is the pleasure model with a pool. (Courtesy of the Richmond Heights Homeowners Association.)

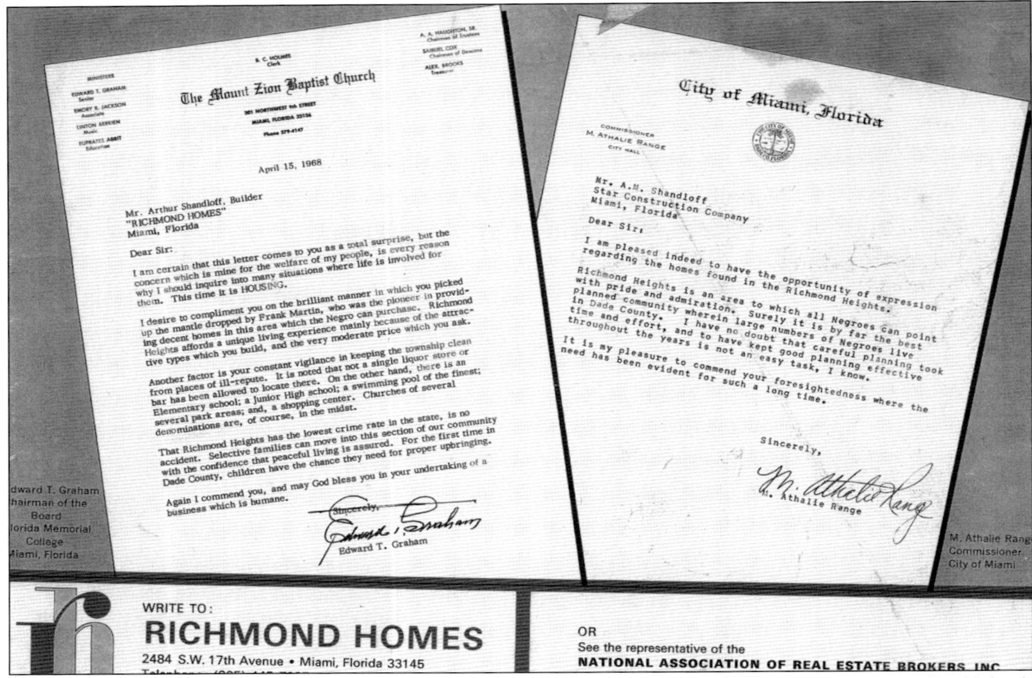

The Mount Zion Baptist Church

April 15, 1968

Mr. Arthur Shandloff, Builder
"RICHMOND HOMES"
Miami, Florida

Dear Sir:

I am certain that this letter comes to you as a total surprise, but the concern which is mine for the welfare of my people, is every reason why I should inquire into many situations where life is involved for them. This time it is HOUSING.

I desire to compliment you on the brilliant manner in which you picked up the mantle dropped by Frank Martin, who was the pioneer in providing decent homes in this area which the Negro can purchase. Richmond Heights affords a unique living experience mainly because of the attractive types which you build, and the very moderate price which you ask.

Another factor is your constant vigilance in keeping the township clean from places of ill-repute. It is noted that not a single liquor store or bar has been allowed to locate there. On the other hand, there is an Elementary school; a Junior High school; a swimming pool of the finest; several park areas; and, a shopping center. Churches of several denominations are, of course, in the midst.

That Richmond Heights has the lowest crime rate in the state, is no accident. Selective families can move into this section of our community with the confidence that peaceful living is assured. For the first time in Dade County, children have the chance they need for proper upbringing.

Again I commend you, and may God bless you in your undertaking of a business which is humane.

Sincerely,

Edward T. Graham

Edward T. Graham
Chairman of the Board
Florida Memorial College
Miami, Florida

City of Miami, Florida

COMMISSIONER
M. ATHALIE RANGE
CITY HALL

Mr. A.M. Shandloff
Star Construction Company
Miami, Florida

Dear Sir,

I am pleased indeed to have the opportunity of expression regarding the homes found in the Richmond Heights.

Richmond Heights is an area to which all Negroes can point with pride and admiration. Surely it is by far the best planned community wherein large numbers of Negroes live in Dade County. I have no doubt that careful planning took time and effort, and to have kept good planning effective throughout the years is not an easy task, I know.

It is my pleasure to commend your foresightedness where the need has been evident for such a long time.

Sincerely,

M. Athalie Range

M. Athalie Range
Commissioner
City of Miami

WRITE TO:
RICHMOND HOMES
2484 S.W. 17th Avenue • Miami, Florida 33145

OR
See the representative of the
NATIONAL ASSOCIATION OF REAL ESTATE BROKERS, INC.

When the community of Richmond Heights was established, there was a counsel of black community leaders formed. One of those leaders was Rev. Edward T. Graham. He was the senior pastor for the Mount Zion Baptist Church. His advisement was still paramount in the community nearly 10 years after its inception, as shown in this advertisement taken from the brochure of Richmond Heights. Commissioner Athalie Range also wrote of her admiration for the community. (Courtesy of the Richmond Heights Homeowner Association.)

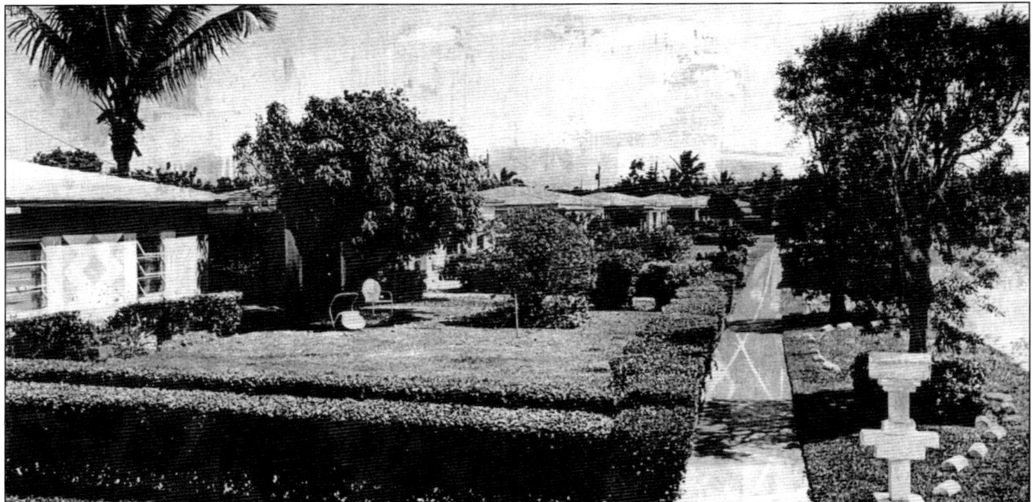

Homeowners took pride in the upkeep of their property. They would have contest to vote on whose lawn was manicured the finest. The perimeter of most homes was lined and sectioned with cherry bushes that served as hedges. This late-1960s photograph of Jackson Street shows how much pride residents took in the upkeep of their community. (Courtesy of the Richmond Heights Homeowner Association.)

Two

School Life

Knowledge is power. This statement was more than a mere sentiment to the residents of Richmond Heights and founder Capt. Frank Crawford Martin. It was a resolve. Captain Martin deeded some 20 acres to the Board of Public Instruction of Dade County for this very purpose. The area was full of promise, purpose, and power.

Captain Martin had a discussion with the Board of Public Instruction of Dade County about the deeded property, and they told Captain Martin that they really were not interested in opening another school for blacks. Captain Martin was a visionary and made it almost impossible for them not to open a school for blacks by adding a fail-safe clause. It stated that if the Board of Public Instruction of Dade County would add a school to the property by the said date, then the land would be deeded without cost. Two days prior to this date, the Board of Public Instruction of Dade County moved portables from Perrine onto the property to begin a school.

This was the first school—Richmond Heights Elementary School. It was located off Boggs Drive, bordering Richmond Heights Park. These six portable classrooms and one lunchroom opened the doors for 190 students on September 4, 1952. After the first week of school, student enrollment increased to over 200 students. This demanded an additional portable classroom, and that first year, the faculty was made up of an all-black staff, including principal Walter A. White and 16 teachers and staff members.

In 1956, the residents of Richmond Heights and the Parent-Teacher Association (PTA) voted to name the school after the community's founder. The school name was changed to Frank C. Martin Elementary. More schools were later added to the community. In 1963, Richmond Heights Junior High opened its doors to the community. Cope South, an alternative school, opened in 1972, and Coral Reef Senior High School opened in 1997.

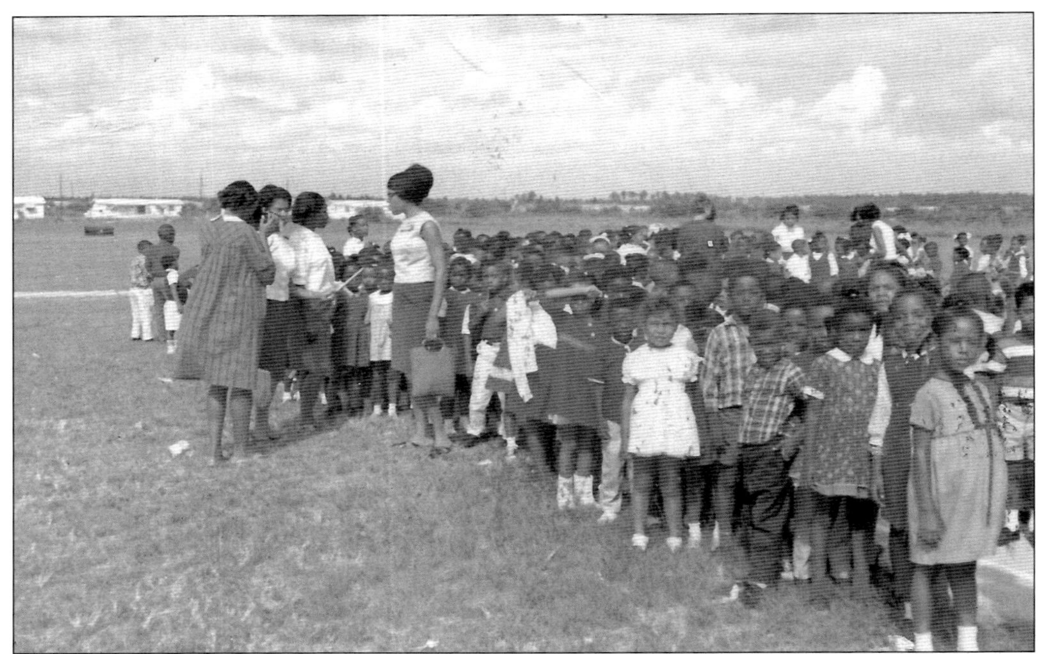

The Richmond Heights community founder, Captain Martin, donated 20 acres of land for a school to be built. On September 2, 1952, an elementary school, named Richmond Heights Elementary School, opened for registration with six portable classrooms. It served the children of the community from kindergarten through the sixth grade. The first school term ended with 202 students enrolled. (Courtesy of the Armstrong family.)

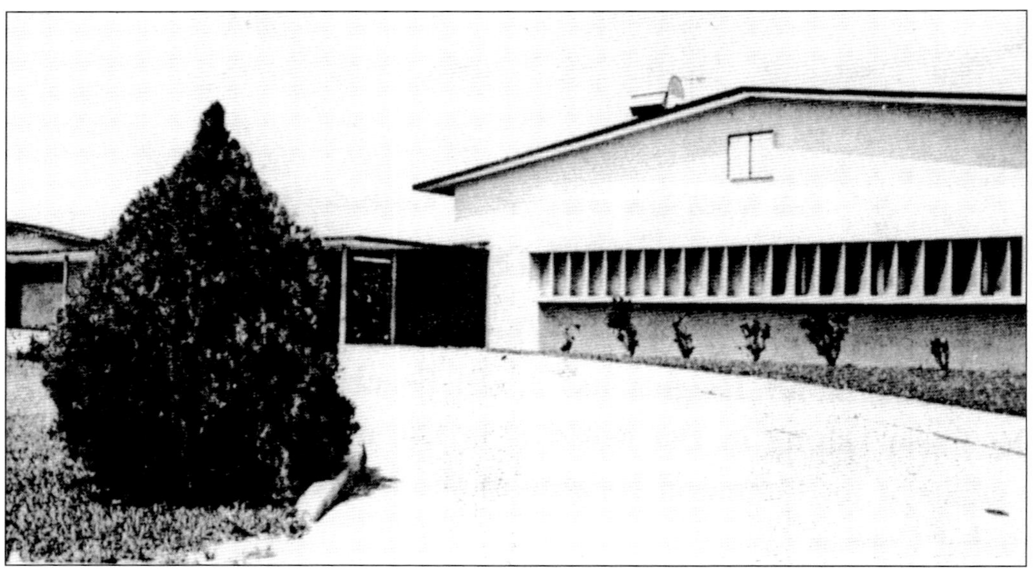

During the 1956–1957 school term, construction of the new school was completed by Clutter Construction Company to replace the portables. At the urging of the PTA, the school board consented to formally change the school's name to Frank C. Martin Elementary. (Courtesy of the Richmond Heights Homeowners Association.)

This is a picture of Frank C. Martin Elementary School principal Walter A. White. White was known for challenging youth and adults. He said, "May no one pass from this school without having been made more courageous and more intelligent." (Courtesy of the Armstrong family.)

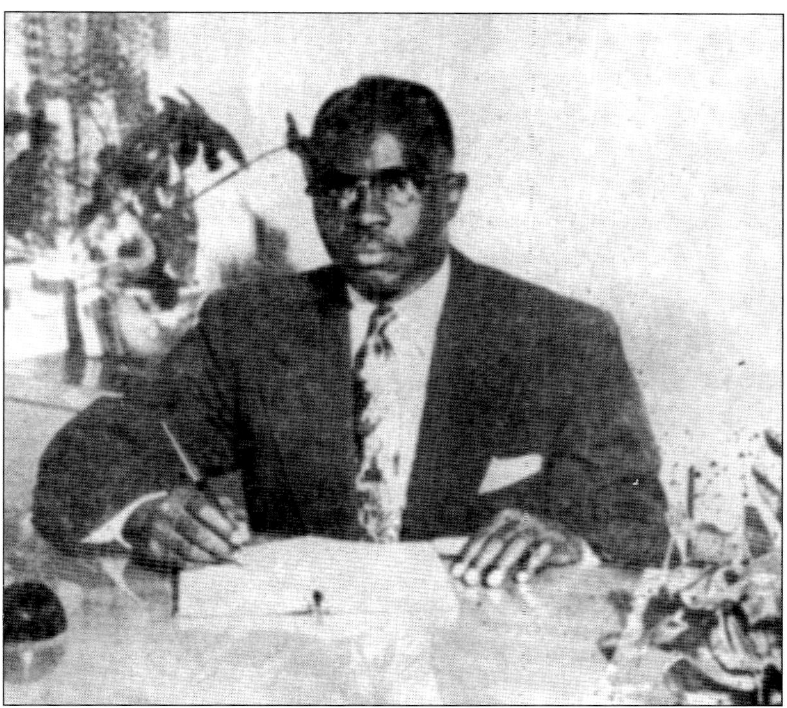

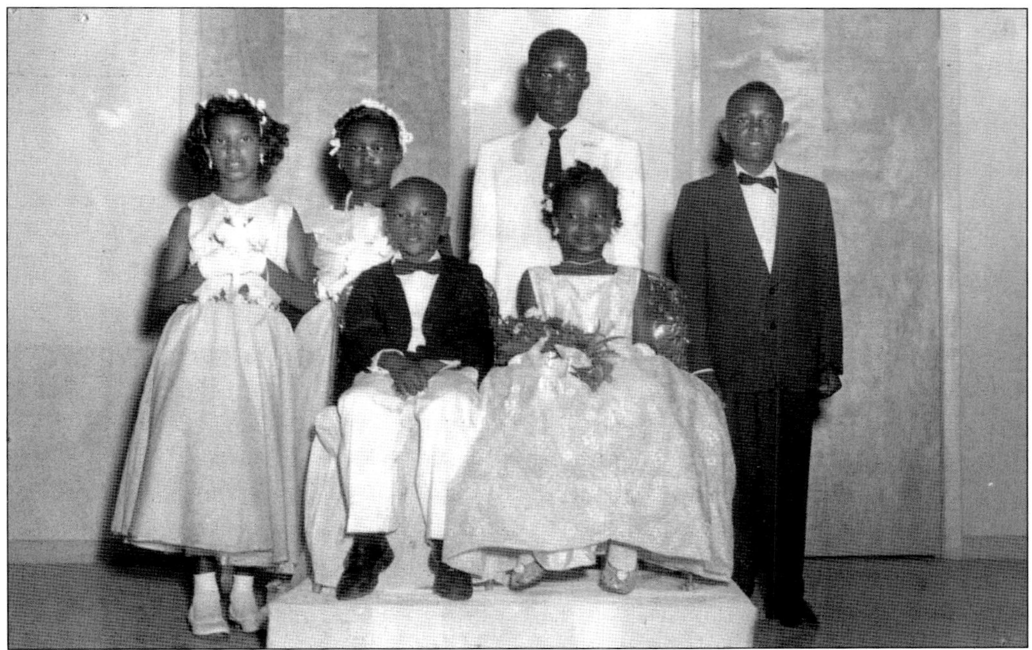

This 1955 photograph captures Frank C. Martin Elementary School students in the cafeteria auditorium for the "Cinderella Wedding," which was sponsored by an organization in Richmond Heights. Photographed are, from left to right, (sitting) Robert Benbow and Phyllis Lee; (standing) M. Gibson, Everlyn Johnson, Wallace Bates, and Clarence Martin. (Courtesy of the Armstrong family.)

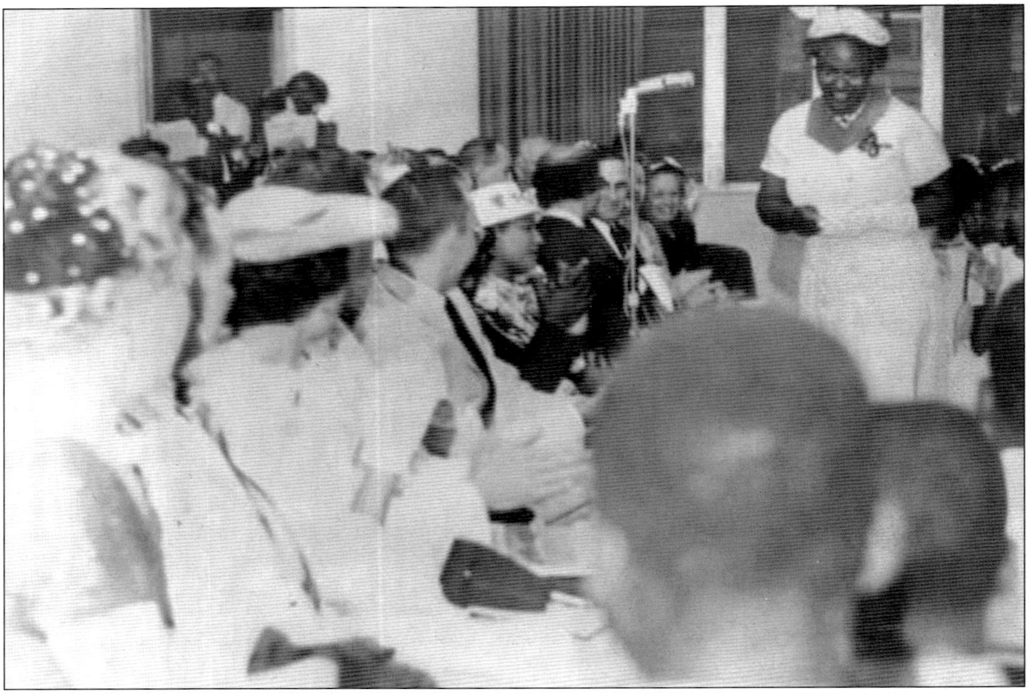

On Friday, April 26, 1957, the community of Richmond Heights was excited to welcome faculty, parents, school board members, and others to the dedicatory program for Frank C. Martin Elementary School. During this time, the school song, "Oh! Frank C. Martin," was officially adopted. Richmond Heights resident Ferrecita Pinder, a member of the graduating class of 1955, wrote it. In the auditorium, Charlotte Ford Clark, zone supervisor for the board of public instruction, is pictured speaking at the microphone introducing the guests. (Courtesy of the Armstrong family.)

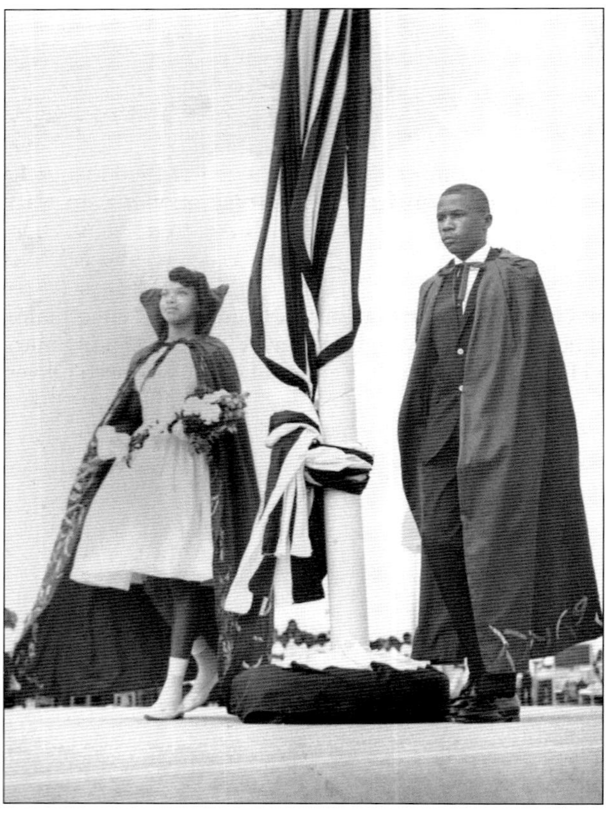

On May 3, 1962, May Day queen and May Day king festivities were held on the campus of Frank C. Martin Elementary School. This photograph shows classmates May Day queen Sandra Stringer and May Day king Gary Young strutting in front of their school's student body. (Courtesy of the Stringer family.)

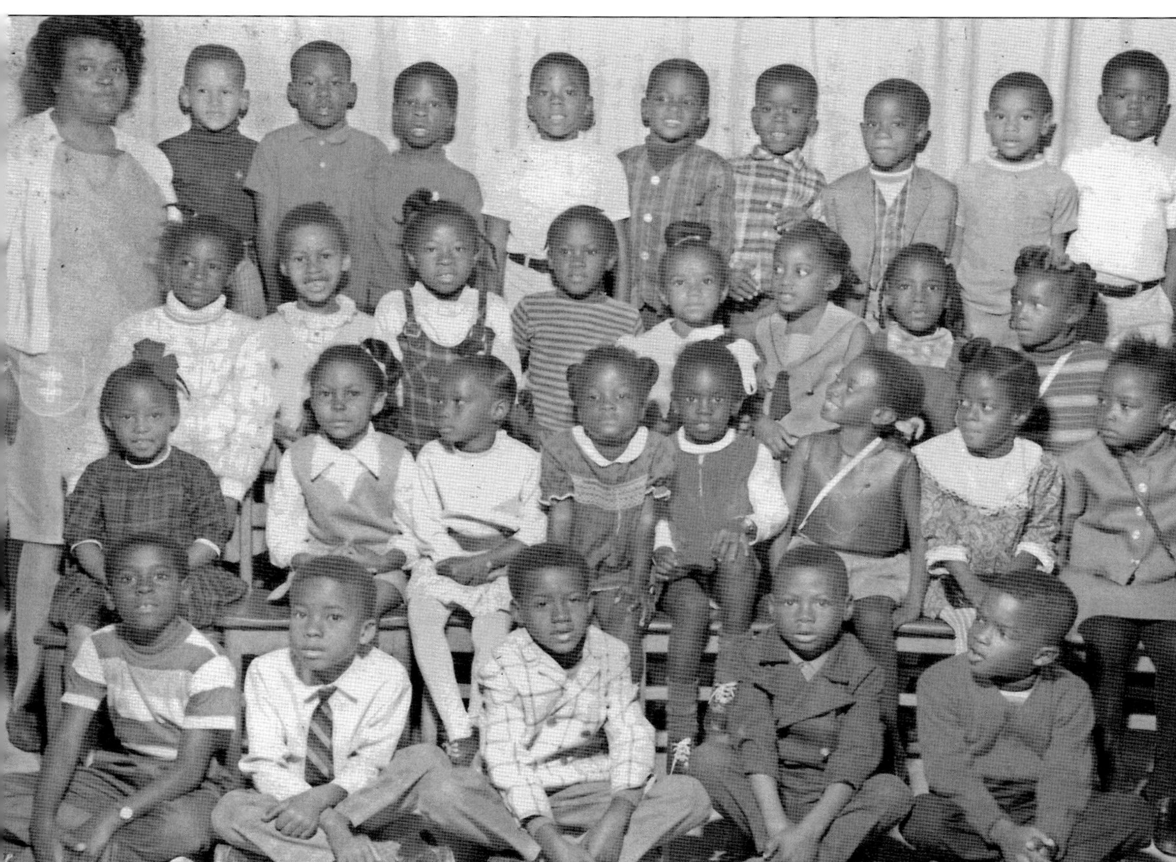

Frank C. Martin Elementary School teacher Bobbie Harper is pictured with her 1968 first-grade class. Harper taught here for 13 years and was later transferred once integration was in place to Banyan Elementary, which was formerly an all-white school. Pictured are, from left to right, (first row) Michael Sutton, Nathaniel Graham, Gary Butler, Clayton Thomas, and Michael Jones; (second row) Annette Synagogue, Gloria Johnson, Candace Williams, Sharon Blash, Patty Bruton, Beverly Delancey, Fayrine Gibson, and Erthia Carter; (third row) Sylvia James, Amanda Chattic, Nancy Causey, Vickie Lucas, Martenar Wright, Karen Williams, Valeria Smith, and Brenda Moore; (fourth row) Bobbie Harper, Dino Powell, Kenneth Powell, Kenneth Oliver, Mathew Lawson, Jerome Mitchell, Lawrence Lee, Dean Gross, Arnold Smith, Gregory Ware, and Jeffrey Mitchell. (Courtesy of the Redding family.)

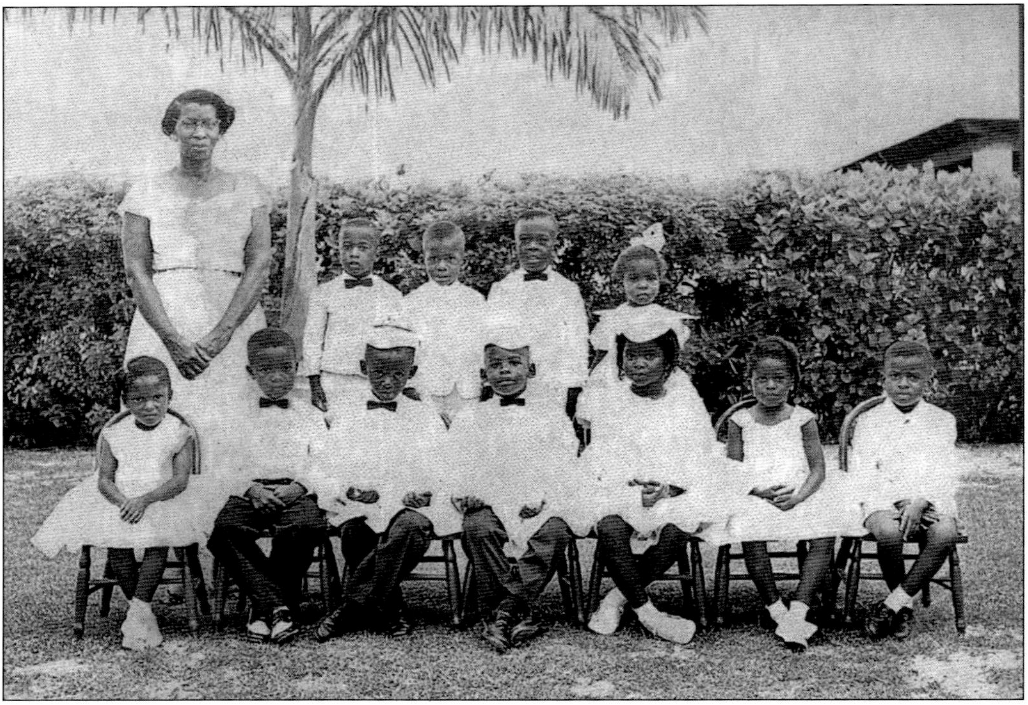

The Bethel Nursery was a community staple for parents. Located on Pierce Street, it is remembered for its Christian environment as well as its encouragement of reading. Myrtle Bethel is pictured with her 1959 class. From left to right are (first row) Audrey Hadley, Xavier Hunter, Michael Hepburn, Clarence Bankston, Barbara Holmes, Gratheryn Chisholm, and Michael Simms; (second row) Myrtle Bethel, Michael Henderson, Tommie Daniels, Gregory Dean, and Roslyn Hunter. (Courtesy of the Bethel family.)

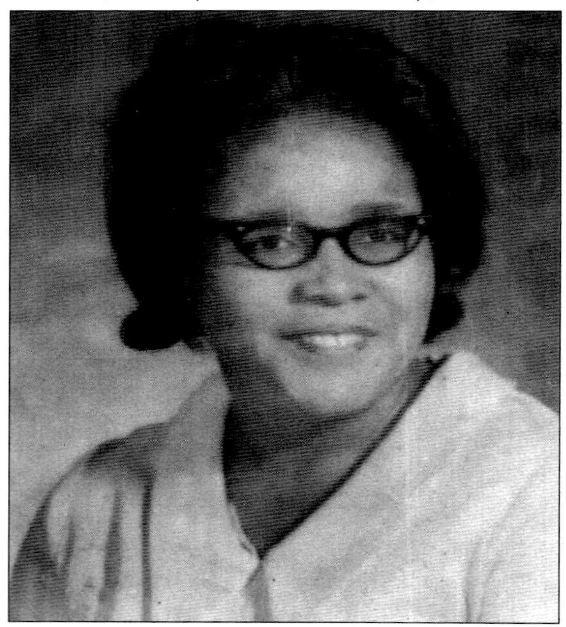

A few years after graduating from Florida Normal and Industrial Memorial College with a degree in education, Jeannean Britt moved to the city of Miami and settled in Richmond Heights on Jackson Street in 1960. She embarked as a teacher for Frank C. Martin Elementary and later retired from Whispering Pines Elementary. She was blessed with a son, Henry Britt. This is a school photograph of Britt at Frank C. Martin Elementary.

PROGRAM

PRAYER	Group
JESUS LOVFS THE LITTIE CHILDREN	Group
APOSTLE'S CREED	Group
SPEAKER - LEADERS OF TOMORROW -	Gra Theryn Chisholm
STFPPING STONES	Xavier Hunter
DIOS BENDIGA AMERICA	Group
A MIRROR	Tommie Daniels
FACE THE SUN	Audrey Hadley
"ES EL LUNES"	Shirlry Haynes
STOP AND THINK	Michael Henderson
FREY FELIPE	Keith Tribble Cassandra Hudson
FINEST THINGS IN LIFE	Clarence Bankston
UNIVFRSAL LANGUAGE	Roslyn Hunter
PRFSENTATION OF CERTIFICATES MR. W. A. WHITF	Michael Simms
RFMARKS REV. L. R. BROWN	Vanya Barkston

GRADUATES

GRA THERYN CHISHOLM — XAVIER HUNTER

MICHAEL SIMMS — MICHAEL HENDERSON

SHIRLEY HAYNES

Before attending Frank C. Martin Elementary School, students most likely graduated from Bethel Nursery. Mrs. Bethel did not take this graduation lightly. Decked out in graduation robes and caps, children walked across the front porch while parents proudly watched from the front lawn. On this day, graduates included Michael Henderson, Xavier Hunter, Gratheryn Chisholm, Shirley Haynes, and Michael Simms. This document is from the 1959 graduating class. (Courtesy of the Bethel family.)

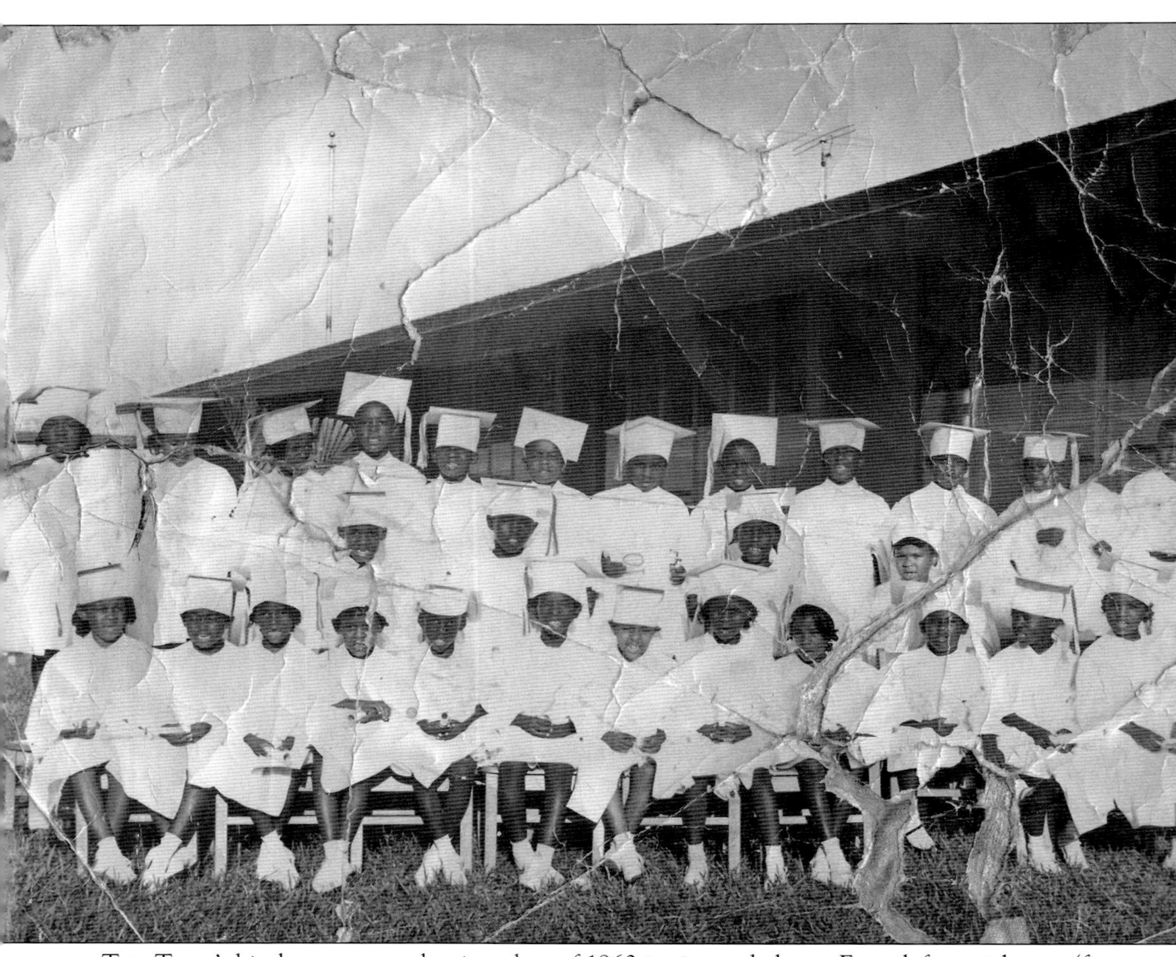

Tots Town's kindergarten graduating class of 1960 is pictured above. From left to right are (first row) Robin Williams, Vanessa Staten, Karen Russell, Diedra Shelton, Betty Williams, Marty Cox, Teresa Shed, Anita Walker, Barbara Hudson, Judith Webb, Cassandra Ramsey, and Angie Askew; (second row) Malachi Green, unidentified, Melody Johnson, and unidentified; (third row) Yvonne Williams, Joshlyn Hall, unidentified, Robert Riley, unidentified, James Burkes, Linda Cox, Alvin Pool, three unidentified, and Gerald Pratt. (Courtesy of the Ramsey family.)

Tots Town is a neighborhood place of learning; its motto is as follows: "As the twig is bent, so grows the tree." Tots Town's 1960 kindergarten graduation, pictured at right, took place in the Frank C. Martin School auditorium. The Tots Town founder, Thelma Aranha, is pictured behind the students. (Courtesy of the Ramsey family.)

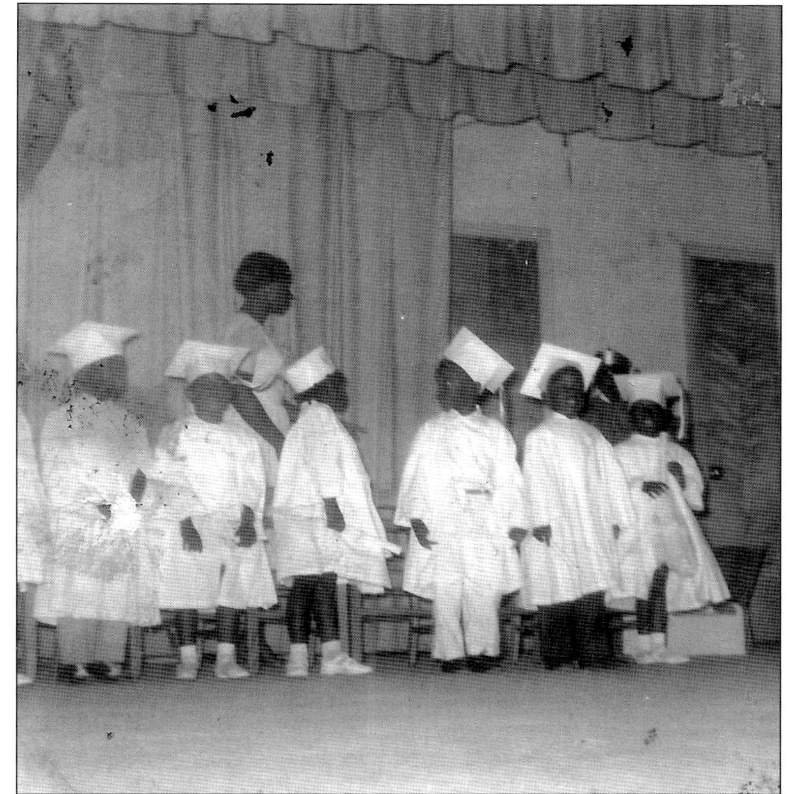

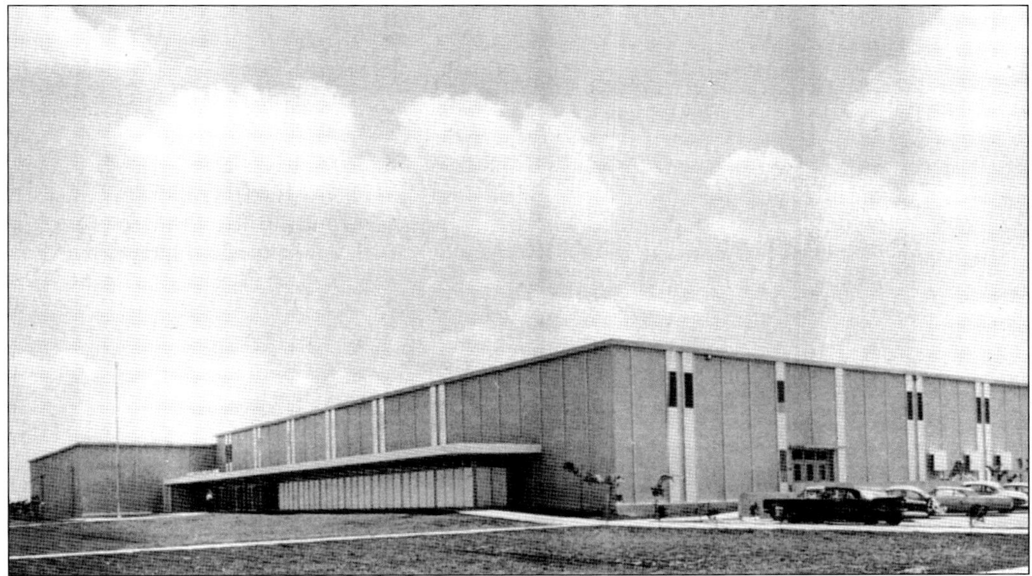

Richmond Heights Junior High School opened its doors to the community in 1963 with Dr. Edward Arahill, a white man, as principal. In 1968, Richmond experienced its first year of student integration. The only white eight-grade students were Robert VanValkenberg and Michelle Green. (Courtesy of Richmond Middle School.)

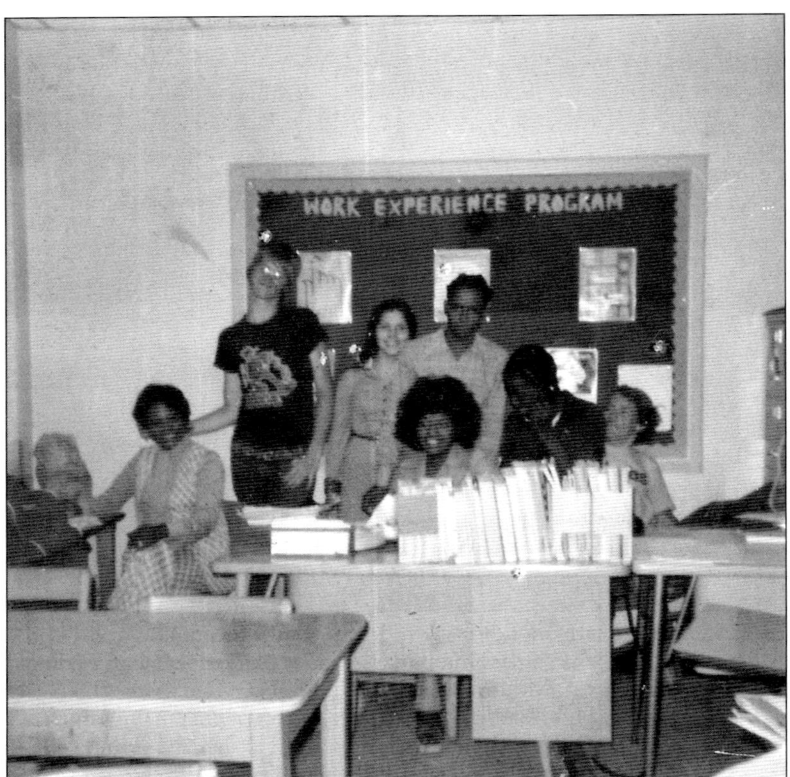

Students are engaged in conversation with teachers Lessie Wells Canada and Patricia Harper Garrett, who taught work experience. Work experience was a class devoted to teaching students about employment. They learned the proper way to fill out an application, how to interview for a job, and what was needed to stay employed.

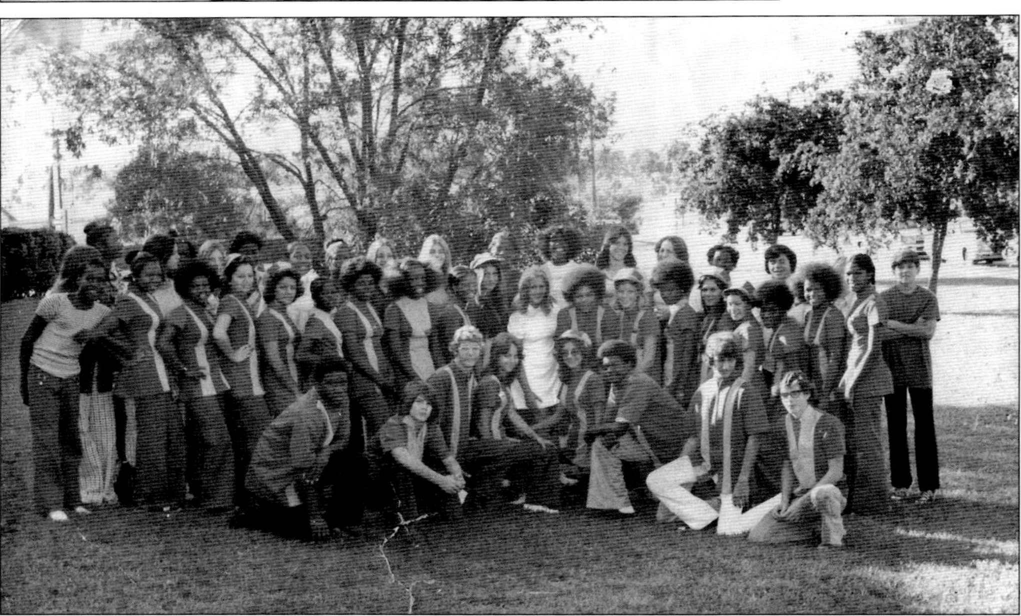

Richmond Junior High School's work experience students strike a pose as most are dressed in their Burger King work uniforms. These students were taught real-life work experience because of the on-the-job training curriculum. Students enrolled in this class would take their core courses in the morning and would head to work in the afternoon.

RICHMOND HEIGHTS JUNIOR HIGH COMMUNITY SCHOOL
15015 S.W. 103RD AVENUE
MIAMI, FLORIDA 33158

MRS. LUCILLE J. BENTLEY
PRINCIPAL
DR. ROSA L. WHITE
Asst. Princ. for Comm. Edu.

DR. LEONARD M. BRITTON
SUPT. DADE COUNTY SCHOOLS

CITIZENS'CRIME WATCH
AGENDA

January 8, 1981

I. Meditation-----------------Rev. T. Roddy
II. Purpose of the meeting-------Mr. W. Redding
III. History Of Crime Watch--------Dr. Rosa L. White
IV. What Is Crime Watch-----------Mr. W. Redding
V. Strategies For Organizing Neighborhood Crime Watch---Mr. W. Redding
   1. Identifying Areas (Map)
   2. Identifying Area Chairpersons

   SMALL GROUP MEETING
   1. Identifying Block Captains
   2. Identifying Block Watchers
   3. Sign-up sheets
   4. Dates for Block Meetings

VI. NEXT STEP

Date for next general meeting ------January 19, 1981--Time_ 7:30 P.M.
GUEST
Crime Watch Officer, Officer Harry Wright
Speaker, Mary Williams

VII. Summary
VIII. Adjournment

Precent No 4 #7

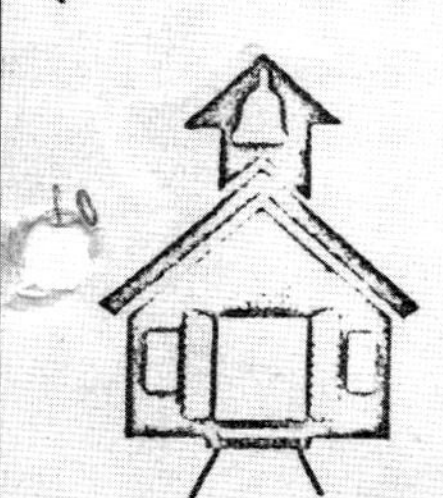

Round the clock, round the year use of our school building.

Richmond Heights Junior High Schools was a formal extension of the community. In fact, many civic organizations held meetings and events in the school's auditorium. This is the agenda taken from a Citizen's Crime Watch meeting in 1981. Community leader Willie Redding told residents the purpose of the meeting as well as strategies for the organization. (Courtesy of the Redding family.)

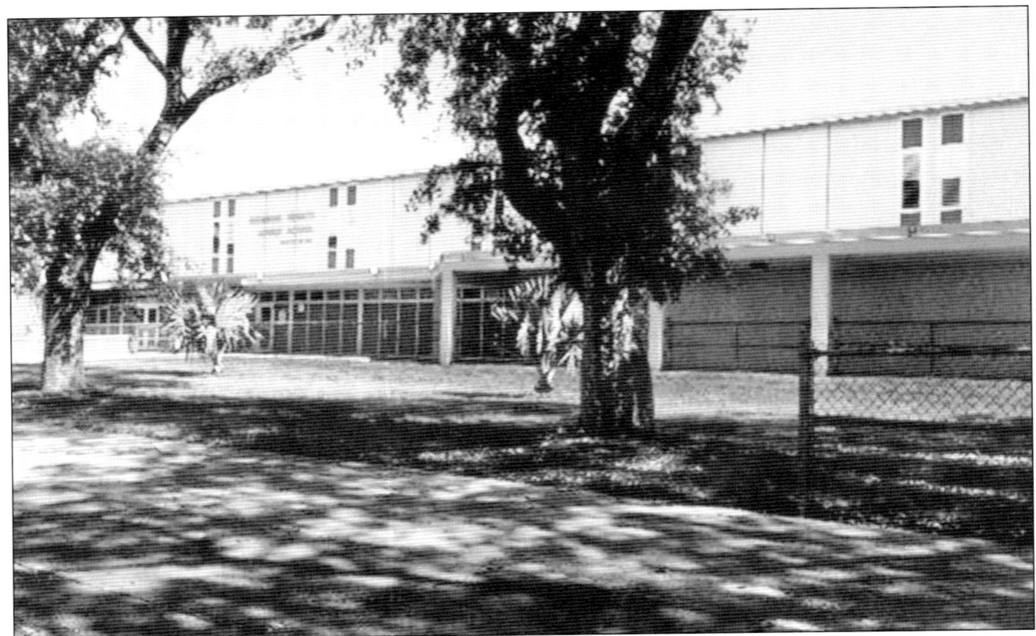

In 1993, Richmond Heights Junior High School went through several changes. The school's name was changed to Richmond Middle School, and ninth-grade students moved up to the senior high school, so that the only grades taught at the school were the sixth through eighth grades. (Courtesy of Shelby Turner.)

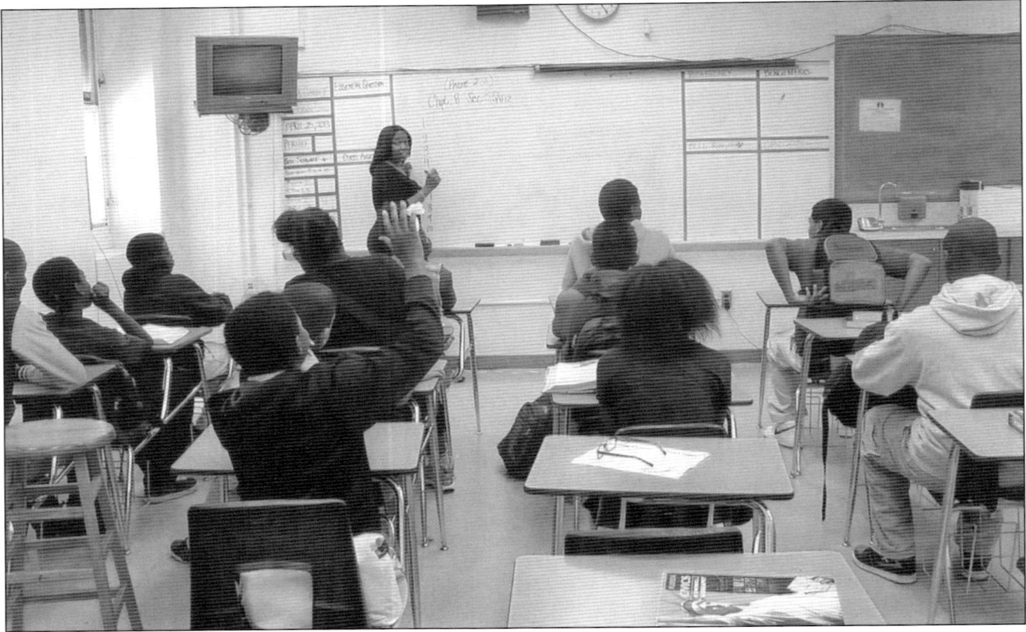

April Garrett enjoyed her neighborhood so much that she decided to go back to work there. She is the school counselor at Richmond Middle School and oversees all student academic criteria. Her love for her neighborhood is her bright horizon and allows her to stay passionate about helping to guide the students. (Courtesy of Shelby Turner.)

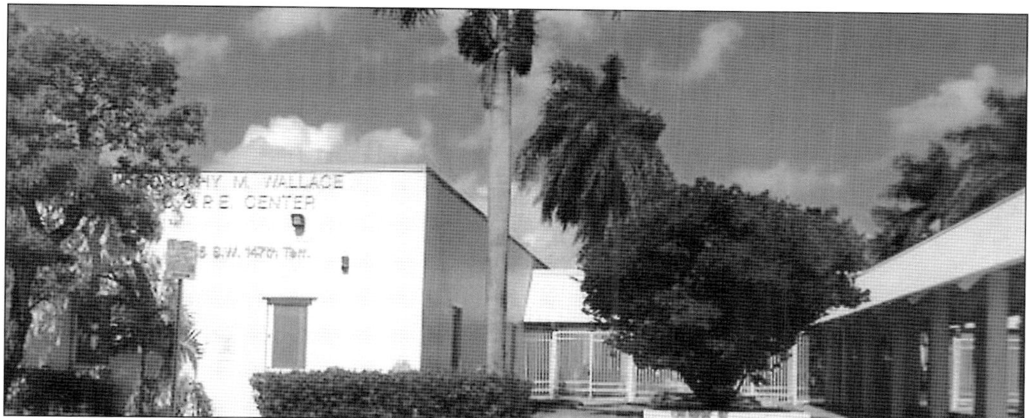

A stork with a baby is the proud mascot of the COPE (Continuing Opportunities for Purposeful Education) Center. The school was founded in 1972. The purpose of the school is to provide for the educational needs of teenage expectant parents as well as teenage parents. The school opened under the leadership of principal Dorothy Wallace. (Courtesy of Shelby Turner.)

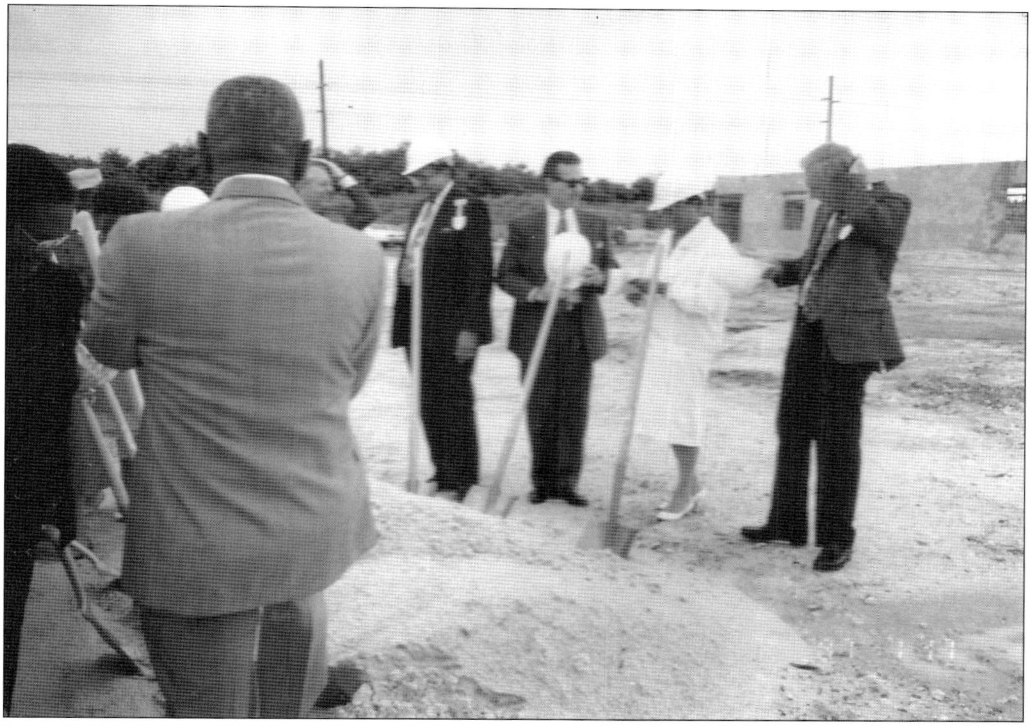

Dorothy Wallace is a history maker, and Miami-Dade County Public Schools agreed. It was in 1997 that they named Cope South in her honor. She was one of the first blacks to earn her master's degree from the School of Education at the University of Miami in 1963. As the chairperson of the guidance department, she opened Richmond Junior High in 1963. She and husband, Harvey Wallace, also owned a home in the Richmond Heights community. This photograph shows Wallace in a hard hat at the 1996 ground breaking for Cope South's new school home. (Courtesy of Dorothy Wallace.)

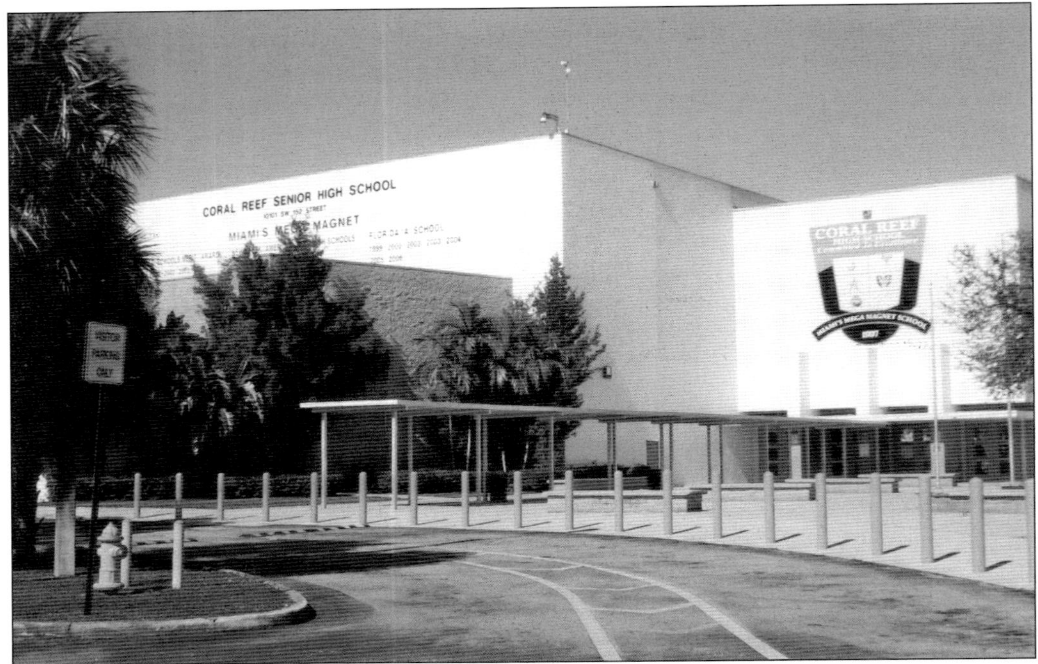

Coral Reef Senior High School opened its doors on August 1997 under the leadership of principal Greg Zawyer. According to *Newsweek* magazine's 2008 list of the top 1,000 schools in the nation, Coral Reef proudly sat at No. 19 in the nation. Coral Reef is a magnet school with six divisions: international baccalaureate, leisure medicine and health science, business and finance, legal and public affairs, agri-science and engineering technology, and visual and performing arts.

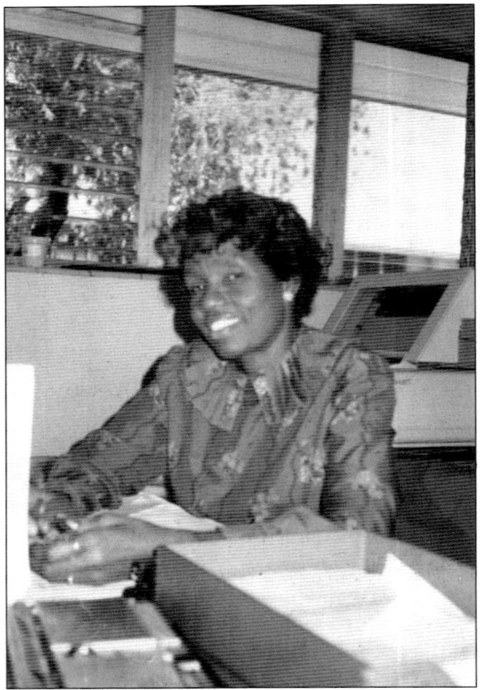

Samuel and Queen Armstrong moved to Richmond Heights in 1950 and raised their five children. In 1962, Queen Armstrong began to serve as Frank C. Martin Elementary School's attendance secretary for the next 25 years. After she retired, she began to concentrate on working in her church and community. (Courtesy of the Armstrong family.)

Three

Religious Life

As the community was envisioned, Capt. Frank C. Martin set aside a few acres to build places of worship. God has always been the foundation for the residents in Richmond Heights, so it is no wonder that residents began worship services in their homes until they were able to officially charter and organize a church under a suitable doctrine. They knew that an official building was not going to stop the gathering of like minds. Religion was going to be instrumental to the way of life in Richmond Heights.

This vision was fulfilled with the first churches, Bethel Missionary Baptist Church and Mount Pleasant African Methodist Episcopal Church, being built in 1951. The churches began in residents' homes and later moved to the community center that sat on the dead end street of Pinkston Drive. They shared this community center for some time until their own facilities were built. On the first and third Sundays of each month, the center on Pinkston Drive was for the worship service of Mount Pleasant AME Church. On the second and fourth Sundays of each month, the Bethel Missionary Baptist Church used the center to worship.

Other churches sprouted as the community grew and interest rose. The community is now fitted with seven churches, Martin Memorial African Methodist Episcopal, the Bethel Church, Second Baptist Church, Macedonia Church of God in Christ, Glendale Missionary Baptist Church, Community Bible Baptist Church, and the Family Worship Center Ministries International. Some of these churches began in residents' homes, the Richmond Heights sales office, the water tower, Richmond Heights Park, or at Frank C. Martin Elementary School. After Hurricane Andrew in 1992, most churches had to rebuild. They are now completely modern and outfitted with vaulted ceilings and elaborate facades.

All of the Richmond Heights church congregations come together for community activities. One event is for the Easter sunrise service, which has been held in Richmond Heights Park as well as the field at Second Baptist Church. Residents who were instrumental in bringing a church to the community were early settlers like Enoch Smith and a Mr. Moore, who served as the first trustees for Mount Pleasant AME Church.

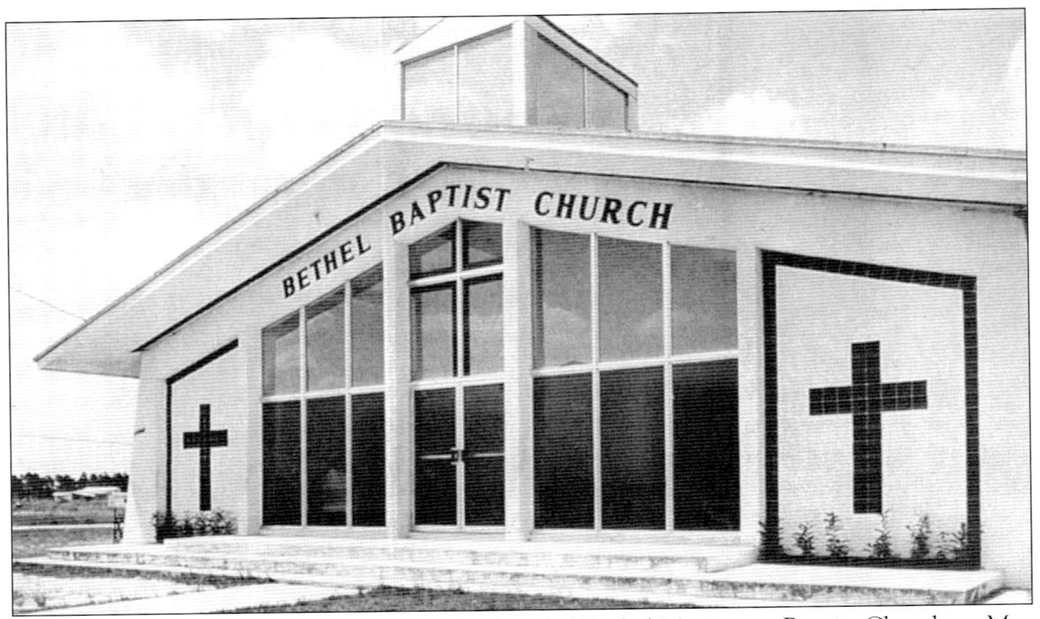

Reverends Butler, Grant, Tanner, and Bailey founded Bethel Missionary Baptist Church on May 4, 1951. Rev. W.H. Faison was called to pastoral leadership in 1953. Two years later, it was Rev. Leroy Ross who took the helm. Rev. Leroy Ross and members broke ground at 14440 Lincoln Boulevard on May 4, 1958. (Courtesy of the Bethel Church.)

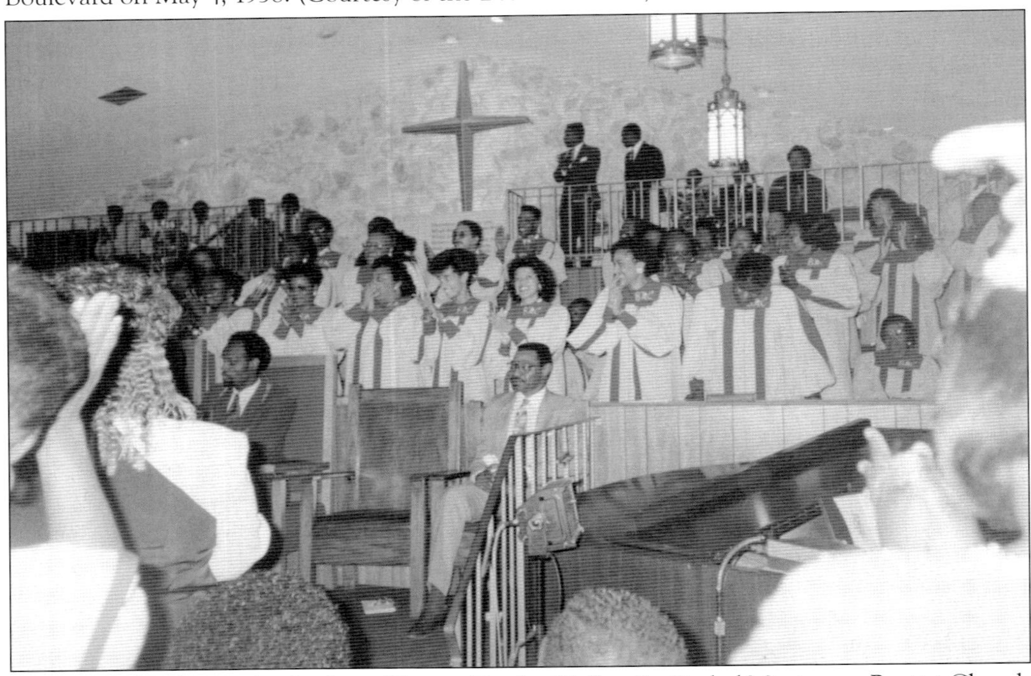

In 1969, under the new leadership of Pastor Charles Walker Sr., Bethel Missionary Baptist Church was renovated to include a large sanctuary, fellowship hall, 12 classrooms, a recording room, two offices, a conference room, and a prayer room. Pastor Walker also instituted the church's motto of "the whole word for the whole world." (Courtesy of the Bethel Church.)

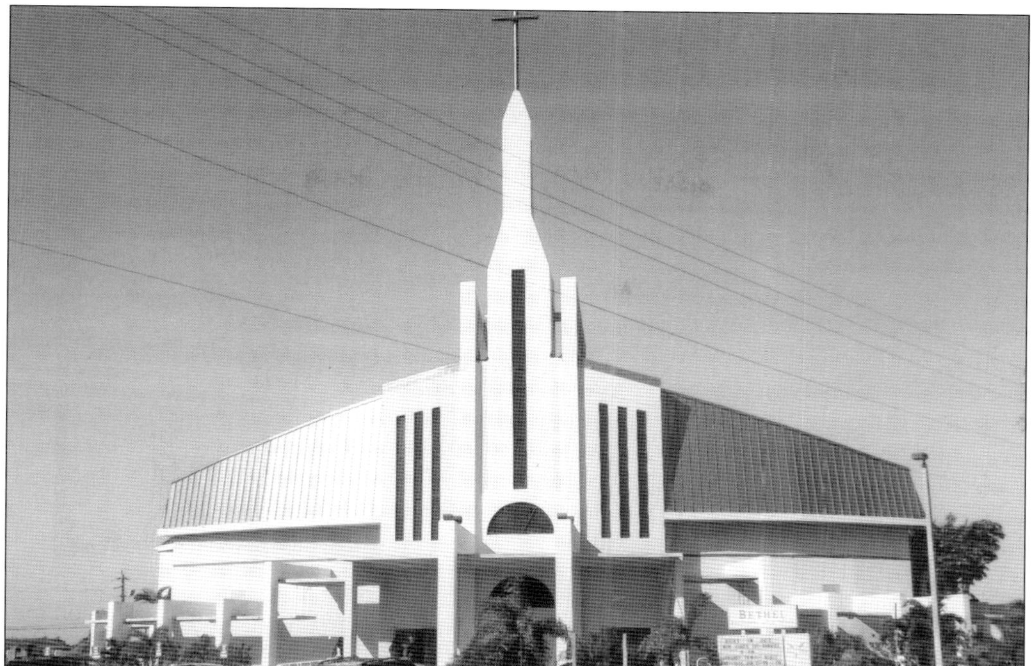

In 1990, Apostle Carlos L. Malone Sr. accepted the call to leadership of Bethel. Under Apostle Malone, membership increased to 748 members, and on October 9, 1994, these members marched down Lincoln Boulevard into their new and current edifice. Also that year, outreach efforts increased to serve the community, and the stage productions for Easter and Christmas led to thousands giving their lives to Christ. (Courtesy of the Bethel Church.)

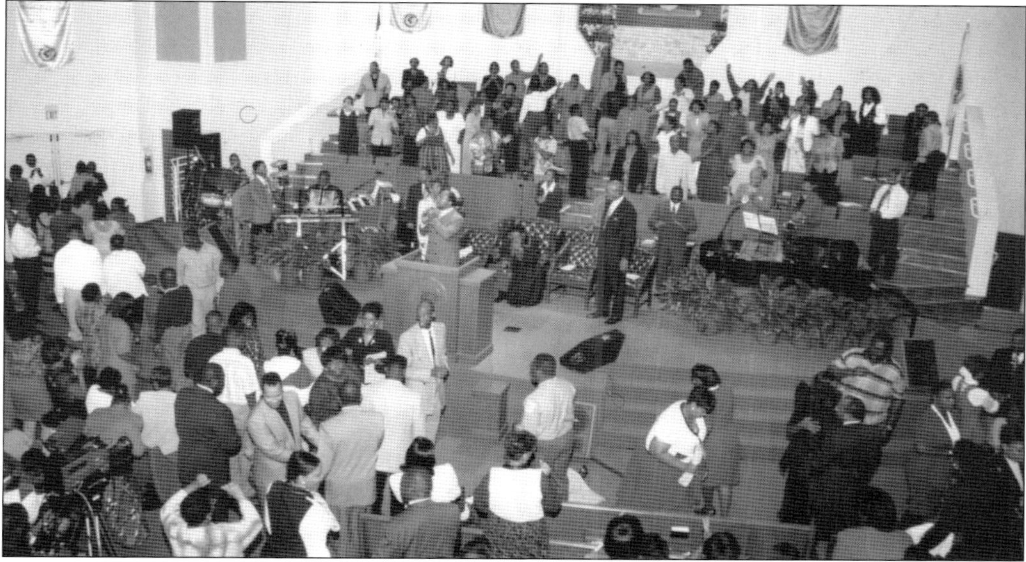

Today, Apostle Malone has taken his ministry into a new dimension. The ministry is no longer identified by a religious denomination but by its God-ordained purpose. As a result, the church name was changed to the Bethel Church with a membership of over 1,500 members. Apostle Malone is seen standing at the podium in the pulpit. (Courtesy of the Bethel Church.)

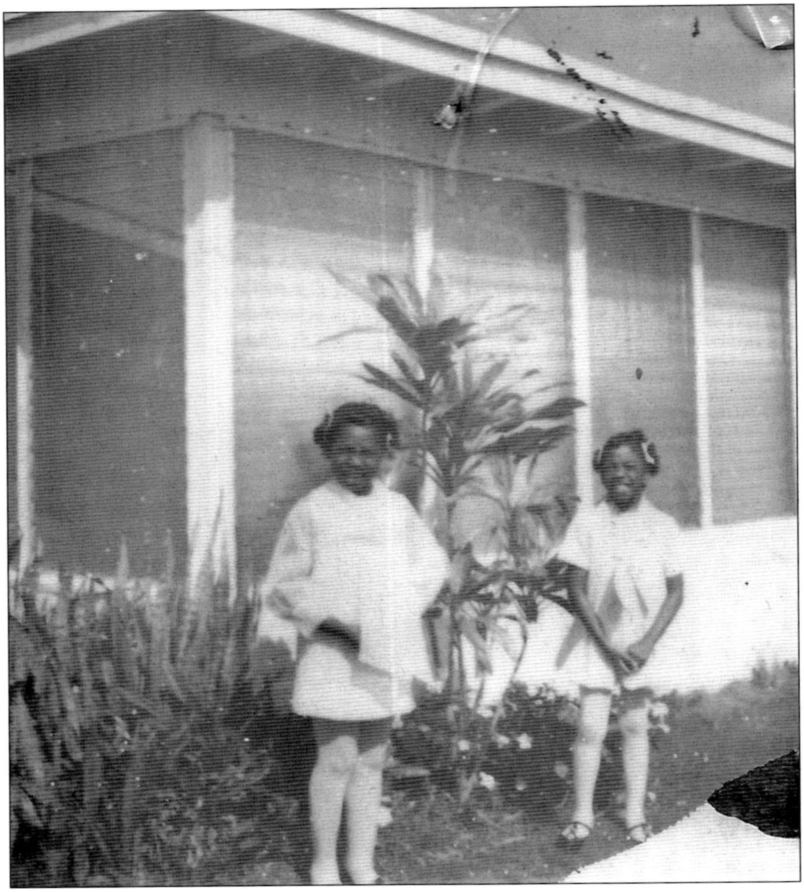

From left to right, sisters Daphne and Kimberly Jackson are pictured dressed in their Sunday best. This duo is ready for Easter service at Bethel Baptist Church. They are pictured in the backyard of their Polk Street home by their Florida room. In this picture, Kim is seven, and Daphne is nine. (Courtesy of the Jackson family.)

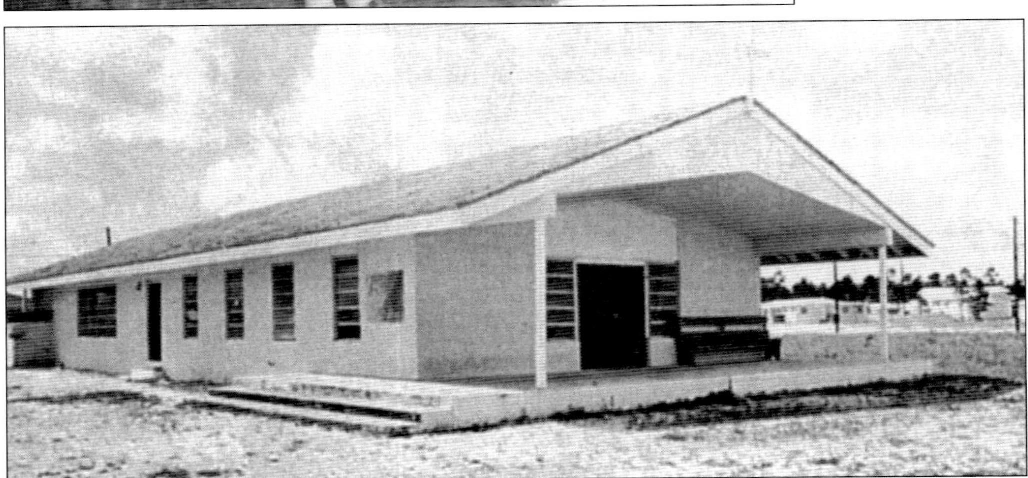

Mount Pleasant AME Church was founded in a model home/sales office in the Richmond Heights community on October 19, 1951. The church changed its name to Martin Memorial AME as a way to pay homage to the community founder, Frank C. Martin. Anthony Palmore was church leader, and Murry James Jr., H.M. Moore, and Enoch Smith were trustees. (Courtesy of Shelby Turner.)

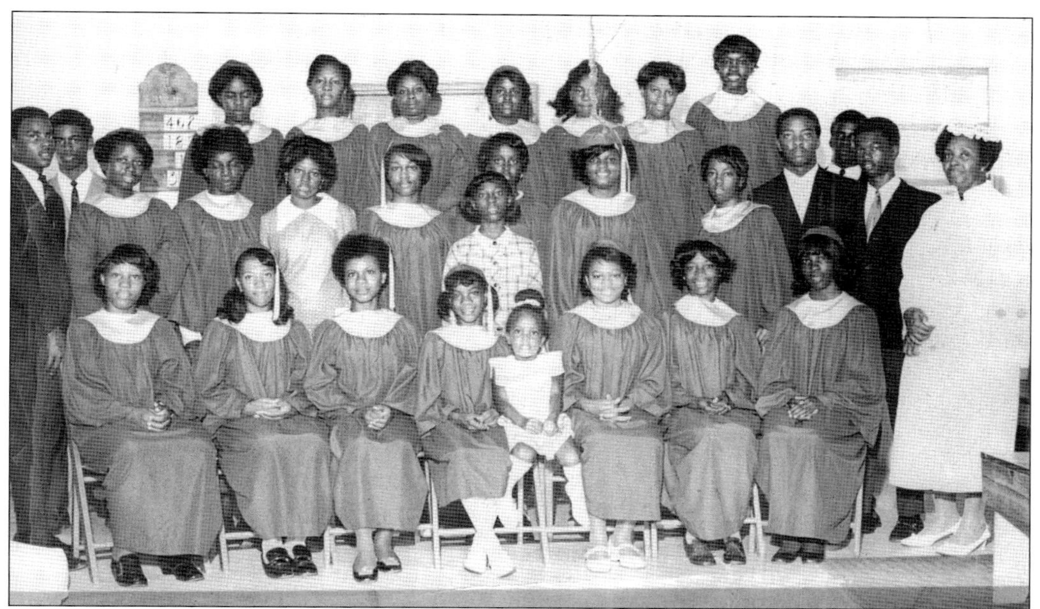

In 1957, members of Martin Memorial AME marched down Carver Drive to their new place of worship, which is still their current location on Lincoln Boulevard. Captain Martin donated this land for the church. The original choir consisted of the following families: the Dixons, Rosses, Kellys, Browns, Wilsons, Littlefields, Turners, and Flunorys. Pictured above are choir director Laura Ann Palmore and other choir members. (Courtesy of the Palmore family.)

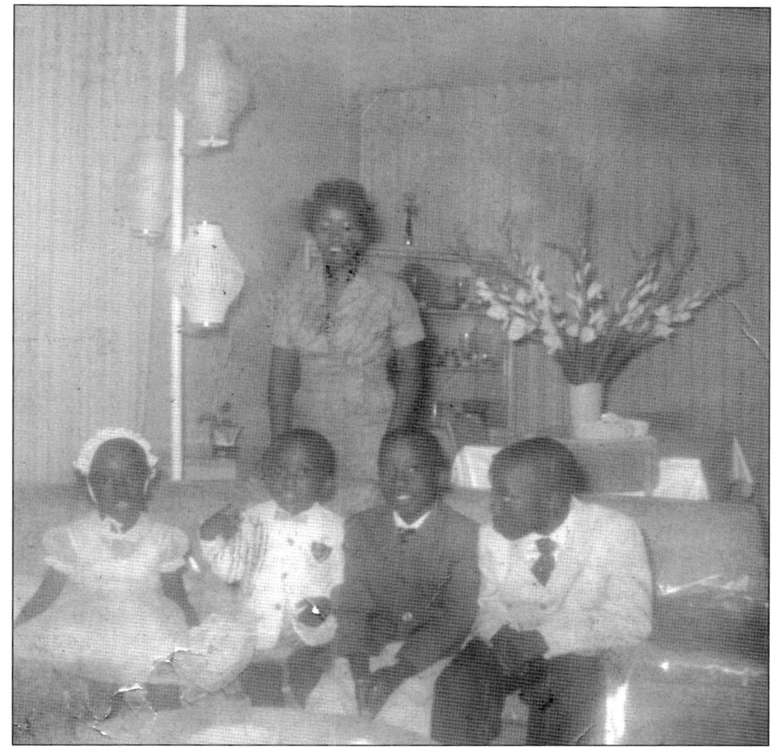

In April 1958, from left to right, Cassandra, Carl, David, and Freddie Ramsey are seen in their Perry Drive home seated on the couch while their mother, Mildred Ramsey, stands in the background. They are headed to celebrate Easter activities at Martin Memorial AME Church. (Courtesy of the Ramsey family.)

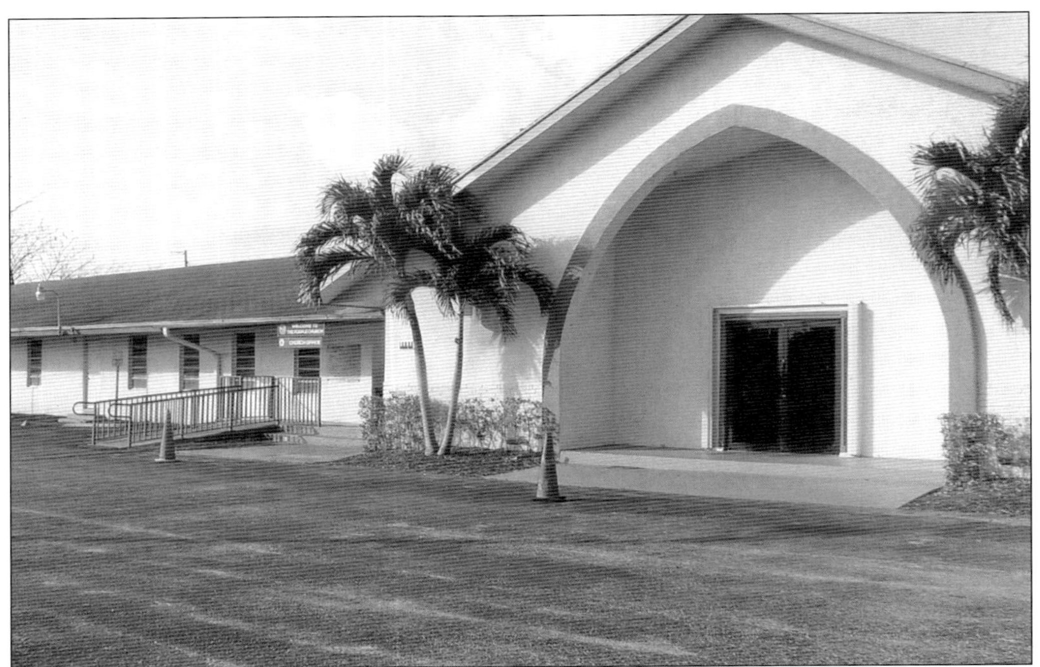

When Martin Memorial AME began, the first officers of the church were Readie Johnson, Ida Ross, Ray Ross, Olive Ware, Roosevelt Dixon, and Maggie Wilson. Anthony Palmore served as the class leader. The trustees were Murray James Jr., H.M. Moore, and Enoch Smith. This is a photograph of the exterior of the church around 2013. (Courtesy of Shelby Turner.)

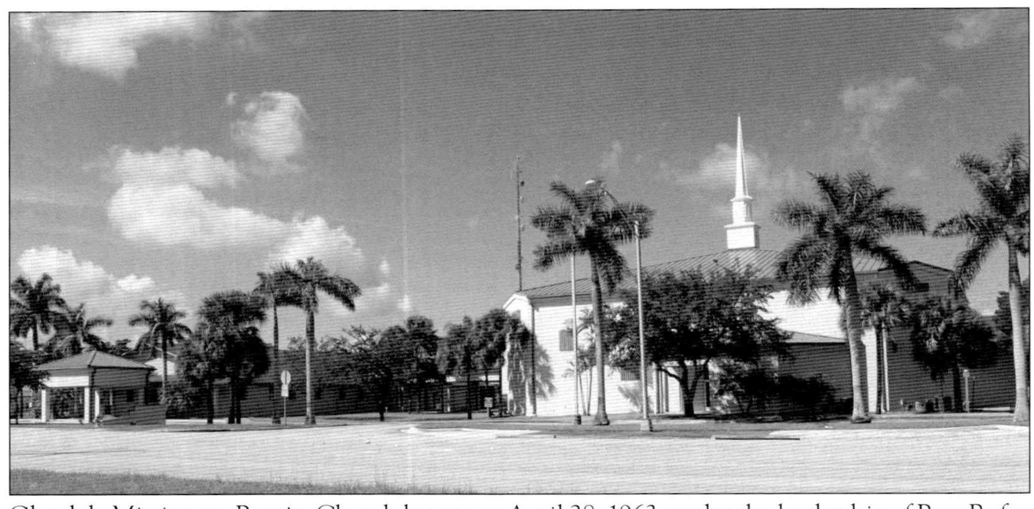

Glendale Missionary Baptist Church began on April 28, 1963, under the leadership of Rev. Rufus Grant. Early worship service was held at Frank C. Martin Elementary School. Dr. James A. Harrington followed Reverend Grant and served from 1963 to 1965. Rev. Bragg Turner was the residing pastor for the next two years. In November 1971, Rev. Joseph Coats Sr. took the helm. (Courtesy of Glendale Missionary Baptist Church.)

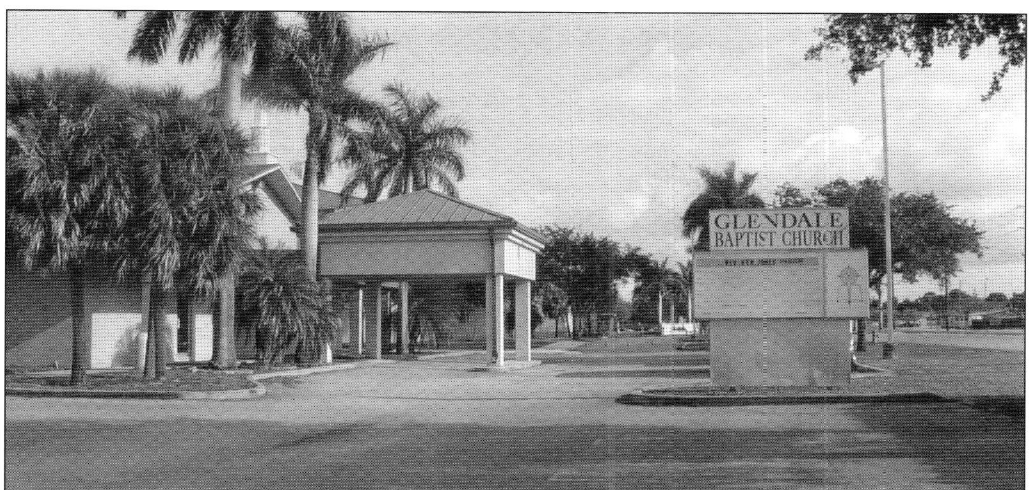

In 1992, Hurricane Andrew hit the South Florida community of Richmond Heights, and Glendale Missionary Baptist Church went through renovations until 1996, when it was dedicated. Reverend Coats's tenure as pastor concluded in 1999. At that time, Rev. Ricky Armstrong became the pastor for Glendale Missionary Baptist Church for the next 10 years. The current pastor, Rev. Kenneth Jones, took over in 2010. (Courtesy of Glendale Missionary Baptist Church.)

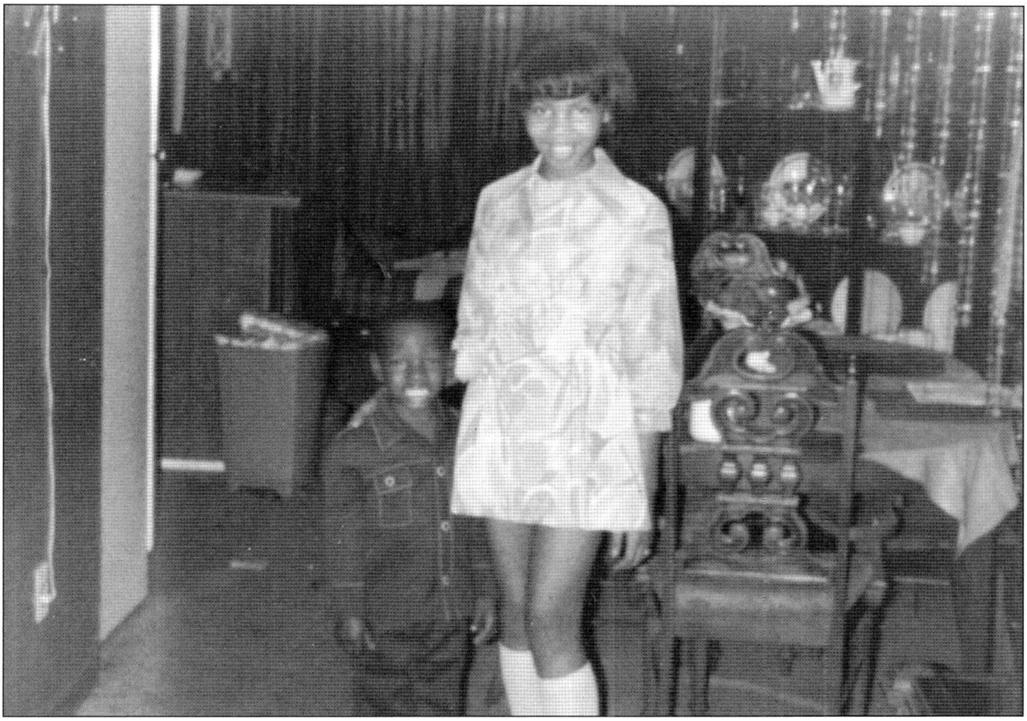

Pictured are Amanda Chattic and her brother Enoch Smiley in the front room of their home on Washington Boulevard. Amanda's Sunday duties were to get brother Enoch dressed to attend church with her. She adored this time with her brother and pretended he was her child. This was a special day because it was the first day of worship at Glendale Missionary Baptist Church on April 28, 1963. (Courtesy of the Chattic family.)

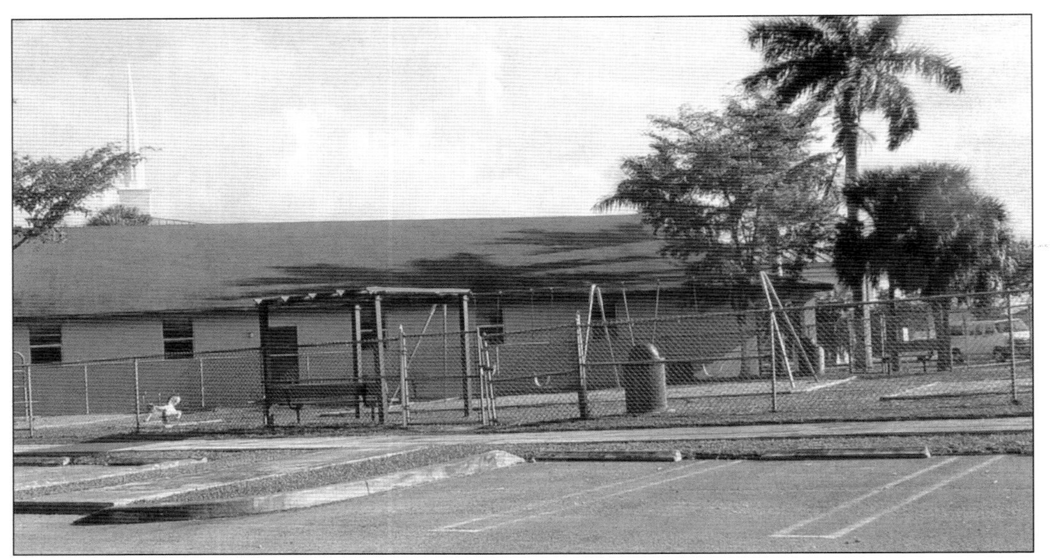

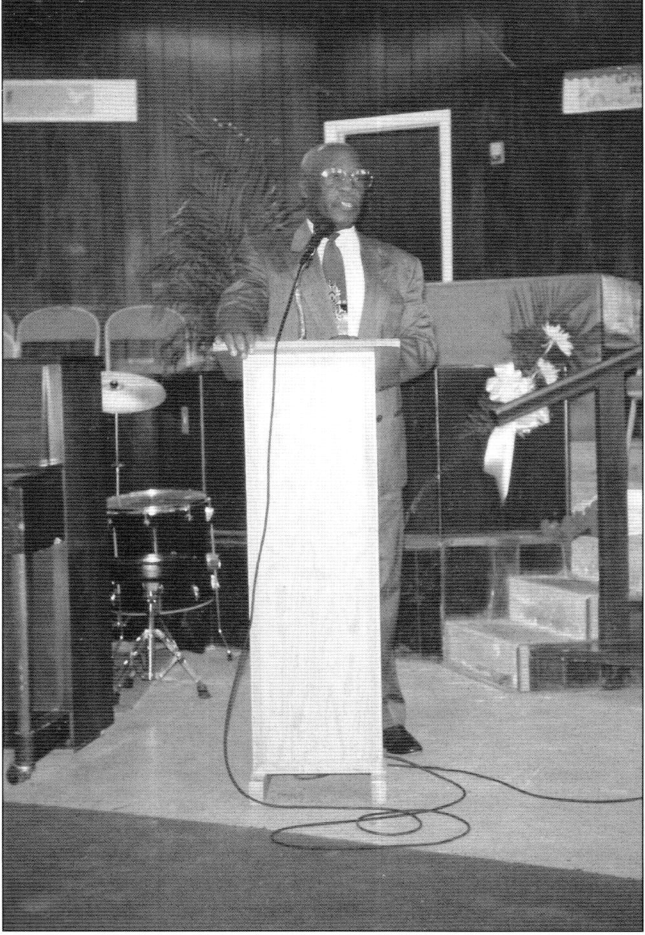

Glendale Missionary Baptist Church is home to Glendale Christian Academy. The school's mission is to glorify God by equipping children with a Christian view of the world, educating them biblically and academically in an environment of excellence and discipline where they learn to serve God and their fellow man. Association of Christian Schools International (ACSI) and the Department of Children and Families license the academy. (Courtesy of Shelby Turner.)

In 1964, thirteen people met in an effort to organize a church. As a result of this meeting, Rev. John A. Ferguson became the founder/pastor of Second Baptist Church. Under his leadership, Israel Benbow, Sherman Clark, Alphonso Thomas, and Amos Larkins Sr. became the first ordained deacons. In this picture, Reverend Ferguson is preaching a message in the original sanctuary. (Courtesy of Second Baptist Church.)

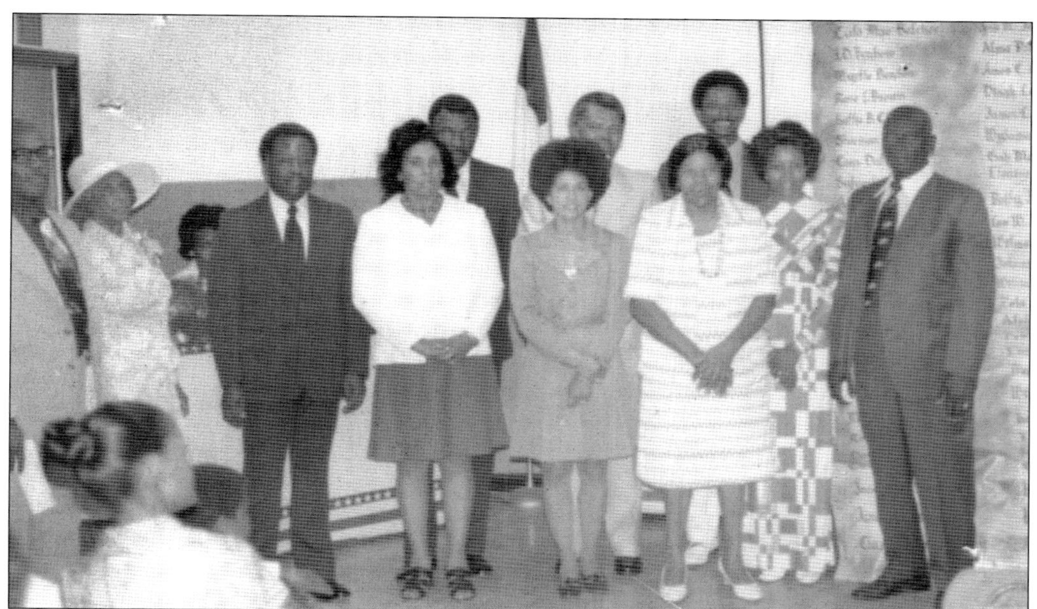

A total of 53 members applied for and received the charter for Second Baptist Church. The official organization with charter was adopted on May 17, 1964. Pictured are, from left to right, (first row) Rev. John Ferguson and charter members Lula Mae Belcher, Burk Jones, Mary Williams, Vivian Greene, Myrtle Benbow, Ossie Hollis, and J.D. Benbow; (second row) Eugene Williams, Dr. Herbert Greene, and Donald Hollis. (Courtesy of Donald Hollis.)

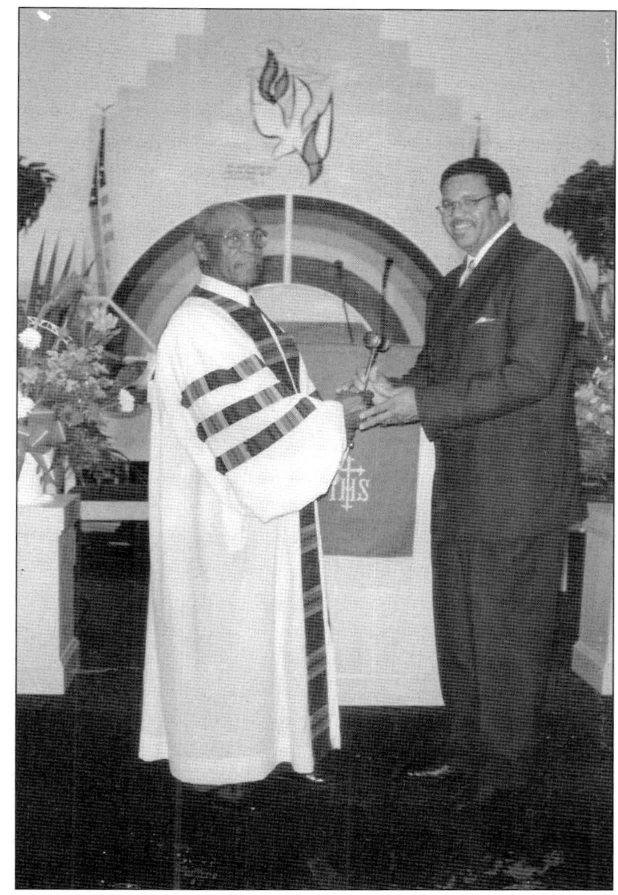

Andrew Green, Donald Hollis, Burk Jones Sr., and James Marshall served on the first board of trustees for Second Baptist Church. On May 9, 1965, Second Baptist congregation moved into a building of worship, which formally operated as the post office. A newly constructed sanctuary was complete in April 1995. After 36 years of leadership, Rev. John A. Ferguson (left) retired and welcomed Pastor Alphonso Jackson Sr. (right) to carry on his legacy. (Courtesy of Second Baptist Church.)

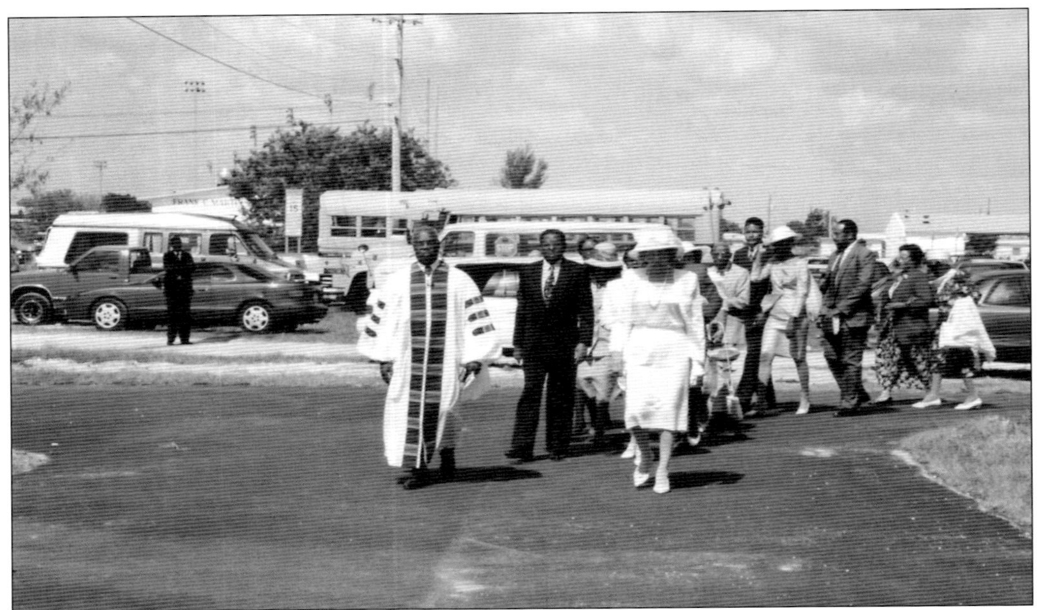

A growth in Second Baptist Church's membership dictated a move from the office space in the water tower where they worshiped. The parishioners moved to the Richmond Heights Community Building at 11111 Pinkston Drive to worship. This was until 1995, when they moved into a larger church. The congregation is shown marching to their new church on April 16, 1995. (Courtesy of Donald Hollis.)

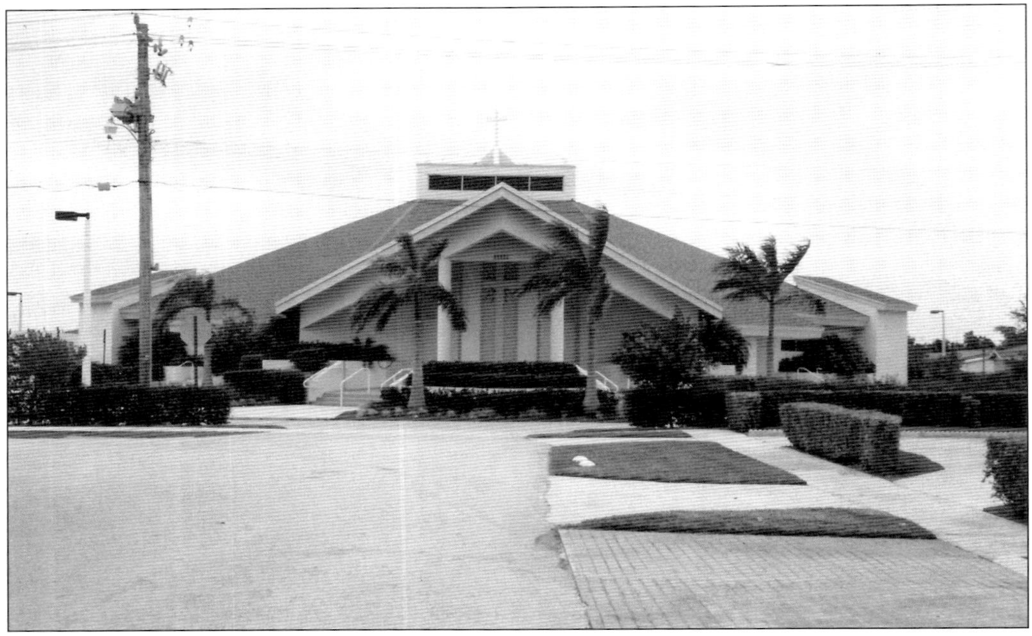

Hurricane Andrew severely damaged the Second Baptist Church building and the day care facility in 1992. Church members repaired the building, but due to the enormous growth in church membership, a new sanctuary was constructed adjacent to the previous facility. This photograph is of the new church that was built. (Courtesy of Second Baptist Church.)

In the fall of 1958, Elder Paul Golatt Sr. started having prayer meetings in the living room of Norman Smith's home on Van Buren Street. These prayer services continued for the next few months, and others opened their doors to hold services until a permanent home would be available. This was the beginning of Macedonia Church of God in Christ. (Courtesy of Macedonia Church of God.)

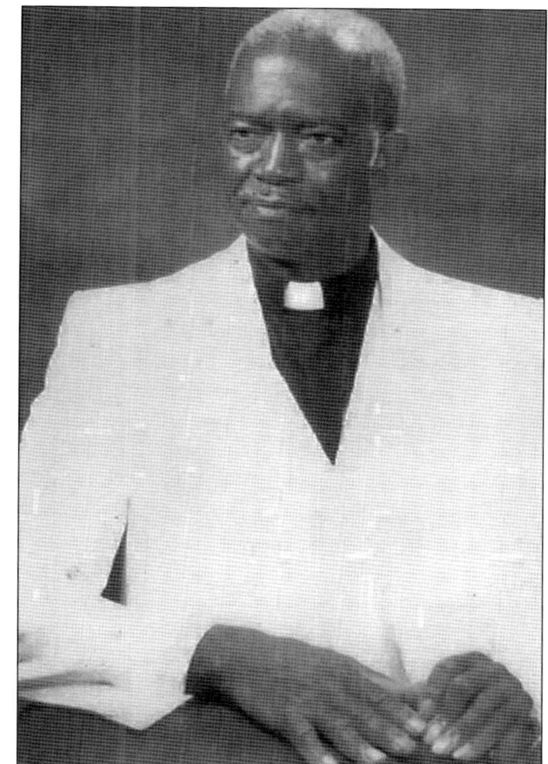

Macedonia Church of God in Christ did eventually get its permanent home. After the passing of Elder Golatt Sr., Elder Paul Golatt Jr. took the helm of the ministry as the pastor. Pictured is the concert choir from 1970. (Courtesy of Macedonia Church of God.)

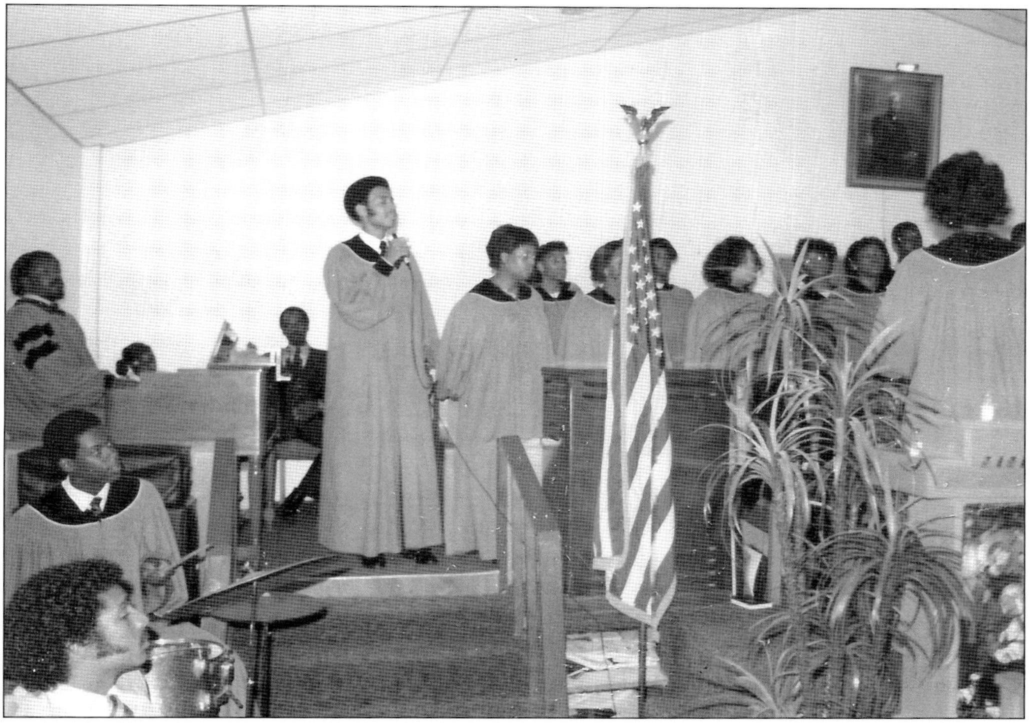

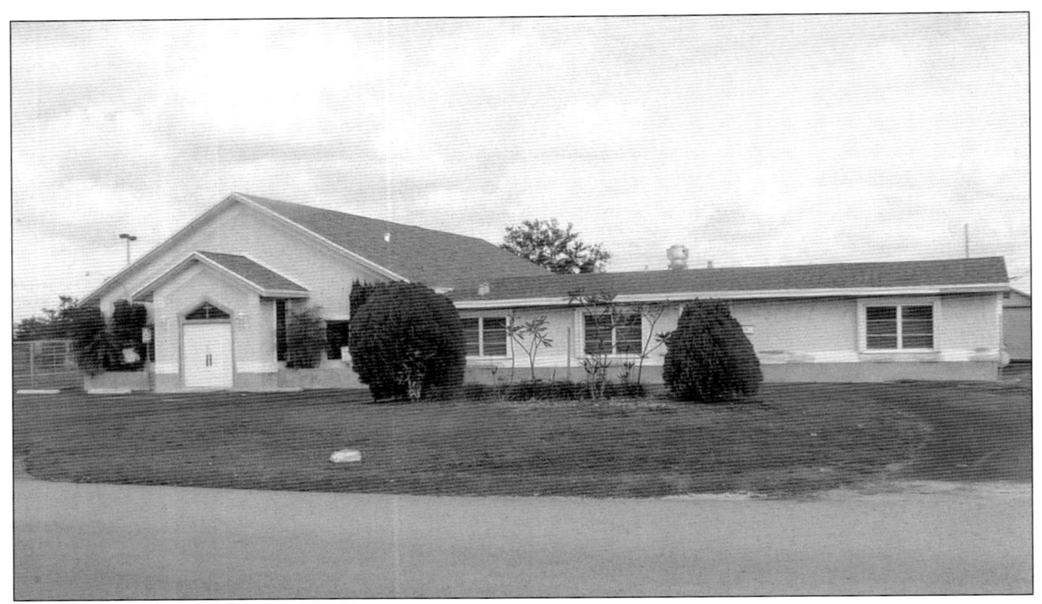

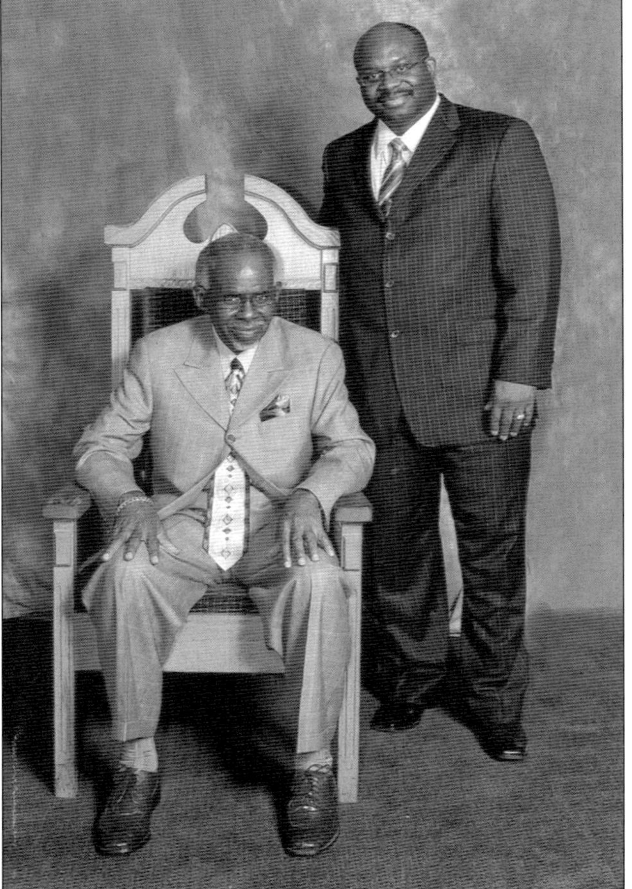

Under the leadership of Elder Paul Golatt Jr., the church became involved with community outreach. The ministry opened its doors during the year for Florida Comprehensive Assessment Test (FCAT) tutorial services and vacation Bible school. The church also hosts clothing give-away drives annually and offers academic scholarships to deserving members of the church. (Courtesy of Macedonia Church of God in Christ.)

Presently, the church is thriving under Pastor Michael Wheeler (standing), seen here with Elder Paul Golatt. It continues to have a spiritual voice in the community. It offers biblical teachings weekly for all ages, along with noonday prayer. Macedonia continues to be a pillar in Richmond Heights by serving the community. (Courtesy of Macedonia Church of God in Christ.)

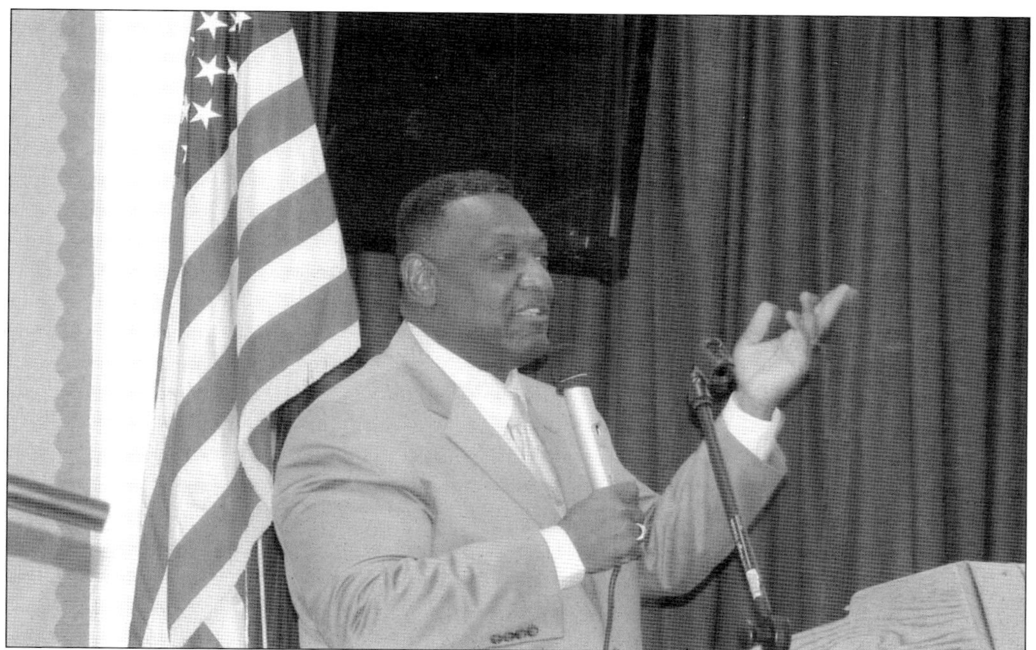

Rev. Ronald A. Smith founded Community Bible Baptist Church after holding a weekly community Bible study at Sgt. Joseph Delancy Park. It was determined that a more formal institution was necessary. In 2001, the church purchased 6.4 acres of land on SW 152nd Street for the future site of its sanctuary, fellowship hall, and day care center. (Courtesy of Ronald Smith.)

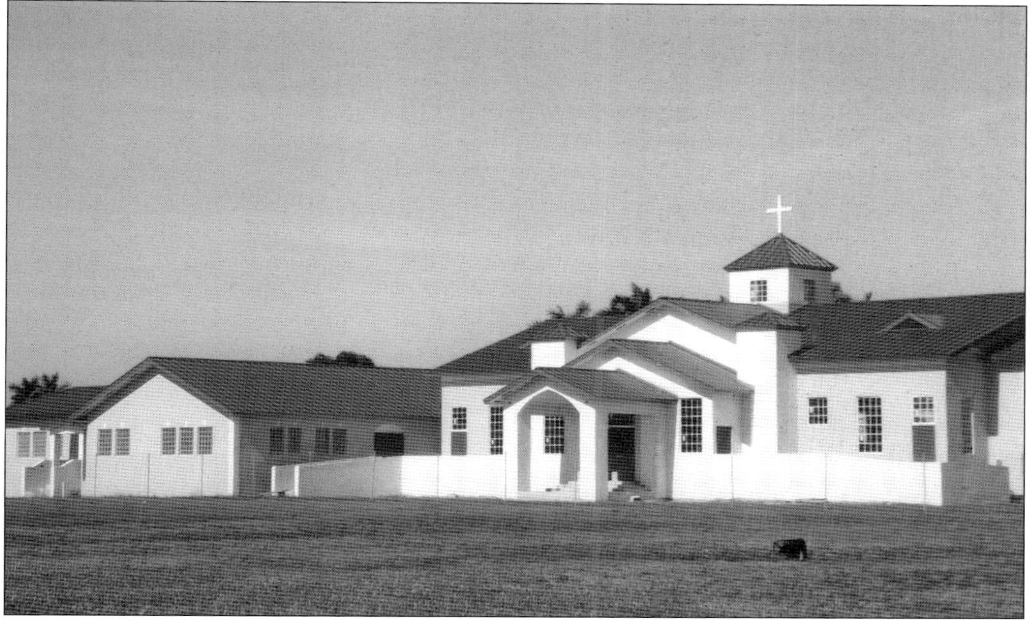

Community Bible Baptist was organized under the leadership of Rev. Ronald A. Smith Sr. The membership at the beginning of the mission was 29. Presently, the membership is 321, with 14 ministries, 16 deacons, and 9 associate ministers. Community Bible Baptist Church is organized under the Miami Baptist Association Church Starter Program. (Courtesy of Ronald Smith.)

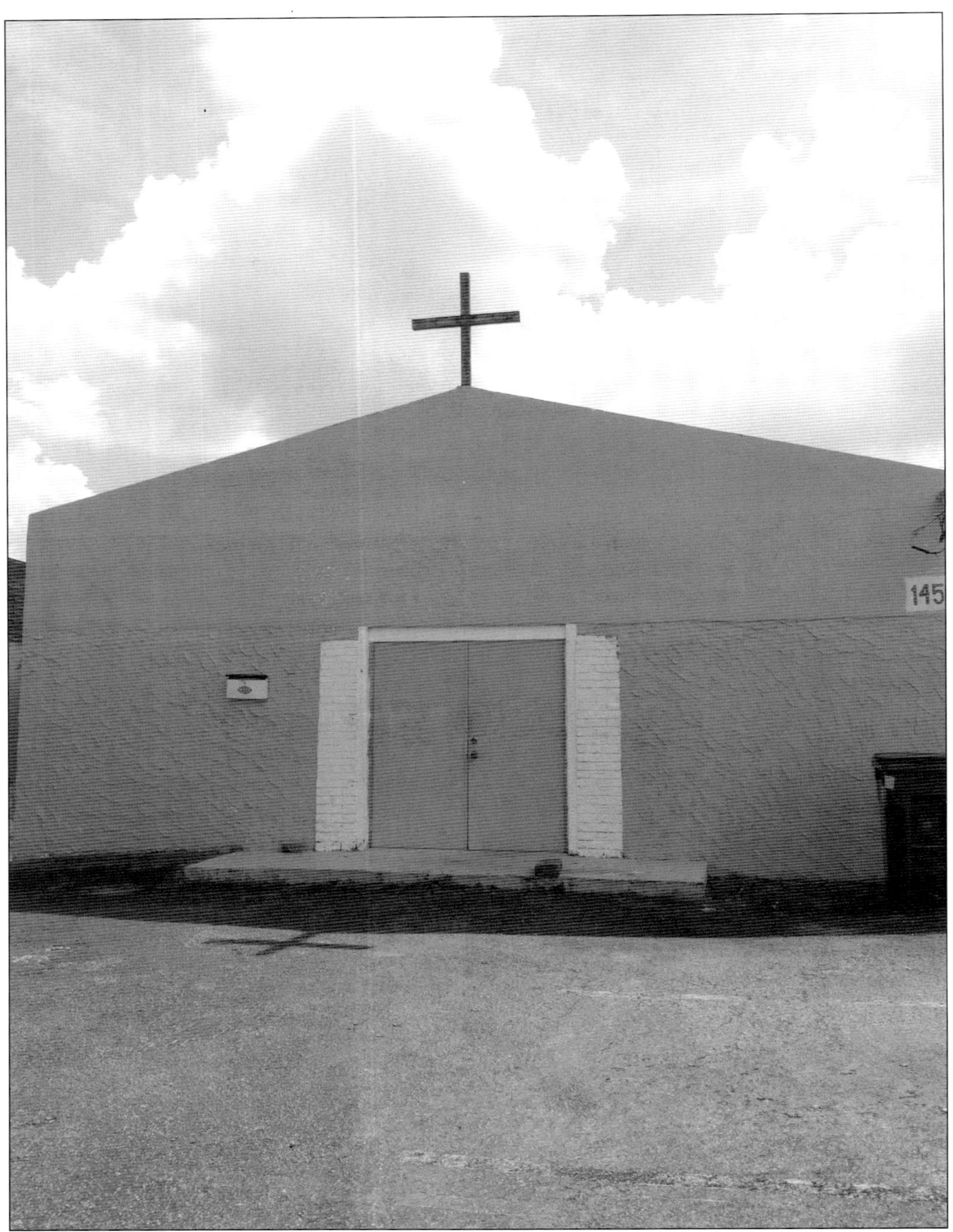

The Family Worship Center Ministries International, Inc., was founded in 1982 by Pastor Alonzo Fraser. This Pentecostal church began by parishioners meeting in the recreation center at Richmond Park. Pastor Fraser founded the church to provide a comprehensive approach to living by incorporating spiritual, economic, and physical wellness. Above, their current church building is photographed off Carver Drive.

Four

Social Life

In the 1950s, when Miami was still segregated, blacks had a nice assortment of social venues to choose from. Black men and women would dress very stylish, and actually, most wore tailored clothing. The women would don beautiful dresses, some being made from *Vogue* patterns. The men would wear pantsuits particularly styled for their body type. Most men would go to King the Tailor and get "T's," which were tailored slacks.

Their social scene was full of theaters, live entertainment, and dancing. The nightlife for blacks in Miami was in two distinct areas, Overtown and Coconut Grove. These two neighborhoods were full of thriving black businesses that people took pride in patronizing. In Overtown, people would frequent "the strip," which was on NW Second Avenue from Sixth Street to Tenth Street. This area was home to the Knight Beat at Sir John Hotel, the Island Club at the Harlem Square Gardens Hotel, the Fiesta at the Mary Elizabeth Hotel, the Elks, and the Nut Club.

In Coconut Grove, the action took place on Grand Avenue. It was home to restaurants, nightclubs, and theaters. For entertainment, blacks would go to the Tiki Bar, the Poinciana, the Gil Spot, and the Ace Theater. This area was also home to the Dew Drop Inn, a drugstore off Grand Avenue.

Once integration occurred and blacks were allowed access onto Miami Beach, they began to go to other venues for entertainment. These locations were Climax, the Castaway's, the Diplomat, Copa City, the Eden Roc, the Playboy Club, the Deauville, and the Fountainbleau Hotel. In addition, other spots opened like Big Daddy's Lounge and the Inferno.

Other social activities for the residents were conducted in the community. There were block parties as well as socializing at Richmond Heights Park.

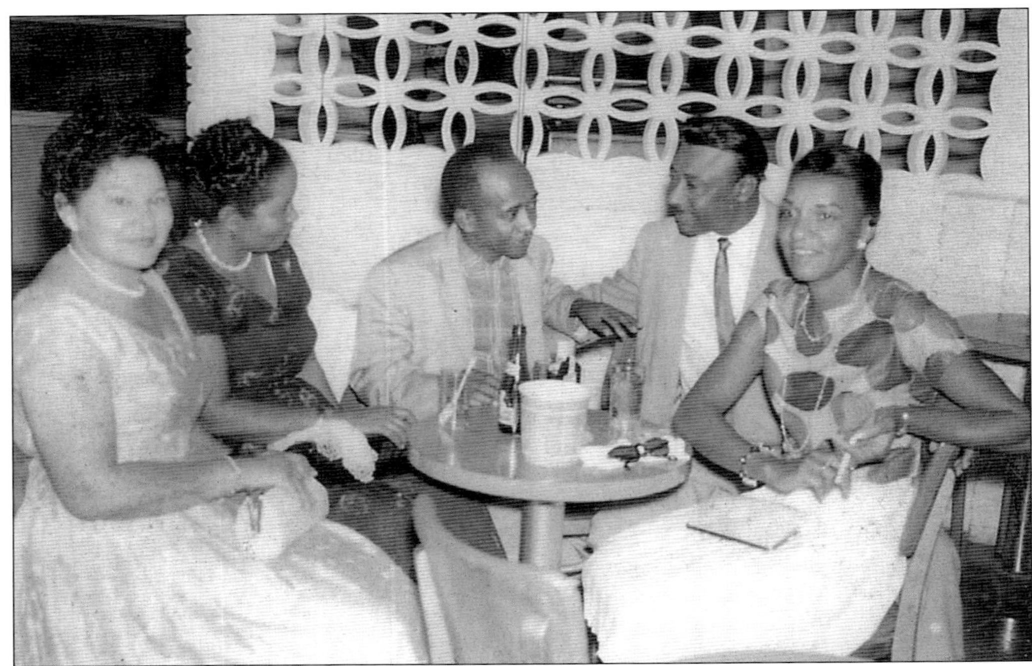

This picture captures the essence of nightlife in Miami in the late 1950s and early 1960s. This photograph is of the Knight Beat nightclub, which was located on NW Second Avenue between Sixth and Tenth Streets. In this photograph are, from left to right. Ella Jones; Frances Palmer; Archibald Pinder, *Miami Times* writer; Clyde Killens, club owner; and a Ms. Jarrett. (Courtesy of Archibald Pinder.)

No 207629 IDENTIFICATION CARD

Name Charlie HARPER, Jr.

Employed Whelan Drug Store

Local Address 3461 Elizabeth St., Coco

Description: Age 30 Height 5-8 Weight 143

Eyes Har. Hair B&K Build Med

This card to be used for Identification Purposes only

MIAMI BEACH POLICE DEPARTMENT

Date NOV 2 1953 By R. J. SHEPARD

In 1953, for blacks to go onto Miami Beach, they had to have special identification from the Miami Beach Police Department that would allow them access. This identification was granted to blacks who worked on Miami Beach. The identification shown is for Charlie Harper, who worked at Whelan Drug Store, and was issued on November 2, 1953.

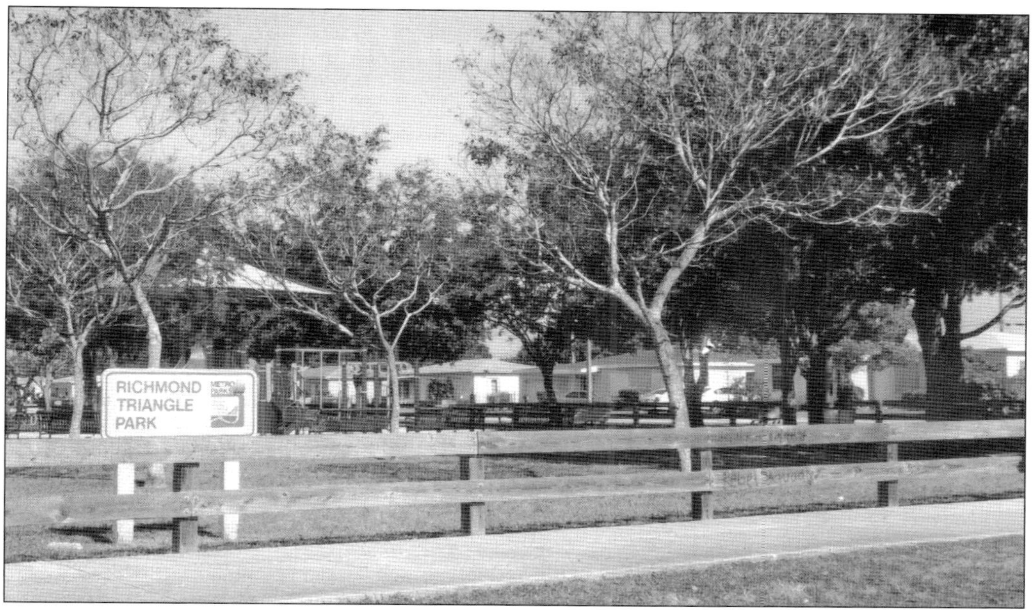

Richmond Triangle Park is located on the intersecting streets of Perry Drive, Graves Drive, and Polk Street. The developer dedicated the park in March 1956. Some 21 years later, a master plan was prepared and landscaping followed and was completed on January 26, 1983. The park is now fully developed with a tot playground, walkway, and landscaping.

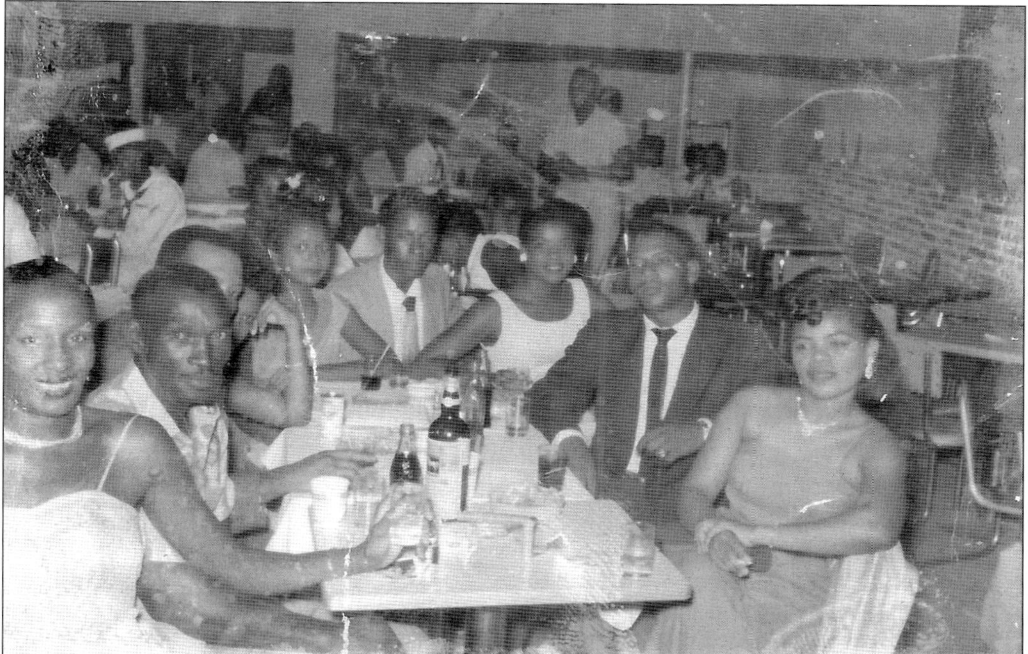

Richmond Heights resident Alice Gaines is shown at a table among many friends at the Tiki Bar in Coconut Grove located off Grand Avenue. This picture was taken around 1956. Alice is seated in the first seat on the right. Also shown in the photograph is a uniformed Navy officer in the background. (Courtesy of Cecilia Gaines Williams.)

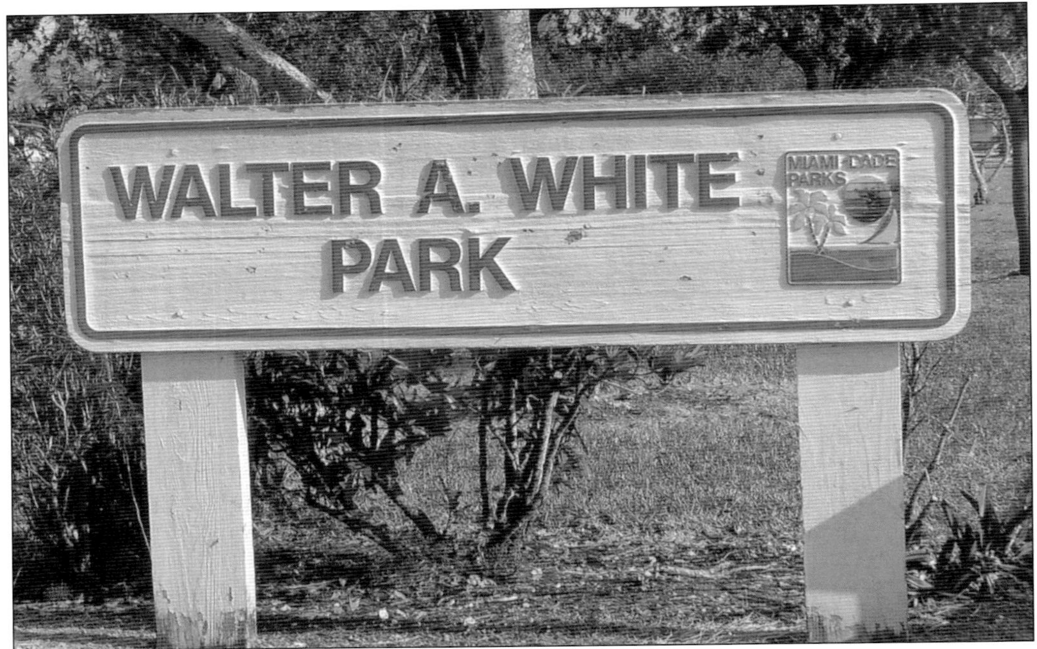

St. Martin Park was dedicated on December 12, 1956. The board of county commissioners renamed the park to Walter A. White Park through Resolution R-170-85, dated February 5, 1985. The master plan for this park was completed on September 22, 1977. The landscape plan was finalized on January 26, 1983. Walter A. White opened Richmond Heights Elementary School on September 4, 1951, as the principal.

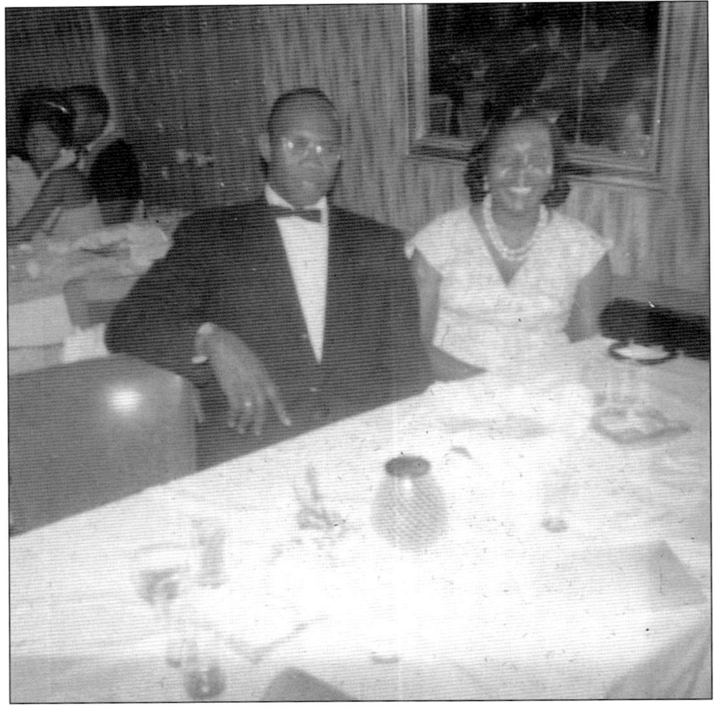

Lt. Taylor Calvin Jackson and Mary Evelyn Jackson met at Tuskegee Institute and were married in Miami, Florida. They settled in Richmond Heights and moved into their home in 1956 on Polk Street. This is a picture of the couple at son Isaac's senior prom for Mays High School. The event took place at the Everglades Hotel in downtown Miami in 1965. (Courtesy of the Jackson family.)

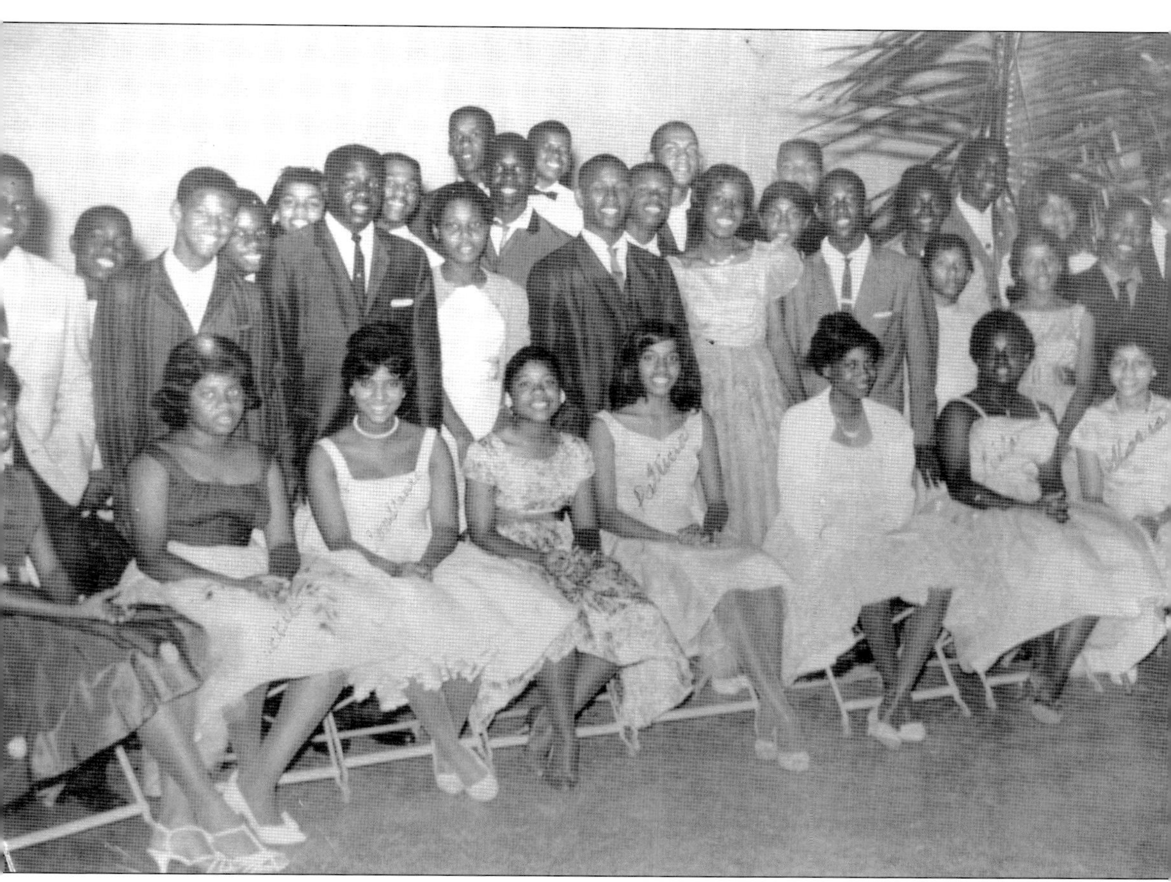

Patricia Ann Harper and friends celebrate at her sweet 16 birthday party at the Richmond Heights Recreation Center in 1961. Some attendees included Arlie Armstrong, Jackie Cambridge, Constance Grant, Clara Nell Stubbs, Beverly Bell, Leila Hobbs, Gloria Dowdell, Wallace Bates, Calvin Grant, Terry Grant, Fleetwood Price, Ernest McArthur Gatewood, Judy Ross, Berry Sweeting, Samuel Mackey, Johnny Jones, Evenlyn Franklin, Lenora Cambridge, Sam Miller, Patricia Hunt, Lloyd Chism, Andrew Greene, and Gwen Armstrong.

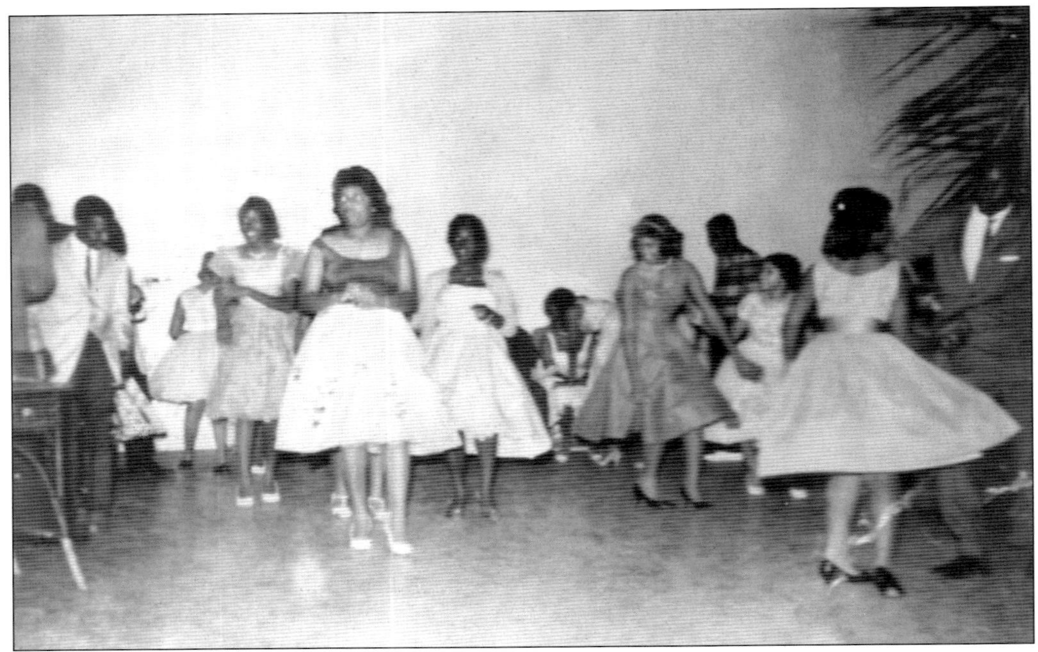

During the 1960s, a black girl's sweet 16 birthday party was her coming-out party. Girls knew to wear a dressy dress with a crinoline slip and a pair of high-heel shoes. Young men would wear a dress shirt, tie, jacket, and dress pants. This event was held in the Richmond Heights Recreation Center and post office.

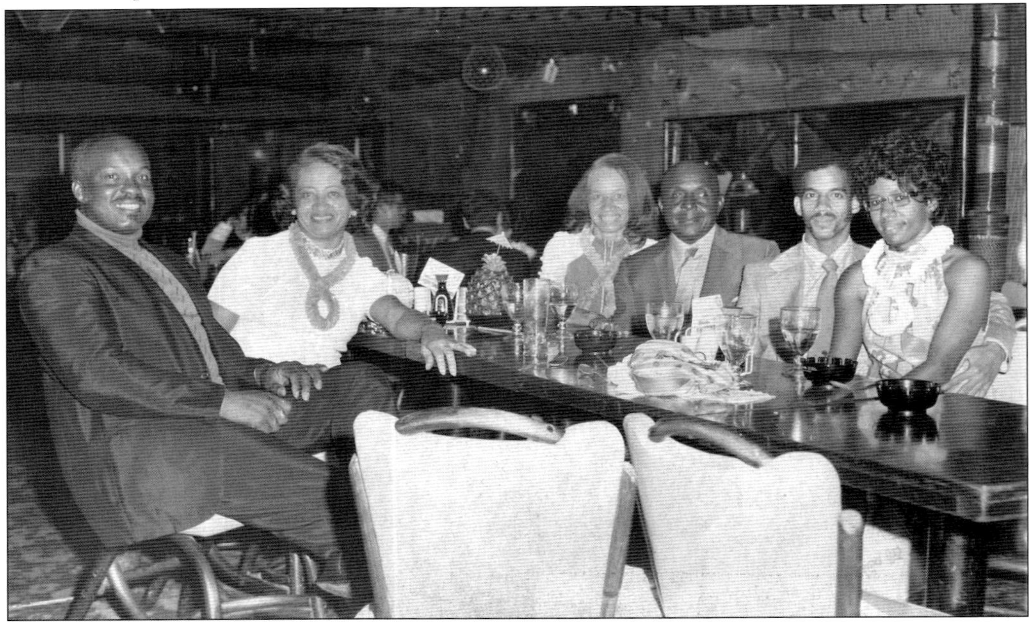

Leroy and Rosemary Stringer Sr. are pictured with two other couples at a Polynesian restaurant in Fort Lauderdale, Florida, in 1970. Pictured are, from left to right, Leroy Stringer Sr., Rosemary Stringer, a Mrs. Williams, Roosevelt Williams, Ronald Davidson, and a Mrs. Davidson. (Courtesy of the Stringer family.)

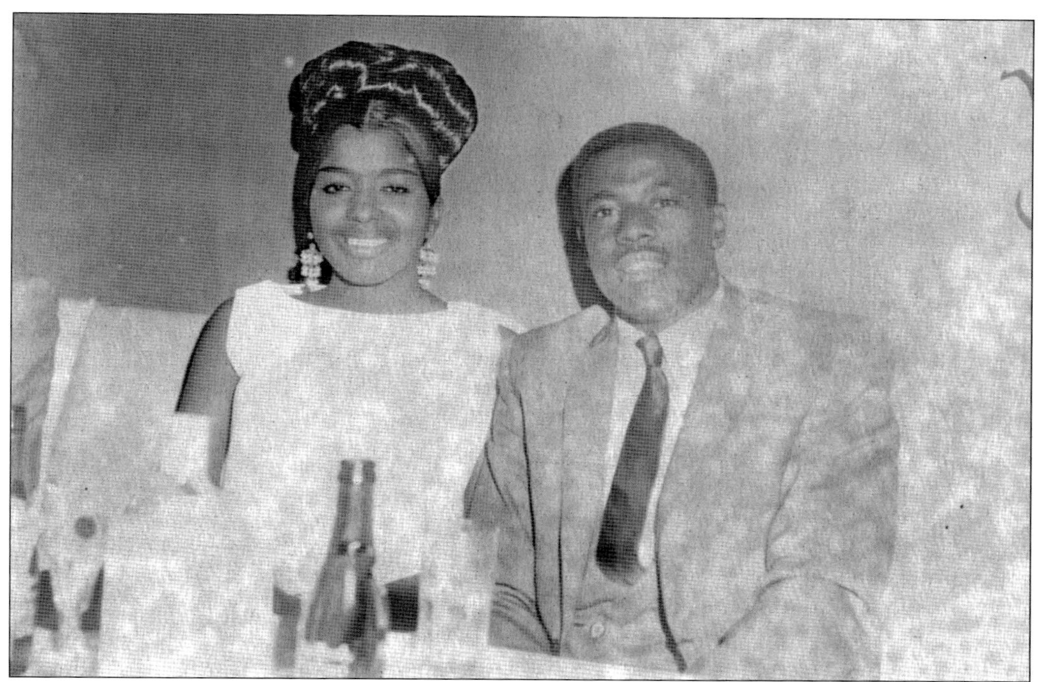

Willie and Patricia Garrett decided in 1969 that they were not going to stick around in their Civic Center apartment for a $20 rent increase. So they decided to plant their roots in Richmond Heights. They were very familiar with this community. Patricia grew up in the neighborhood on Monroe Street, Willie's aunt Jeannean Britt also lived in the neighborhood, and they were married there. It was only fitting that the two would call Polk Street home. They both retired from Dade County Public Schools. Patricia is currently the Florida Democratic committeewoman for Precinct No. 802. This picture was taken on their first date at the Dupont Hotel in 1968.

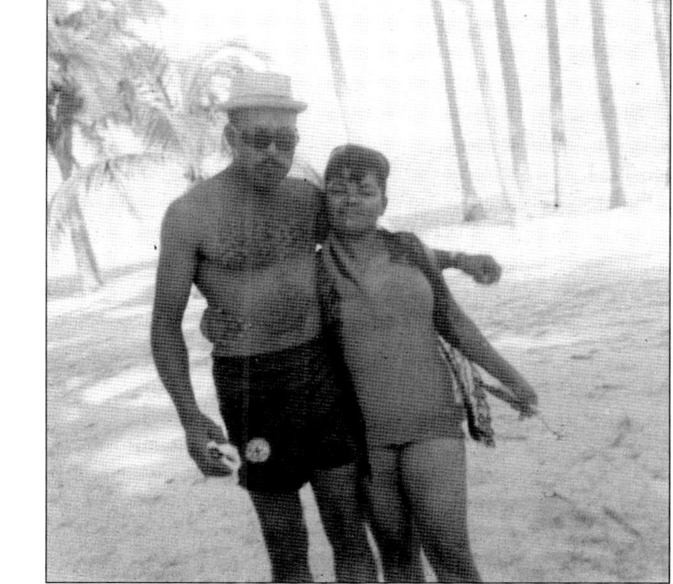

George Gaines served in the US Army during World War II. After retiring, George found comfort in helping at Richmond Heights Park as the first lifeguard for the pool. George is pictured with wife, Alice, at the only black beach, Virginia Key Beach. (Courtesy of Cecilia Gaines Williams.)

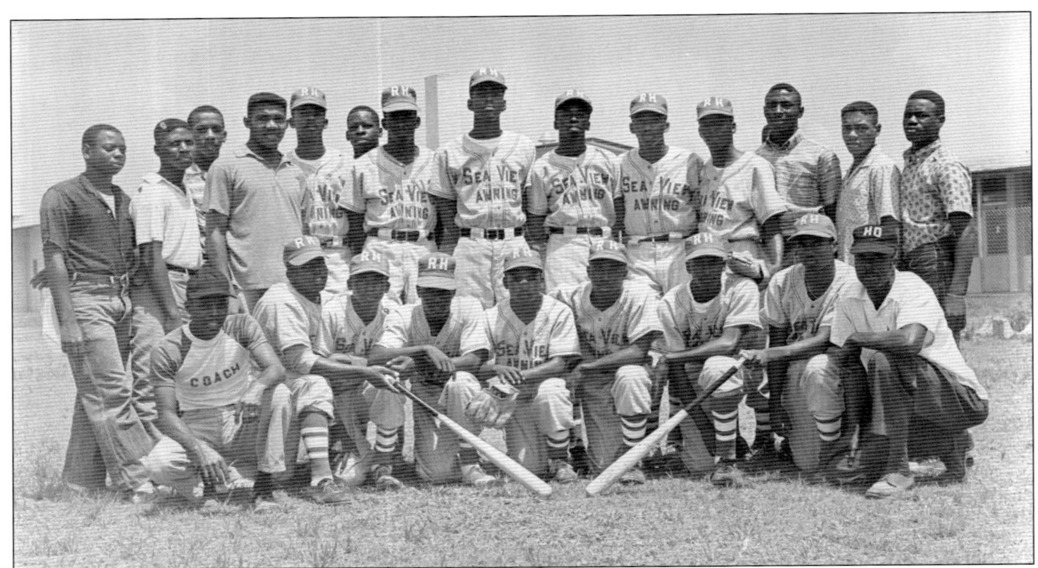

The first baseball team was the Richmond Heights Red Sock team for Martin Memorial Youth Council. Sea-View Awnings sponsored the team. Pictured are, from left to right, (first row) Gad Mays, Enoch Dukes, Ronald Wims, Carl Crawford, Nelson Roberts, Otis Caldwell, Charles Hankerson, Charles Randolph, and Eddie Townsend; (second row) Cornelius Knowles, Alfred Young, Frederick Anderson, Sam Miller, Roy Bentley, Ronald Ferguson, Solomon Hedgemon, Arvis Bethel, Fuellen Vaughan, Andrew Greene, Nathaniel Brooks, Jimmy Douglas, Ira Knight, and Isaiah Hill. (Courtesy of the University of Miami Libraries Special Collection.)

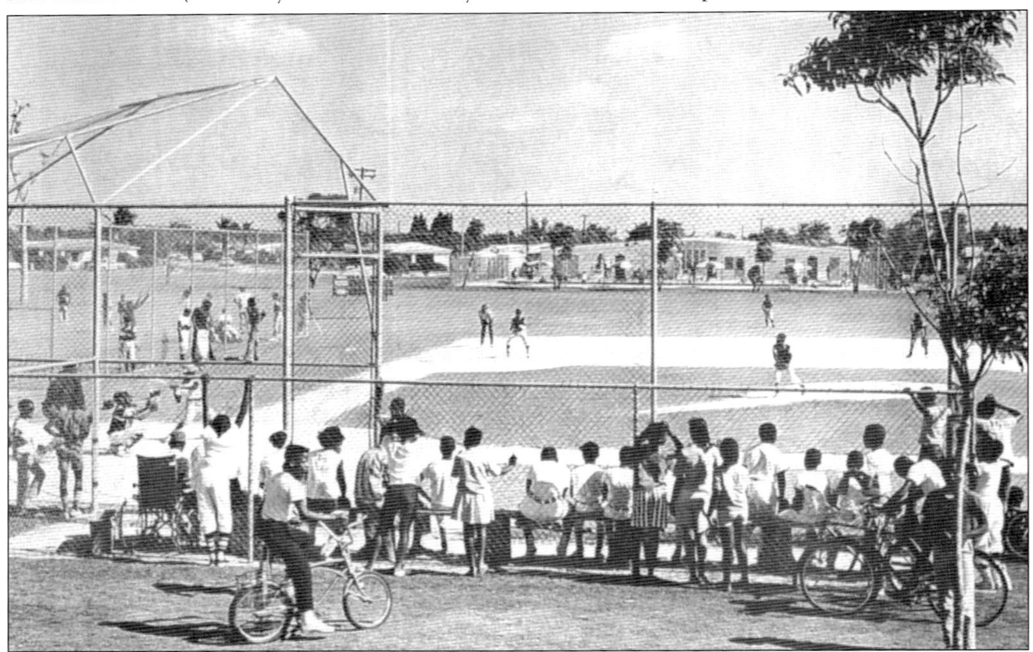

Although acreage was set aside to build a park, it was just a thought in 1949 when the community began. This photograph captures a Little League baseball game toward the end of the 1950s and early 1960s. (Courtesy of the Richmond Heights Homeowners Association.)

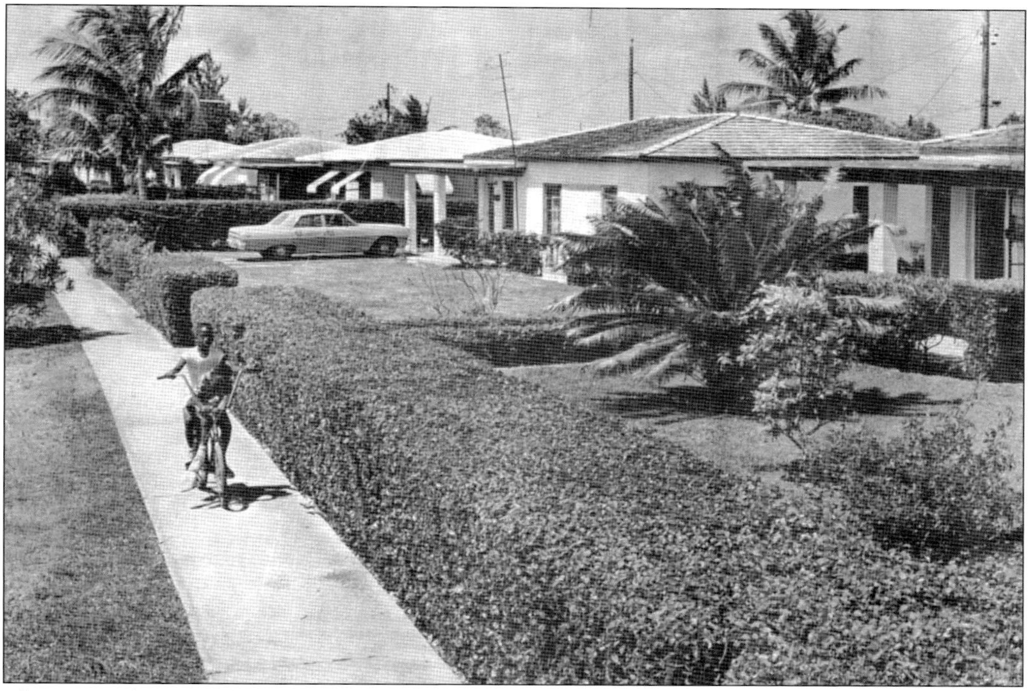

This 1960s photograph encapsulates the essence of life in Richmond Heights for the time. Residents describe it as carefree. Parents did not fret over their children playing outside and would even leave their homes unlocked. This photograph shows Randy Butler riding his bike on Jackson Street. (Courtesy of the Richmond Heights Homeowners Association.)

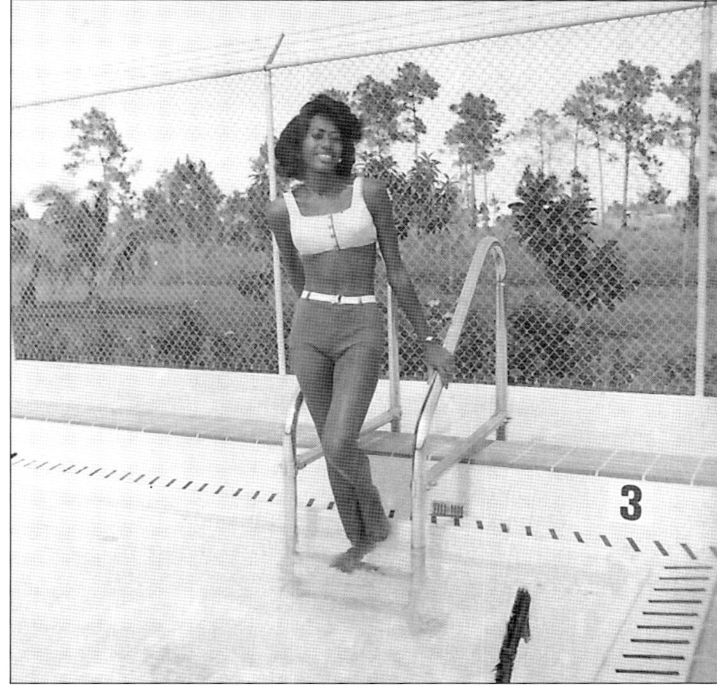

For fun, blacks in Miami would go to Virginia Key Beach to go swimming until Richmond Heights park was developed. It provided a place for people to play tennis and basketball. It also was home to the first public pool in a community where black people were able to swim. By November 1, 1976, the Richmond Heights Recreation Center, tot lot, and pool bathhouse were complete and ready for public use. This is a photograph of the Richmond Heights swimming pool. (Courtesy of Mays Senior High School Alumni Association.)

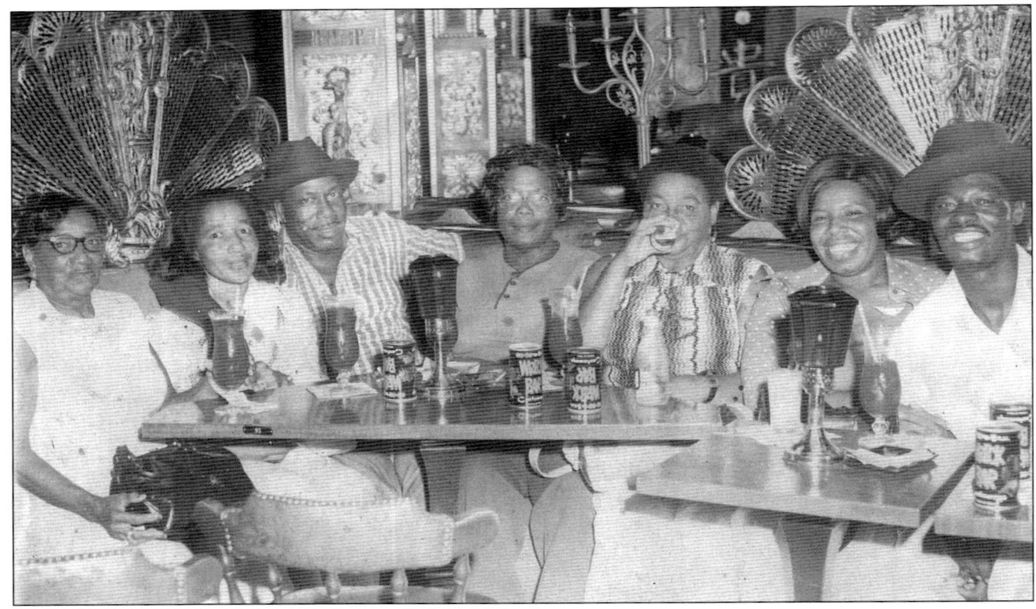

The Castaway's was located on 163rd Street and Collins Avenue in Miami Beach. This was the spot to go to in the late 1960s and early 1970s to meet up with friends and listen to music. It was sure to be a payday week for Richmond Heights' resident Dorothy Chattic and friends. Pictured are, from left to right, Mandy Smith, Emma Gene Ferguson, Mutt Thompson, Gertrude Thomas, Virgia Davis, Dorothy Chattic, and Enoch Smiley. (Courtesy of Amanda Chattic.)

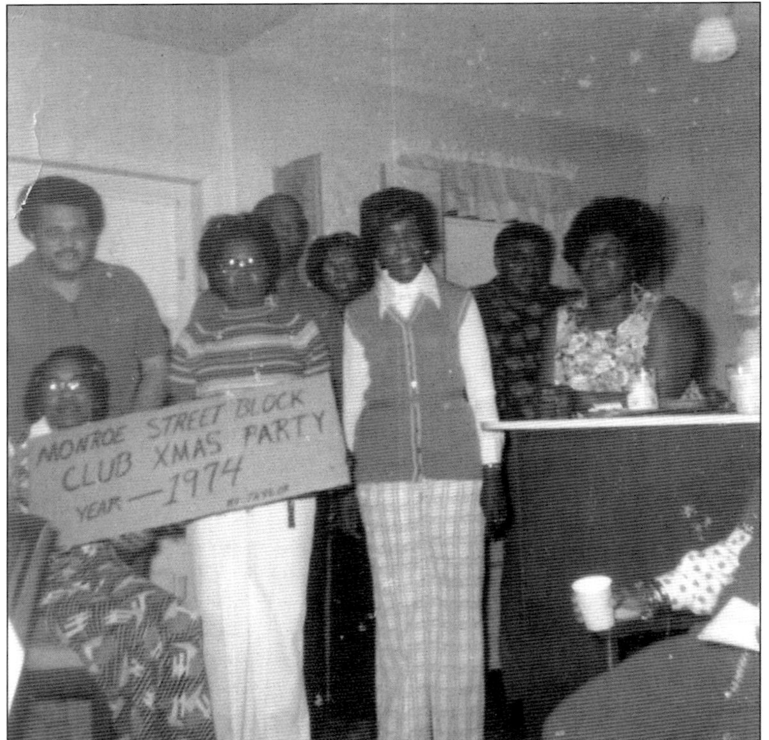

The Monroe Street Block Club would gather weekly to serve as an extended family unit. Members would always find reasons to celebrate and get together. From going on vacations together to gatherings at each other's homes, the families on Monroe Street had a true bond that spread to other streets. Pictured at left is the club gathering to celebrate Christmas 1974 at the Taylors' home on Monroe Street. (Courtesy of Taylor family.)

George and Inez Swain signed their contract for lot 4, block 25 on December 13, 1949. George was in the Navy and worked as a skycap at Pan American Airlines. Inez worked at Frank C. Martin Elementary as a maid. This photograph is of their daughter and nephews at a family gathering. Pictured are, from left to right, (first row) Cameron Payne and Harold Raymond Payne; (second row) Michael Payne, Alfreda Payne, and Betty Swain Askew.

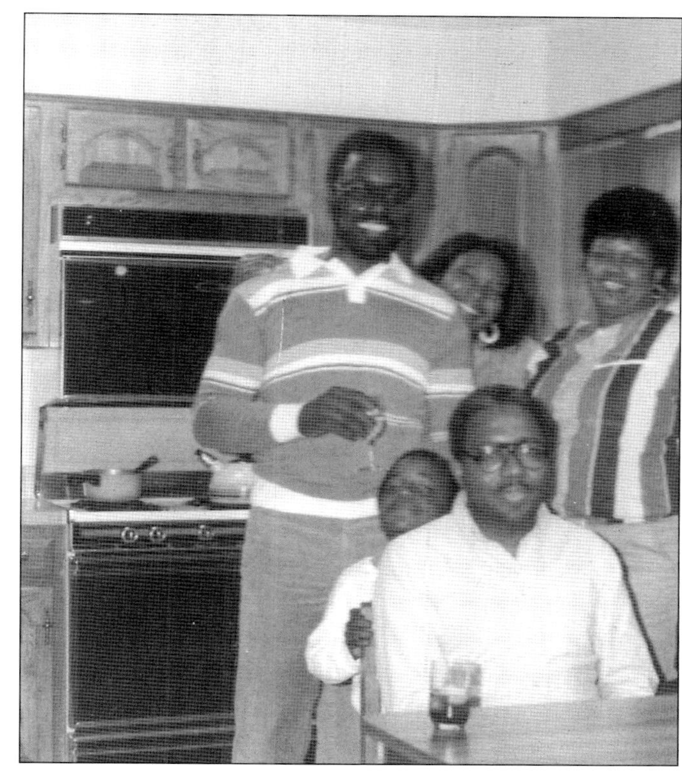

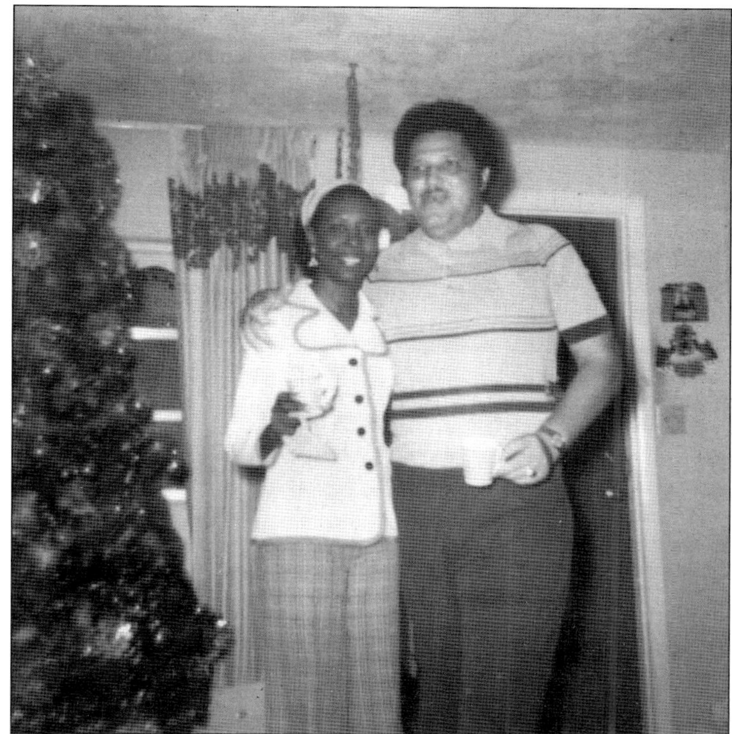

Robert and Ida McKay moved to Richmond Heights in 1956 and purchased a home on Monroe Street. They have three children, Lissette, Robert Jr., and Ivan. They both retired from Miami-Dade County Public Schools. Pictured are Ida and Robert at the Taylors' home for a Christmas party in 1974. (Courtesy of the Taylor family.)

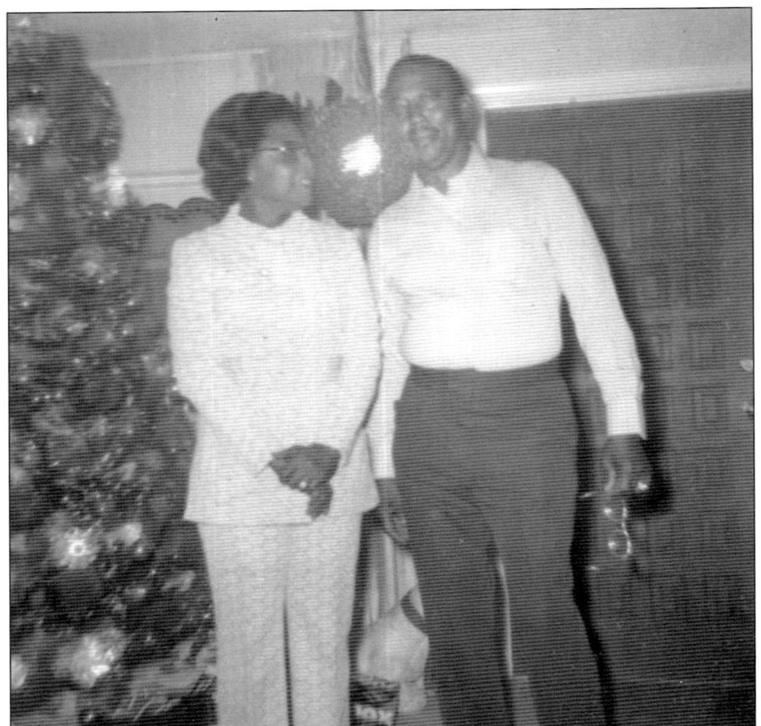

"Christmas just ain't Christmas without the one you love," sang the O'Jays. It is Christmastime in Richmond Heights, and who better to spend the time with other than family and friends. Pictured are, from left to right, Ernestine Chism and Welton Chism Jr. in 1974 at the Taylors' home on Monroe Street. (Courtesy of Taylor family.)

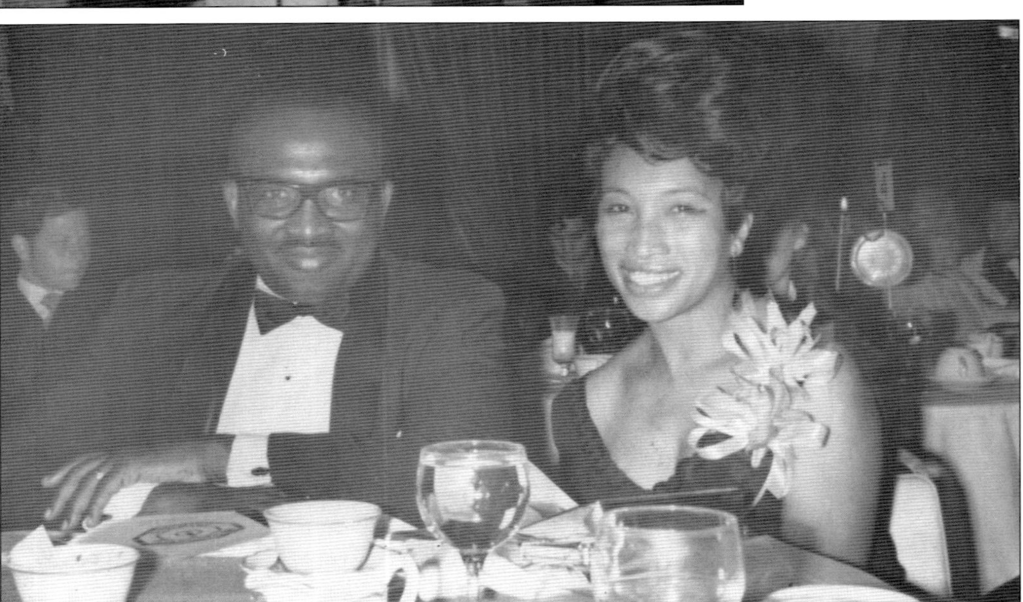

The Marshalls are shown here in the 1960s. James Marshall retired in 2003 from the field of education. He was an administrator for Miami-Dade County Public Schools and an adjunct professor at Nova University. Dr. Wylamerle Glover-Marshall retired from Miami-Dade County Public Schools as an administrator. They both serve the community of Richmond Heights by overseeing the Richmond Heights Homeowners Association and the Neighborhood Resource Center. James Marshall is the founding member of both corporations. (Courtesy of Marshall family.)

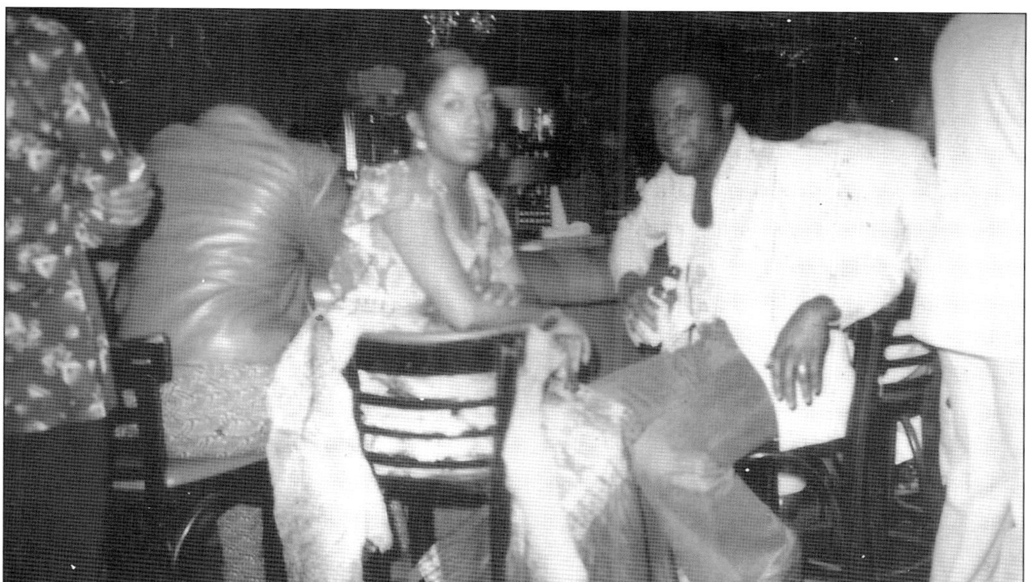

Patricia Harper Garrett and Willie Garrett Jr. would meet up with friends on the weekends to enjoy Miami's nightlife. This photograph captures the couple lounging at the Jet-Away, December 1975. The Jet-Away was off Thirty-sixth Street in Brownsville. People would gather to have drinks, listen to live music, dance, and eat the Caribbean dish called souse.

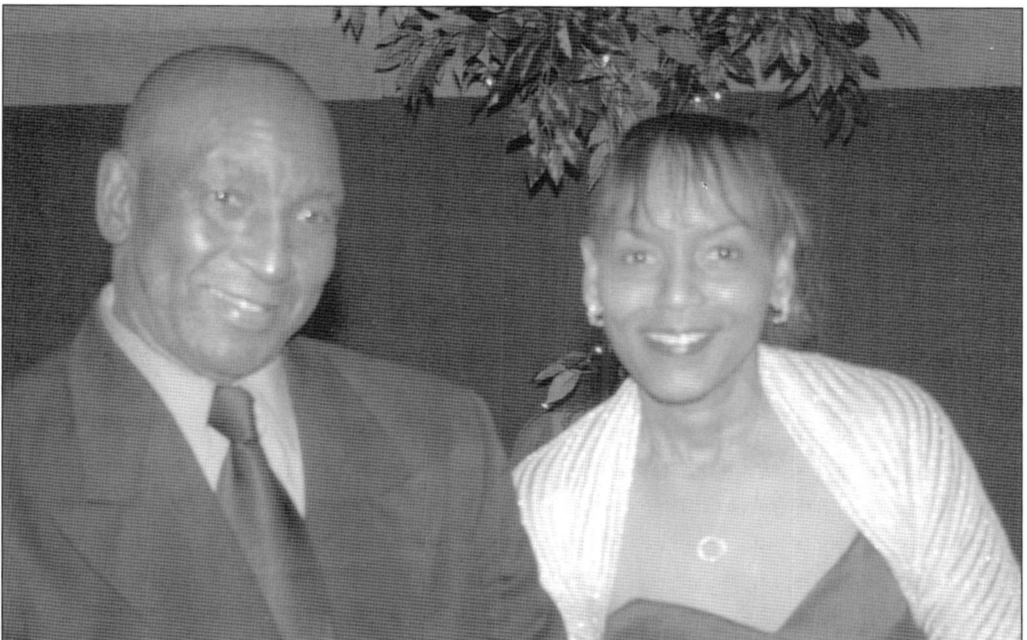

Ken and Mona Jackson are shown celebrating Richmond Heights' 60th anniversary at Signature Gardens. Ken and Mona retired from Miami-Dade County Public Schools. Mona Jackson actually grew up in Richmond Heights and was in the first graduating class from Frank C. Martin Elementary School. Her last assignment with Miami-Dade County Public Schools before retiring was to serve as principal for Richmond Middle School.

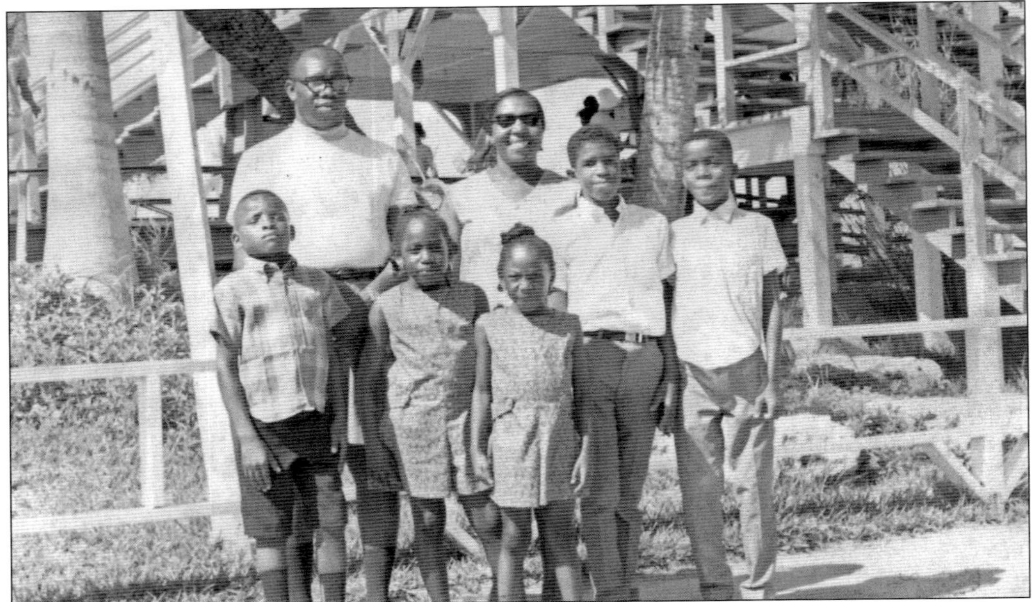

Mary Evelyn Jackson was a teacher for Miami-Dade County Public Schools, and often she would take students on outings with her family. This is a picture of Mary with her students and family at Pirates World in Hollywood, Florida. Pictured from left to right are (first row) unidentified, Daphne Jackson, Kim Jackson, and two unidentified R.R. Moton Elementary students; (second row) Lt. Taylor Jackson and Mary Jackson. (Courtesy of the Jackson family.)

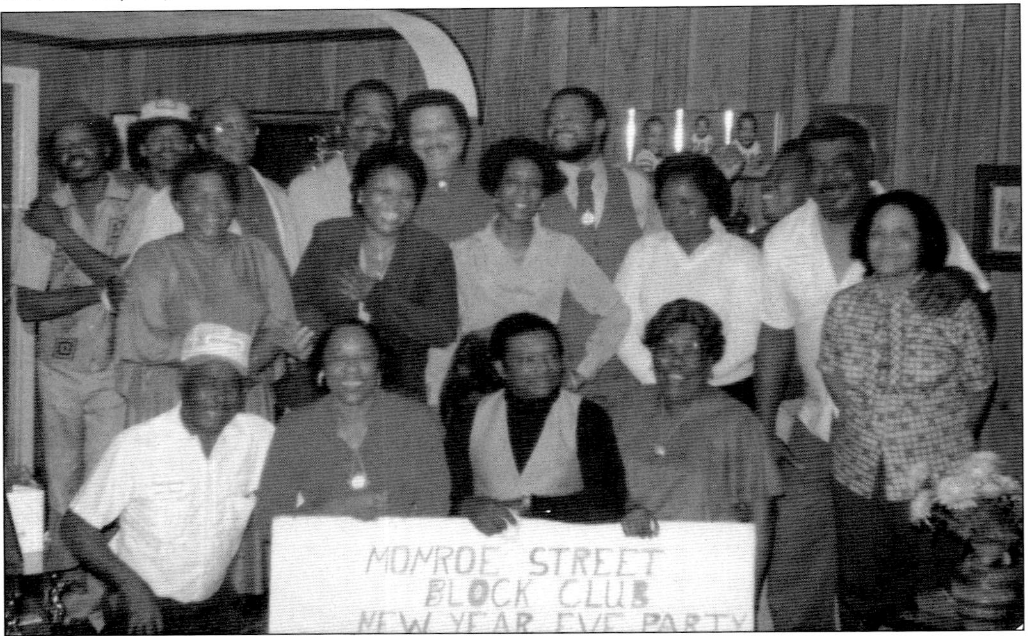

Pictured is a 1980 New Year's Eve celebration at the Taylors' home on Monroe Street. The routine for New Year's Eve was set in stone: families would agree to go to a host home and the guests would bring the food and drinks. After years of get-togethers, the neighbors on Monroe Street are still at it. (Courtesy of Taylor family.)

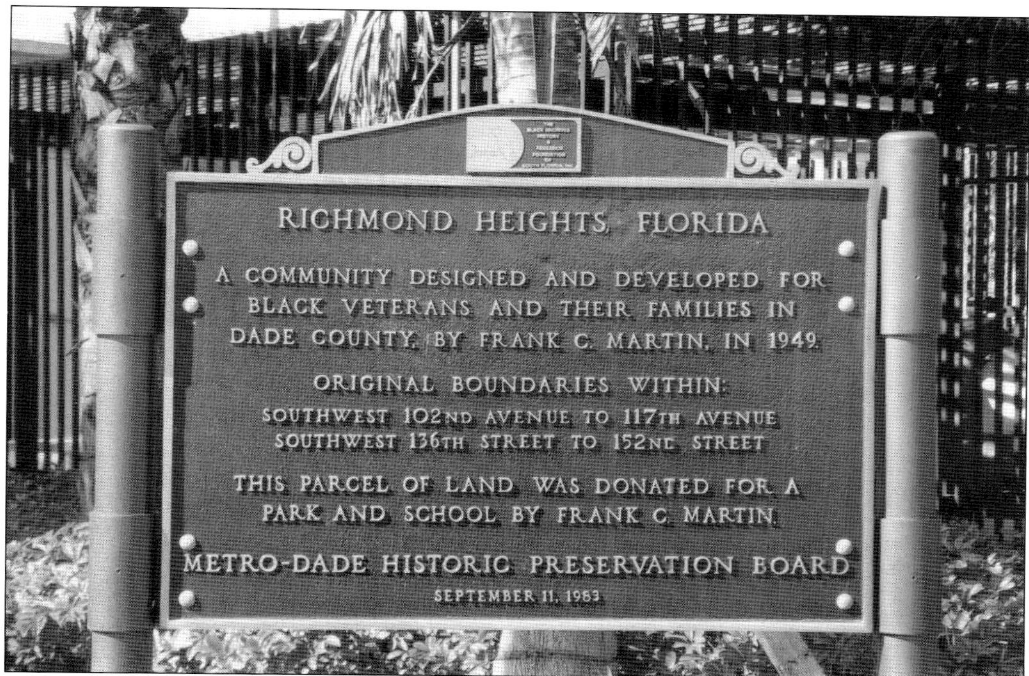

The Richmond Heights marker permanently resides at Sgt. Joseph Delancy Park. It was in 1977 that Janice Aranha Chillis submitted the proposal to have the unique neighborhood included in Dade County's historical records. On September 11, 1983, the marker was finally unveiled by Commissioner Dennis Moss with a full day of events surrounding the unveiling.

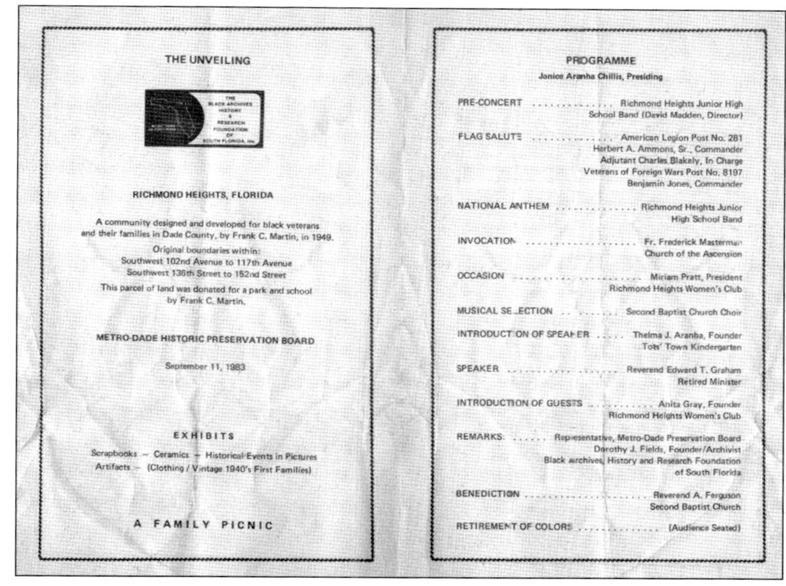

THE UNVEILING

THE BLACK ARCHIVES HISTORY & RESEARCH FOUNDATION OF SOUTH FLORIDA, Inc.

RICHMOND HEIGHTS, FLORIDA

A community designed and developed for black veterans and their families in Dade County, by Frank C. Martin, in 1949.

Original boundaries within:
Southwest 102nd Avenue to 117th Avenue
Southwest 136th Street to 152nd Street

This parcel of land was donated for a park and school by Frank C. Martin.

METRO-DADE HISTORIC PRESERVATION BOARD

September 11, 1983

EXHIBITS

Scrapbooks – Ceramics – Historical Events in Pictures
Artifacts – (Clothing / Vintage 1940's First Families)

A FAMILY PICNIC

PROGRAMME

Janice Aranha Chillis, Presiding

PRE-CONCERT .... Richmond Heights Junior High School Band (David Madden, Director)

FLAG SALUTE .... American Legion Post No. 281
Herbert A. Ammons, Sr., Commander
Adjutant Charles Blakely, In Charge
Veterans of Foreign Wars Post No. 8197
Benjamin Jones, Commander

NATIONAL ANTHEM .... Richmond Heights Junior High School Band

INVOCATION .... Fr. Frederick Masterman
Church of the Ascension

OCCASION .... Miriam Pratt, President
Richmond Heights Women's Club

MUSICAL SELECTION .... Second Baptist Church Choir

INTRODUCTION OF SPEAKER ..... Thelma J. Aranha, Founder
Tots' Town Kindergarten

SPEAKER .... Reverend Edward T. Graham
Retired Minister

INTRODUCTION OF GUESTS .... Anita Gray, Founder
Richmond Heights Women's Club

REMARKS: ...... Representative, Metro-Dade Preservation Board
Dorothy J. Fields, Founder/Archivist
Black archives, History and Research Foundation of South Florida

BENEDICTION .... Reverend A. Ferguson
Second Baptist Church

RETIREMENT OF COLORS .... (Audience Seated)

At the urging of Janice Aranha Chillis, the Metro-Dade Historic Preservation Board made it possible to add a historic marker acknowledging Richmond Heights as a community designed and developed for black war veterans and their families. This is the program from the dedication event. (Courtesy of Eddie Redding.)

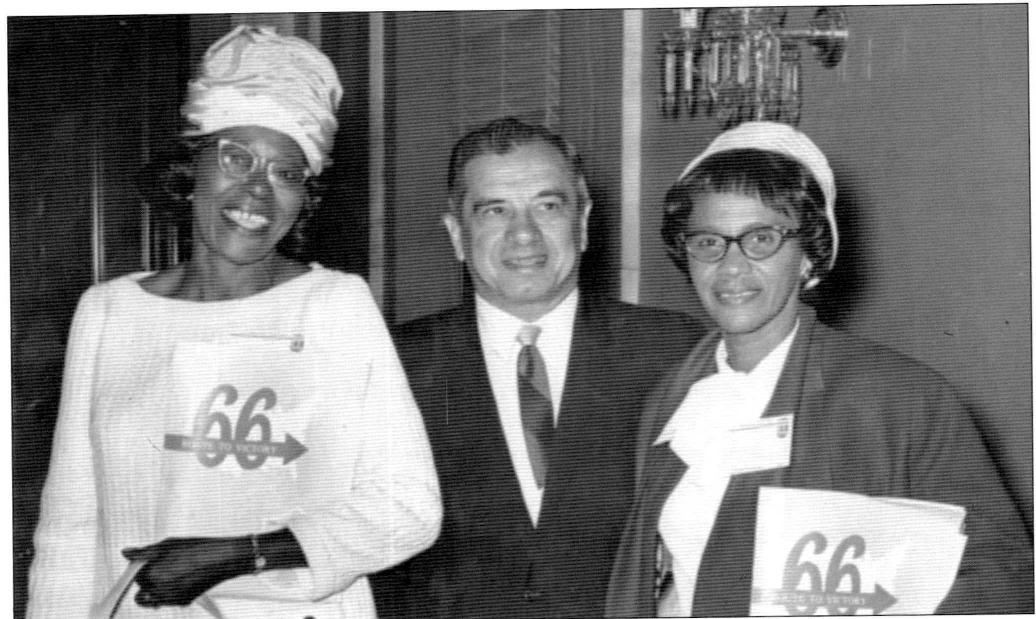

Dante Fascell was a Florida congressman who took pride in serving his Richmond Heights constituents. Yearly, Congressman Fascell would invite residents to join him for the annual Labor Day cookout. He is credited with being the force behind getting residents hired by the government in Washington. His tenure in politics was from 1984 to 1993. He retired as the chairman of the House Committee on Foreign Affairs. This photograph shows Congressman Fascell with two Richmond Heights' residents at a political function. From left to right are Valuda Waters, Dante Fascell, and Louise Bird. (Courtesy of Lee Waters family.)

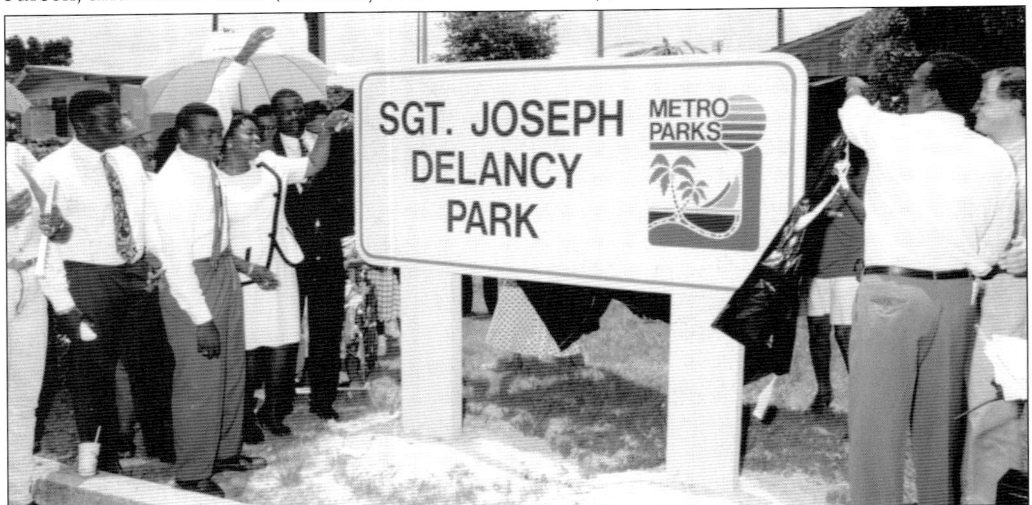

Richmond Heights Park changed its name to Sgt. Joseph Delancy Park pursuant to the board of county commissioner Resolution R-626-93, dated May 18, 1993. Commissioner Dennis Moss was instrumental in having the name changed because of the commitment made to the community by Sgt. Joseph Delancy before his death; Delancy worked for the Miami-Dade Police Department. The park was dedicated with a day of activities orchestrated by local politicians and police officers. (Courtesy of Lee Waters.)

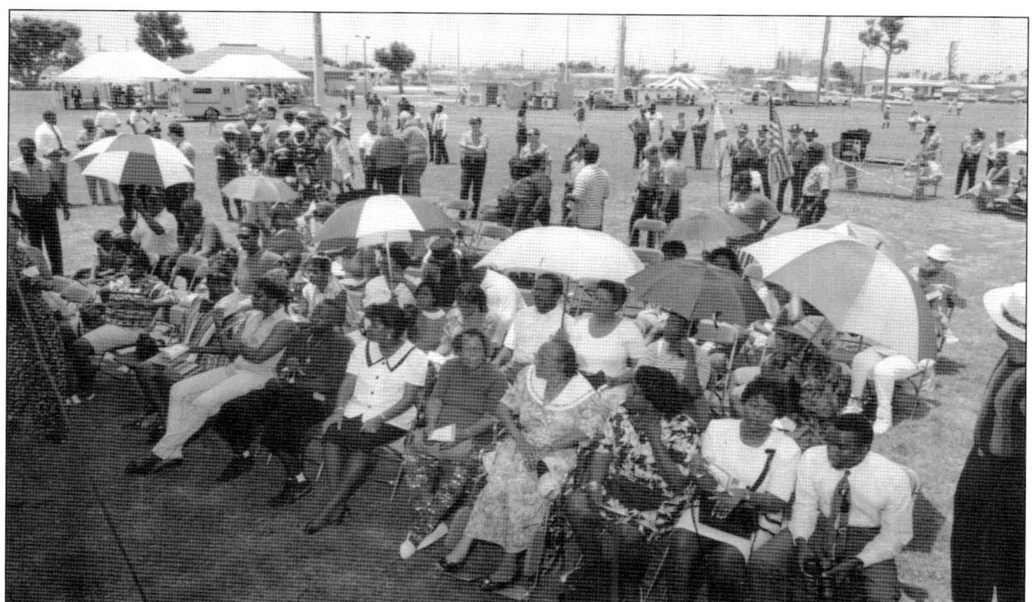

A day of events was set for May 18, 1993, including apple bobbing, clown visits, step teams, and a performance by Tre Songs. The Metro-Dade Police Department was on duty to demonstrate safety awareness. Onlookers are pictured listening to presenters during the dedication ceremony when the park's name changed from Richmond Heights Park to Sgt. Joseph Delancy Park. (Courtesy of Lee Waters.)

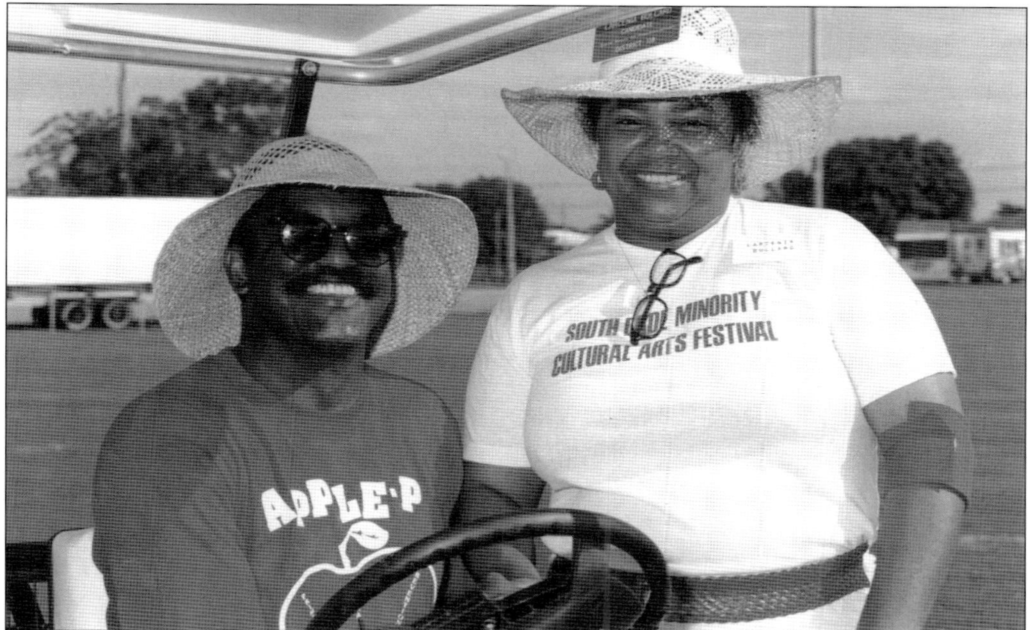

On May 18, 1993, the community came out to support the unveiling for the Richmond Heights Park name change dedication ceremony. Families gathered to participate in a day set for fun. It was all thanks to Commissioner Dennis Moss and Sen. Larcenia Bullard, who are pictured, respectively, from left to right. (Courtesy of Lee Waters.)

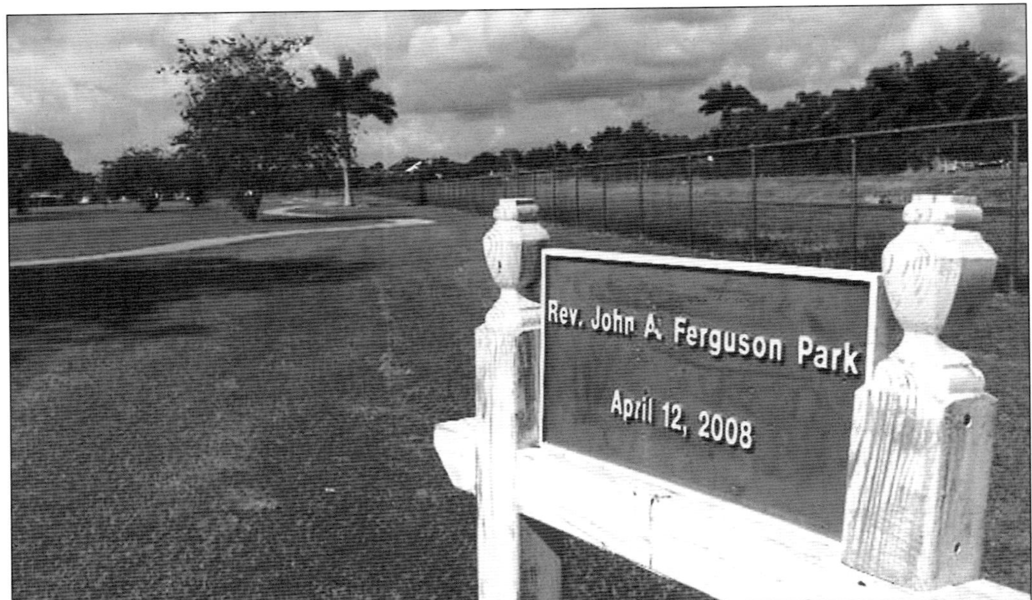

Rev. John A. Ferguson Park was dedicated on April 12, 2008. It sits adjacent to Coral Reef Senior High School and borders SW 103rd Avenue. Rev. John A. Ferguson was the founding pastor of Second Baptist Church, where he pastored for over 36 years. Second Baptist Church is located in Richmond Heights off Pinkston Drive.

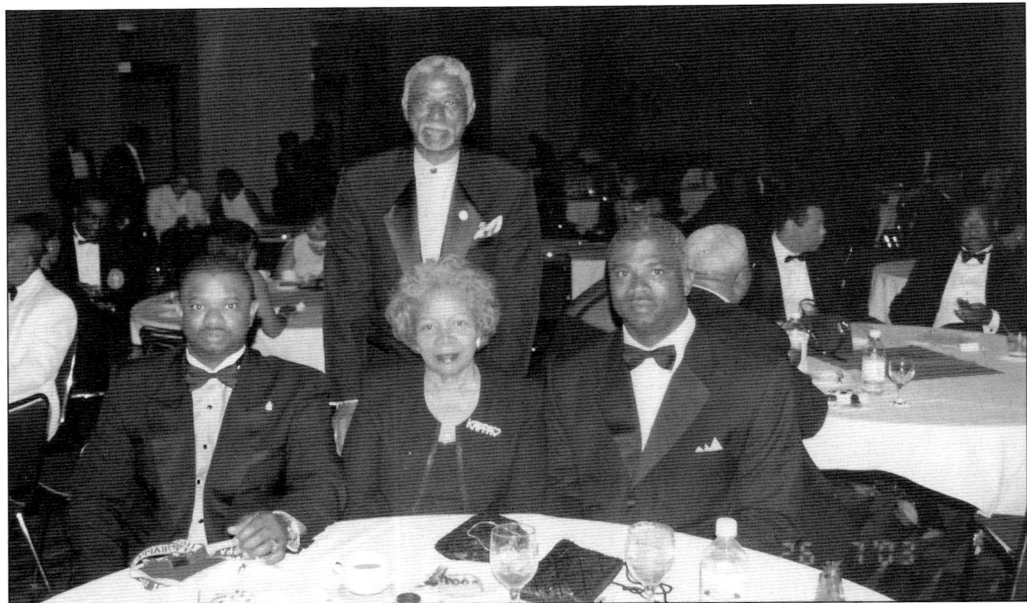
Donald Hollis Sr. and his wife, Ossie, met while in college at Alabama A&M. After several encounters, the two were smitten with each other and married. Donald and Ossie had three children, Deborah, Donald Jr., and Ronald. Pictured are, from left to right, (sitting) Ronald, Ossie, and Donald Jr.; (standing) Donald Sr., who credits George Sparks, a Richmond Heights resident, with mentoring him and being very instrumental in his move to Richmond Heights from Alabama in 1958. (Courtesy of the Hollis family.)

Five

Professional Life

Richmond Heights has been home to many black professionals and black businesses; there were grocery stores, barbershops, drugstores, doctor's offices, dentist's offices, diners, convenience stores, and gas stations. There were all things needed to allow for a self-sufficient community. Captain Martin envisioned a shopping center for entrepreneurs, so that once money got into the community, it stayed in the community.

Richmond Heights Citizen's Committee officially began to serve Richmond Heights' residents on November 13, 1954. The sole purpose of the business was to provide a unified voice for the community in areas of development in an effort to sustain the spirit in which the neighborhood was built. This nonprofit business was established by Fr. Theodore Gibson, who served as the president; Samuel Monour was vice president; Rev. Edward Graham was the business manager; William Taylor was the treasurer; Maude Dias was the financial secretary; and Susan Harris was the recording secretary.

Clarence and Olivia Edwards were the owners and pharmacists for the drugstore in the Richmond Heights community. They were known for helping others and opened Richmond Heights Drugstore, which was commonly called "the drugstore" or "Mrs. Edwards's," in 1955 off Lincoln Boulevard. This street name was later changed in Olivia Edwards's honor to Olivia Edwards Boulevard.

A total of 10 black investors decided to provide space for retailers to service the area. The investors included a Mr. Alexander, Elijah Childs, Clarence Cryer, Dr. Linkston Cryer, George Demeritt, Dr. Herbert Greene, Donald Hollis, a Mr. Wilson, and Willie Redding. 7-Eleven was the anchor store in their strip mall, known to residents as "The Front."

Other memorable local businesses were Barrett-Fryar-Thompson Funeral home, located off Lincoln Boulevard; the Dorsey's Pure Oil gas station, owned by community residents Mantley and Mary Dorsey; Taylor's Service Station, managed by Bill Taylor with everything from bodywork to painting; and Stylecraft Cleaners, the go-to cleaners for dry cleaning, laundry service, and shoe repair.

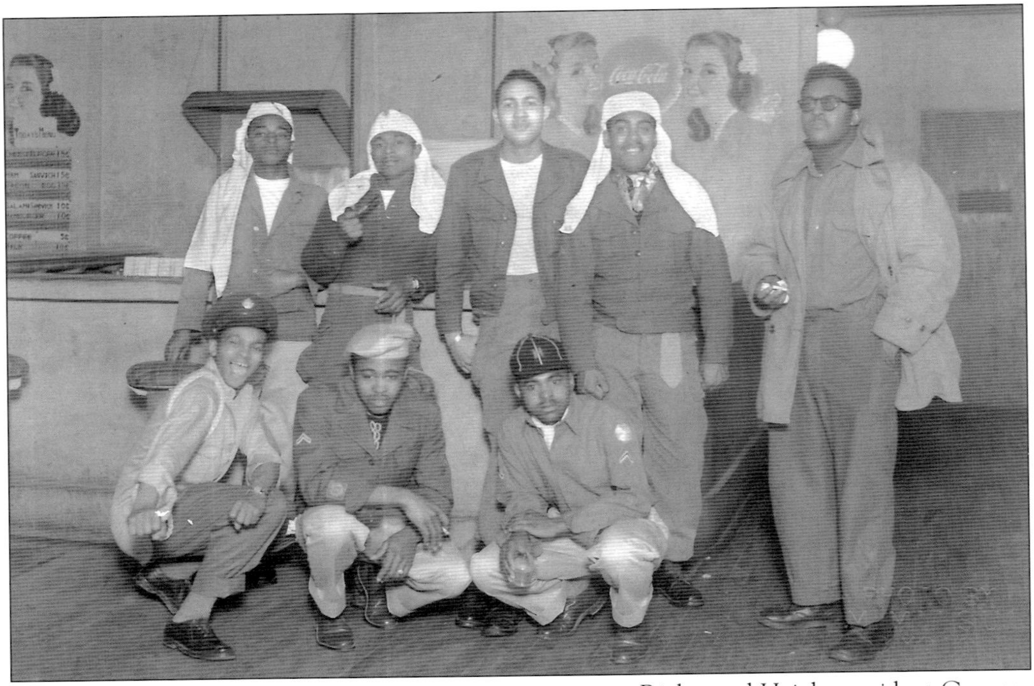

Richmond Heights resident George Gaines, standing at far right, is photographed with unidentified troops in Japan on April 13, 1949. In 1949, a cup of coffee and a cheeseburger only cost 20¢. George received his honorable discharge from the US Army on August 5, 1952, as a private first class. (Courtesy of the Gaines family.)

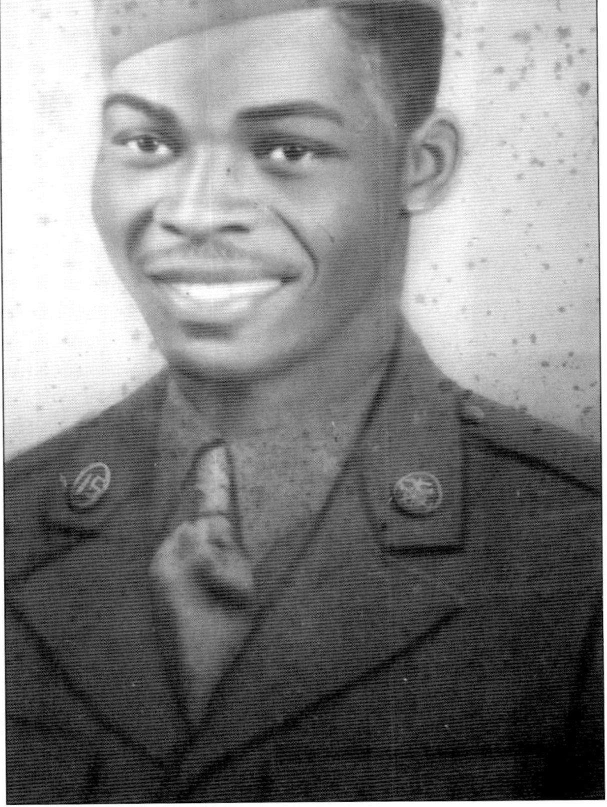

Gladstone Taylor Sr. served in the Army as a US sergeant during World War II. He received his honorable discharge in 1946 and moved to Richmond Heights. He was a member of Martin Memorial African Methodist Episcopal Church. While there, he was a member of the mass choir. He also worked for the US Postal Service. (Courtesy of the Taylor family.)

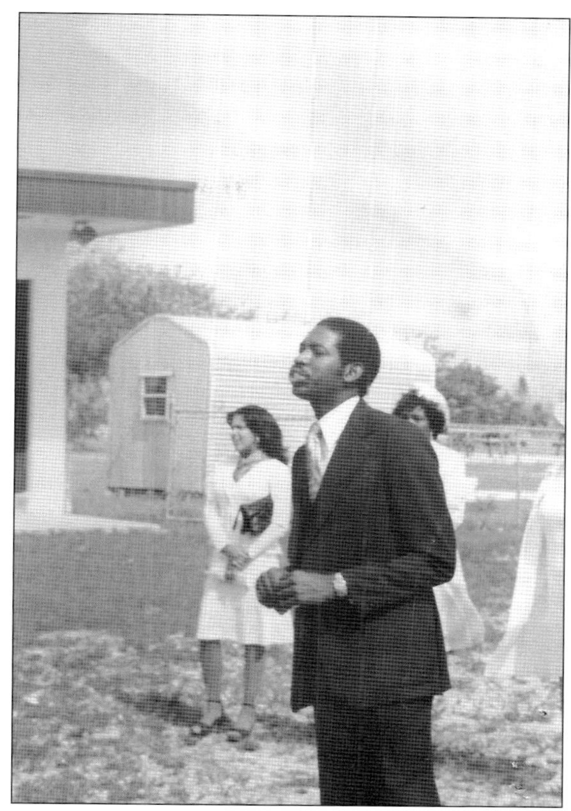

Second Baptist Church founder Rev. John Ferguson licensed and ordained Rev. Walter T. Richardson. Reverend Richardson served the Second Baptist family from 1977 to 1983. He held various positions, such as minister of music and minister of Christian education and preached at least once a month. In October 1983, he became the pastor for Sweet Home Baptist Church in Perrine, Florida. (Courtesy of Donald Hollis.)

This late-1940s photograph is of Ruth Broadnax, a nurse at Kendall Hospital. The medical staff at Kendall Hospital took care of the medical needs of black people in South Dade during this time. The hospital was located on SW 107th Avenue. Ruth met her husband, Warren Porter, while at work at Kendall Hospital. He worked there as an orderly after serving in World War II. They later married and moved to Fillmore Street in Richmond Heights. (Courtesy of the Porter family.)

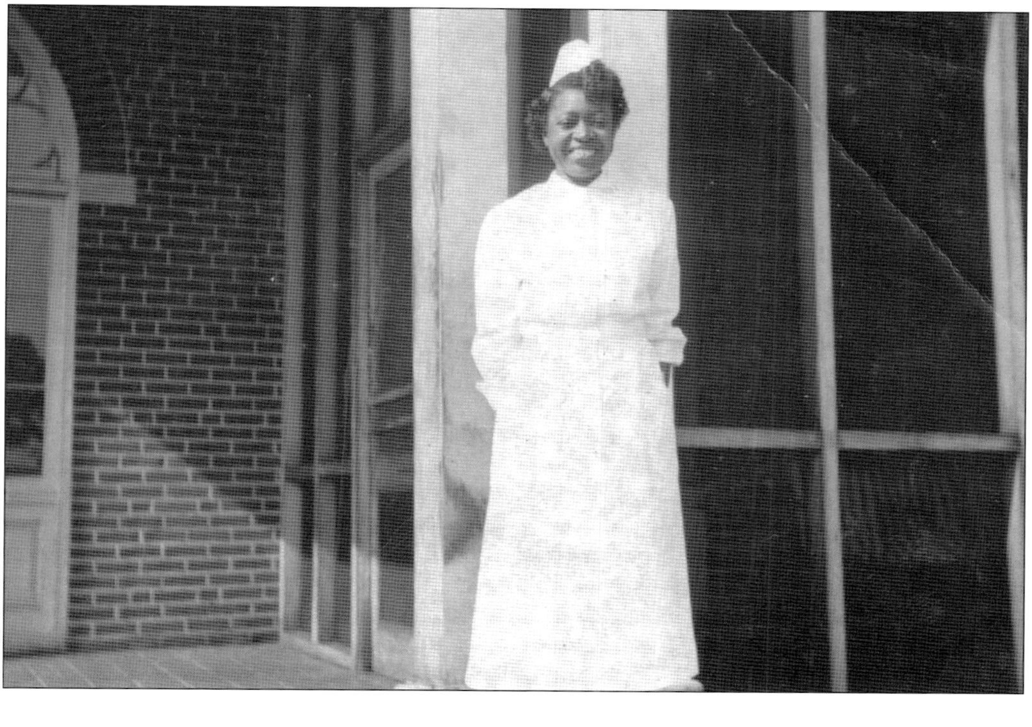

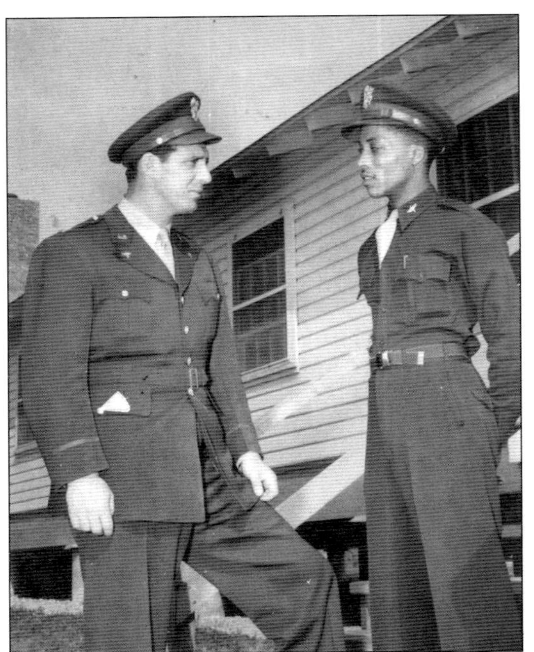

Eldridge F. Williams moved to Miami while still serving the country. He was chosen to attend Officer Candidate School in Miami Beach, Florida. Training was done in order to gain a commission as an officer in the Armed Forces. As the only black in the unit, he had special permission to go to Overtown to get his hair cut and lived at Collins Plaza Hotel on Twenty-first Street and Collins Avenue. While in school, he was classmates with actor Clark Gable, from *Gone with the Wind*, and Hank Greenberg, who was elected into the Baseball Hall of Fame. He graduated on October 28, 1962. Pictured are, from left to right, Hank Greenberg and Eldridge Williams while serving in the Air Force. (Courtesy of Lt. Col. Eldridge Williams.)

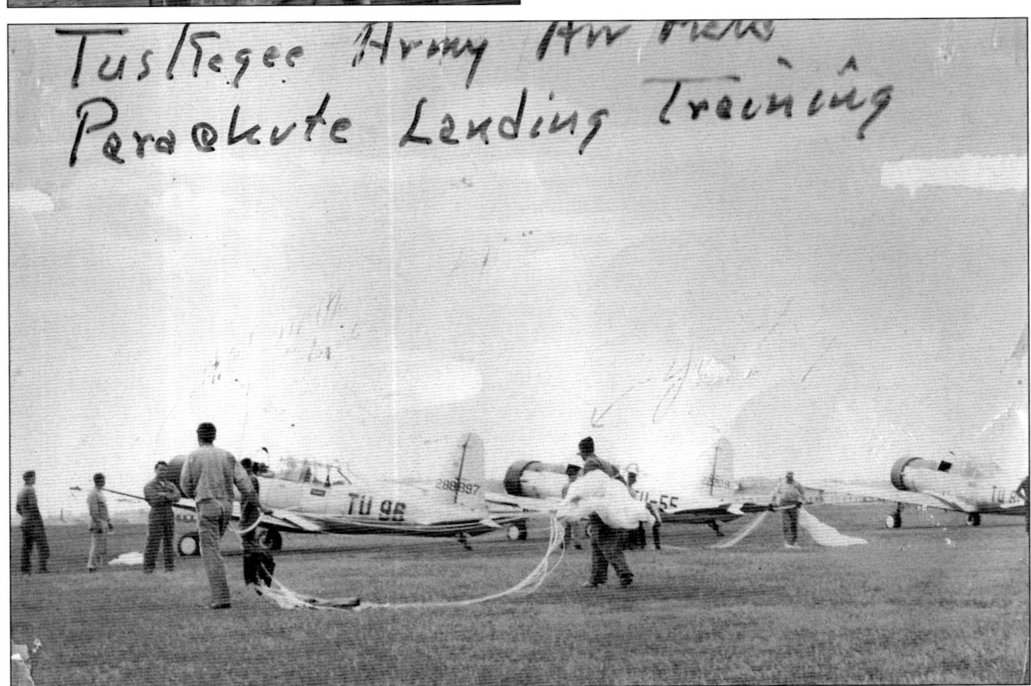

After graduation from Officer Candidate School in Miami Beach, Florida, Eldridge Williams was assigned to Tuskegee Army Airfield in Tuskegee, Alabama. He served as the director of physical fitness, survival training, and parachute landing training. He was responsible for training the Tuskegee Airmen cadets prior to going off to war. This photograph shows parachute landing training at Tuskegee Army Air Field. Williams went on to be the head basketball coach at North Carolina A&T State University. (Courtesy of Lt. Col. Eldridge Williams.)

After retiring from the Army, Lt. Col. Eldridge Williams began working at Richmond Junior High on January 24, 1964, as a teacher. He went on to work for the governing board of Miami-Dade County Public Schools as the director for the office of equal educational opportunity. In this role, he worked to desegregate schools. Public opposition to busing led to his plan being implemented over a period of time. He and his wife purchased their home at 14560 Jackson Street, and he retired from the school system in 1985 as the director for the office of equal educational opportunity. (Courtesy of Lt. Col. Eldridge Williams.)

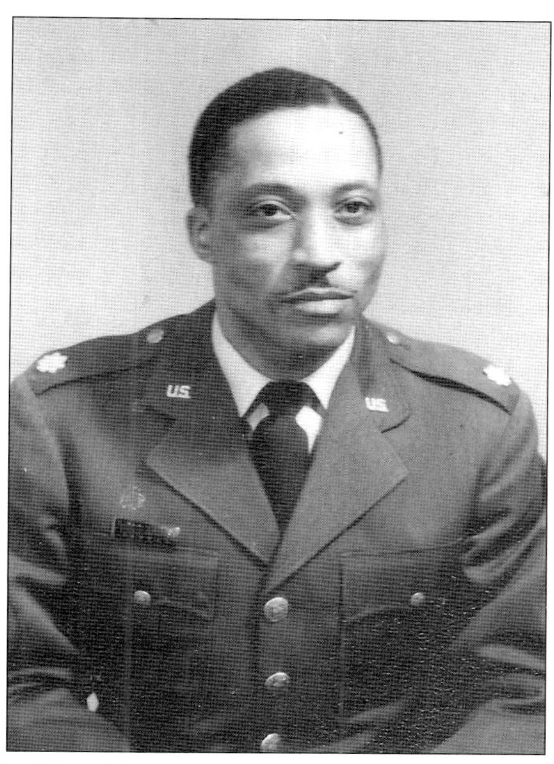

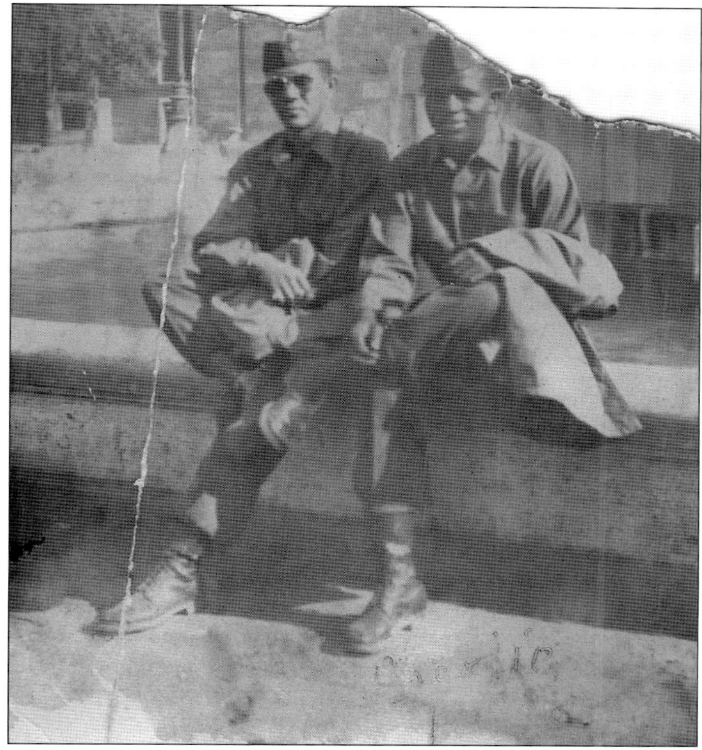

Charlie Harper (right), a World War II veteran, is photographed while stationed in Germany with an unidentified man. In 1952, Harper moved his wife, Bobbie, and their children, Larry and Patricia from Jacksonville, Florida, to Coconut Grove. In 1956, Harper decided to purchase a home in the newly developed community of Richmond Heights. Charlie retired from National Airlines and raised his family on Monroe Street.

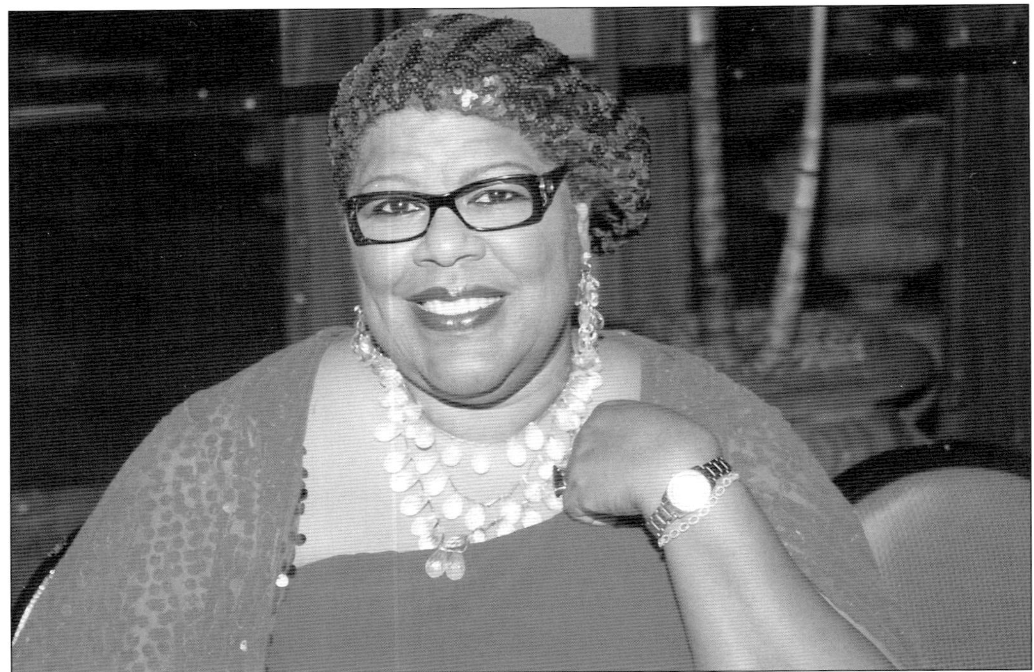

Kristal Bentley Hickmon is the current principal at her alma mater Richmond Middle School. She found her calling for education shortly after graduating from Florida State University, where she majored in biology. She remembers winning the fifth-grade spelling bee at Frank C. Martin Elementary. Her tenacious yet enduring spirit has led Kristal to guide the Zoo Magnet School as its principal.

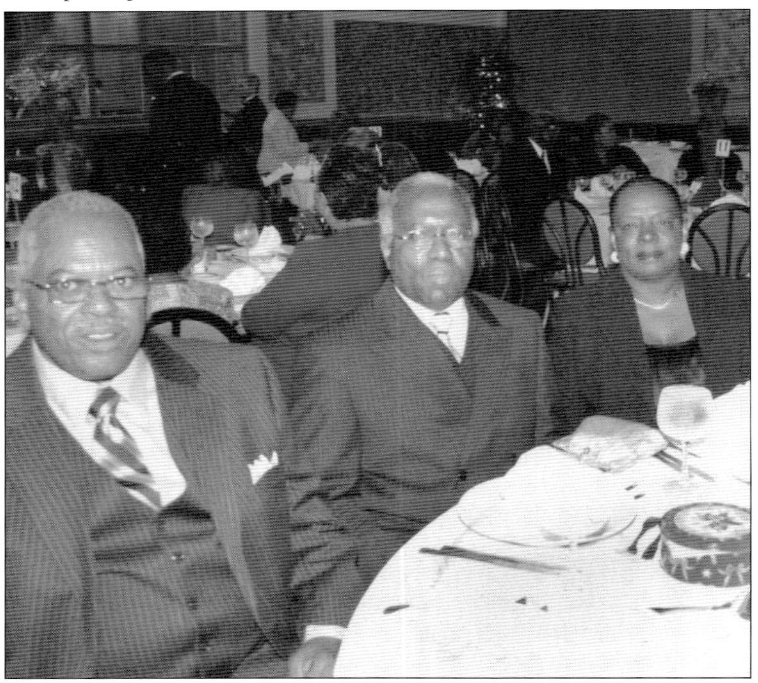

Longtime Richmond Heights' community residents are photographed celebrating Richmond Heights' 60th anniversary at Signature Gardens. From left to right are Monroe Street resident Larry Harper, flight attendant for Pan American Airlines; Harrison Street resident Raymond Payne, retired lieutenant commander in the US Navy; and Polk Street resident Minister Twila Payne, attorney.

This mid-1940s photograph captures World War II veteran Charles Edward Bethel after serving his country. He and his wife, Olga Goodman Bethel, purchased a home in Richmond Heights. They lived at 14460 Buchanan Street, lot No. 10. He went on to work for Pan American Airways as a skycap and was also a member of the American Legion Post in Richmond Heights. Charles and Olga had two children, Ellen and Mona. (Courtesy of Mona Bethel Jackson.)

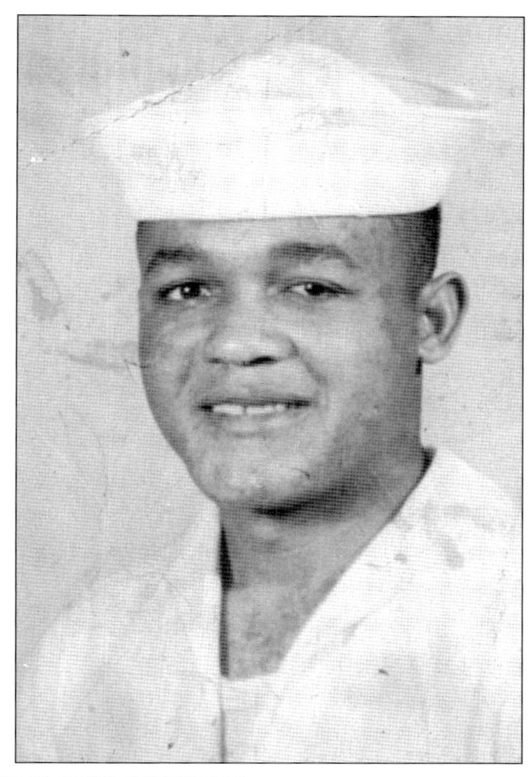

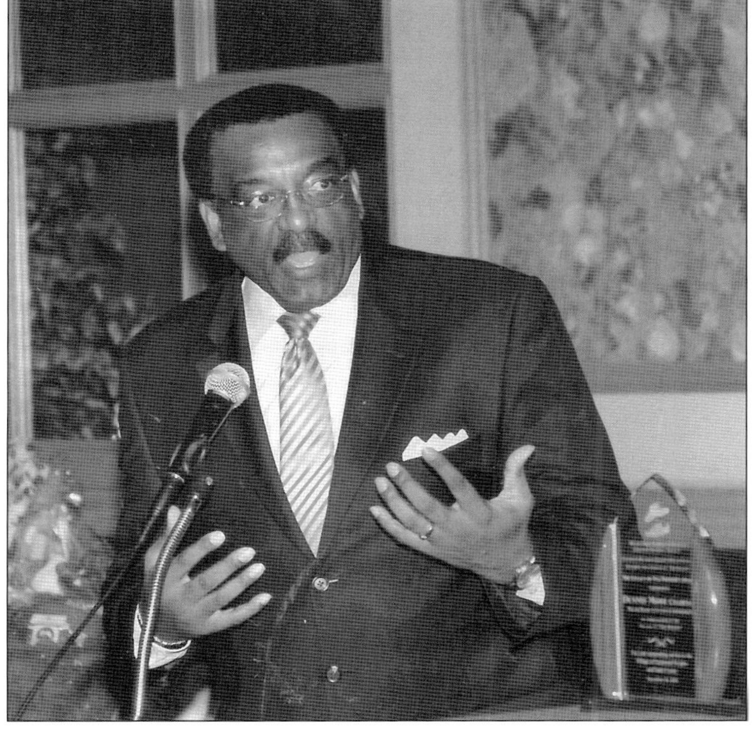

County commissioner Dennis Moss has been serving the community of Richmond Heights for 20 years in an official capacity. His vision for serving the people has resulted in yearly grants for small businesses and rebuilding the community. For over 25 years, he has been the executive director for the Richmond Perrine Optimist Club. He was raised on Jackson Street.

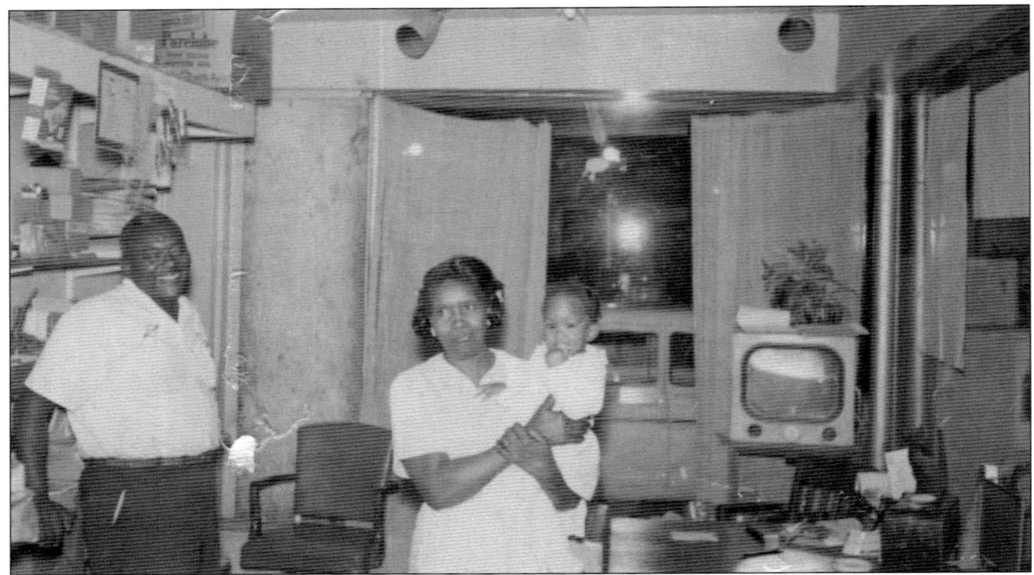

Mantley "Mack" Dorsey Sr. is photographed in this 1965 picture with his wife, Mary Dorsey, and their first grandchild, Wanda Dorsey. They are standing in the service office area of their Richmond Heights' gas station. This was not the couple's first business venture. Prior to the gas station, they owned a restaurant in Coconut Grove. (Courtesy of the Dorsey family.)

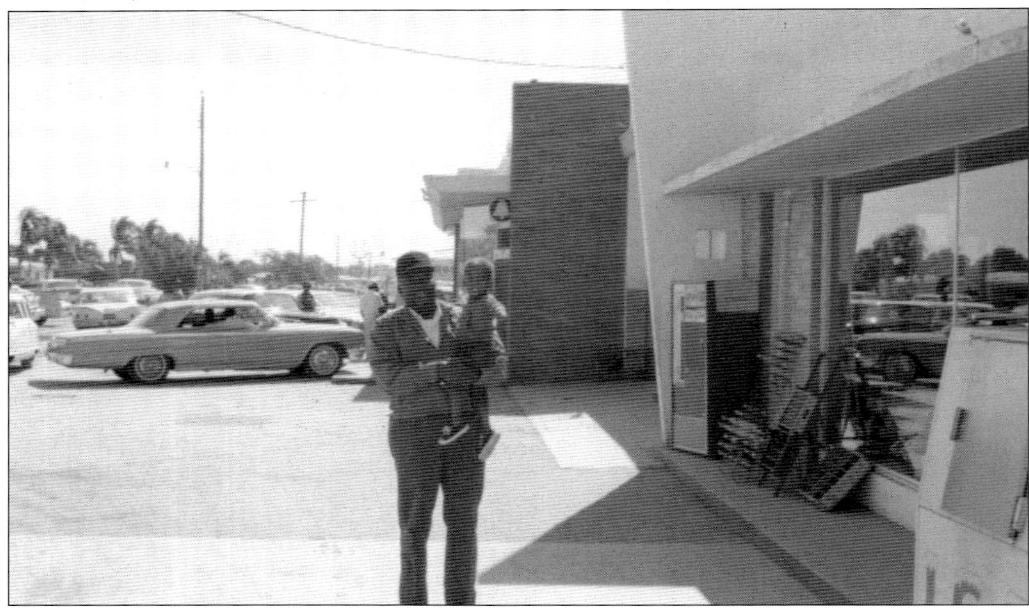

Dorsey's Pure Oil gas station was located inside of the Richmond Heights Plaza as an anchor store. It sat on the corner of Bethune Drive and Lincoln Boulevard. The Richmond Heights Plaza was home to many staples in the neighborhood, like Stylecraft Cleaners and Harry's Sweet Shoppe. During the holiday season, the huge glass window would be painted to depict the black Nativity. Each year, it was drawn by the art teacher for Frank C. Martin Elementary School, Ernest Dawkins. Mantley Dorsey Sr. is pictured holding his granddaughter Wanda Dorsey in front of his gas station in 1966. (Courtesy of the Dorsey family.)

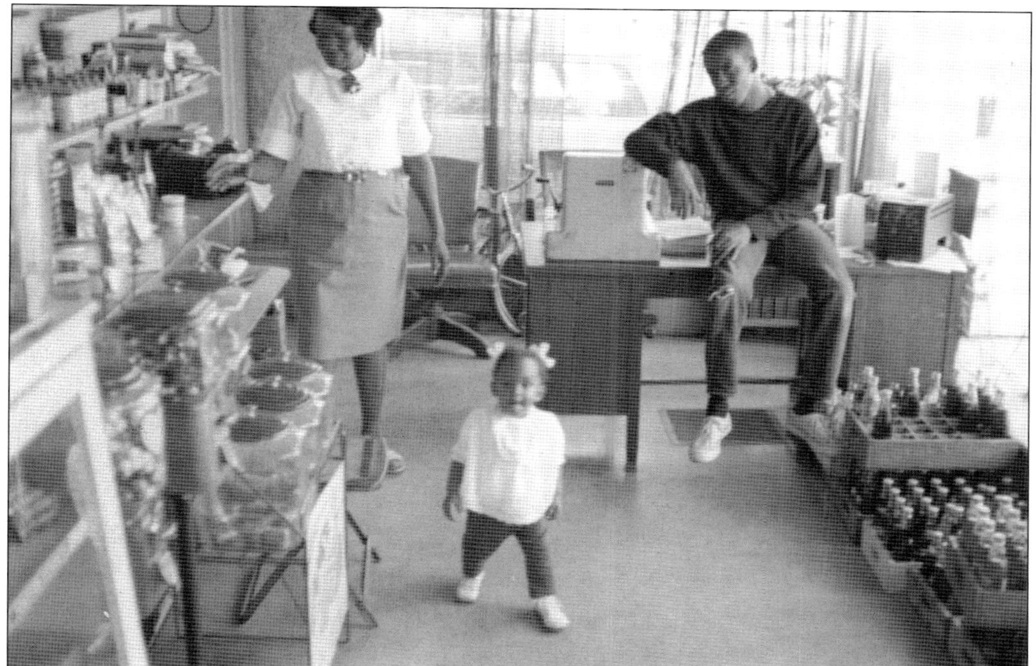

Mary Dorsey and husband, Mantley Dorsey Sr., owned the Dorsey's Pure Oil gas station off Lincoln Boulevard. They were also community residents who lived on Pierce Street. In this 1964 picture are, from left to right, Mary Dorsey, granddaughter Wanda Dorsey, and cousin David "Mister" Payne. The gas station prominently featured a Coca-Cola bottling machine out front. One could also purchase various kinds of candy and bubble gum. (Courtesy of the Dorsey family.)

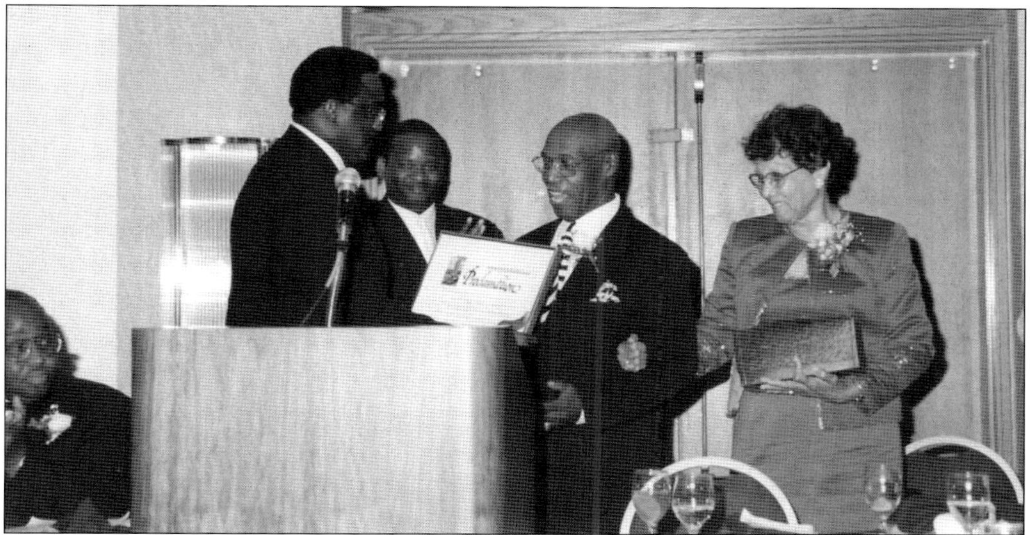

Rev. John A. Ferguson, founding pastor for Second Baptist Church, was born July 23, 1923, in Miami, Florida, and graduated from George Washington Carver High School. He served the country for some 21 years in the US Navy as a chief petty officer. He served during World War II, the Korean War, and the Vietnam War. He is photographed here receiving a proclamation. (Courtesy of Second Baptist Church.)

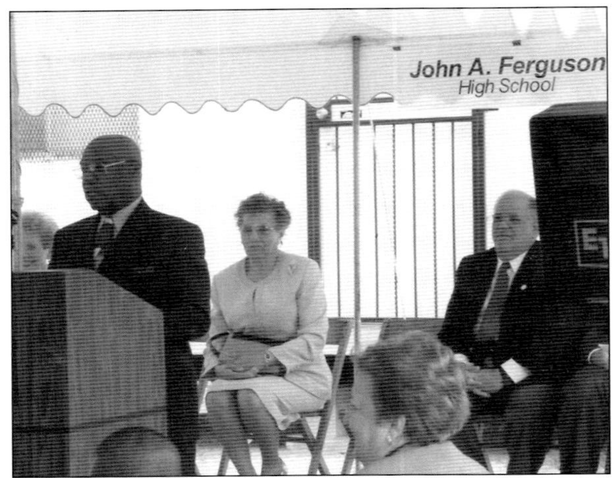

Rev. John A. Ferguson, who served as the founding pastor for Second Baptist Church for 36 years, was extremely instrumental in the Miami race relations during the Liberty City riots of the 1980s and the desegregation of all public schools. Reverend Ferguson was able to do this serving on the Dade County Community Relations Board as well as the school desegregation committee. His countless hours of service led to Dade County Public Schools naming a high school in his honor in 2003. (Courtesy of Second Baptist Church.)

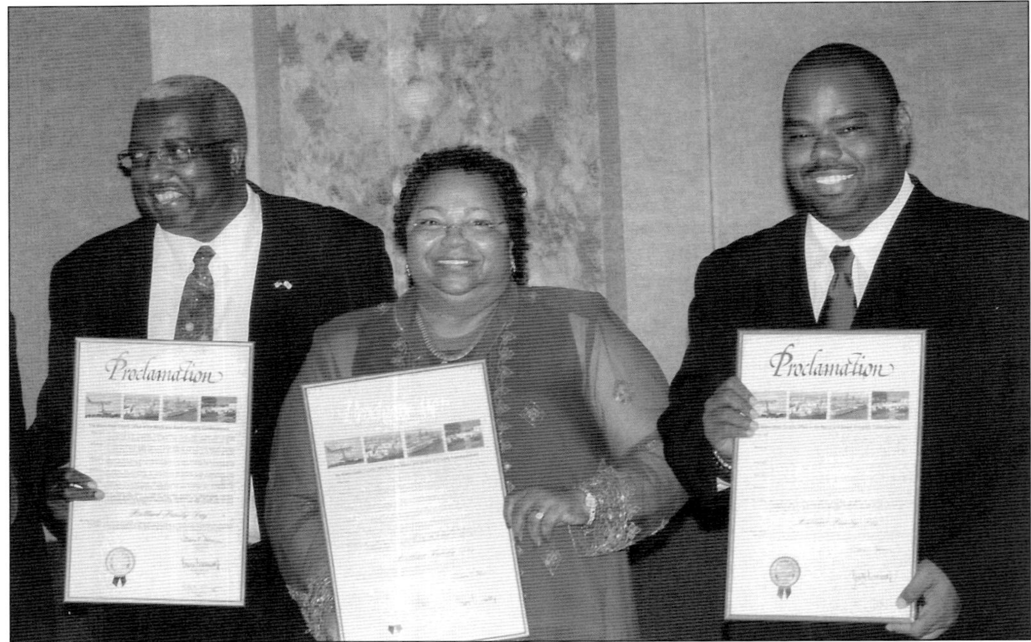

The Bullards are dedicated to community service. Ed Bullard grew up in Richmond Heights on Harrison Street. He later went on to marry Larcenia Dunbar, and they began their family in Richmond Heights off Robinson Street. Ed served as a member of the Florida House of Representatives from 2001 to 2009, while his wife, Larcenia, served as a member of the Florida House of Representatives from 1992 to 2000 and then served as a member of the Florida Senate from 2002 to 2012. Their son Dwight Bullard served in the Florida House of Representative from 2002 to 2012 and then picked up the torch in 2012 from his mom. He is currently a member in the Florida Senate.

Robert Randolph and his wife, Rena, moved to Richmond Heights in 1951 after a tour of duty with the US Navy. The couple had three children, Robert, Brenda, and Rodney. Randolph worked for Gulf Life Insurance as an insurance agent and was assigned the Richmond Heights community. Pictured at right is their son Rodney Randolph, who was one of the four residents selected to work on Capitol Hill as a US Capitol police officer from 1973 to 1998. (Courtesy of the Patterson family.)

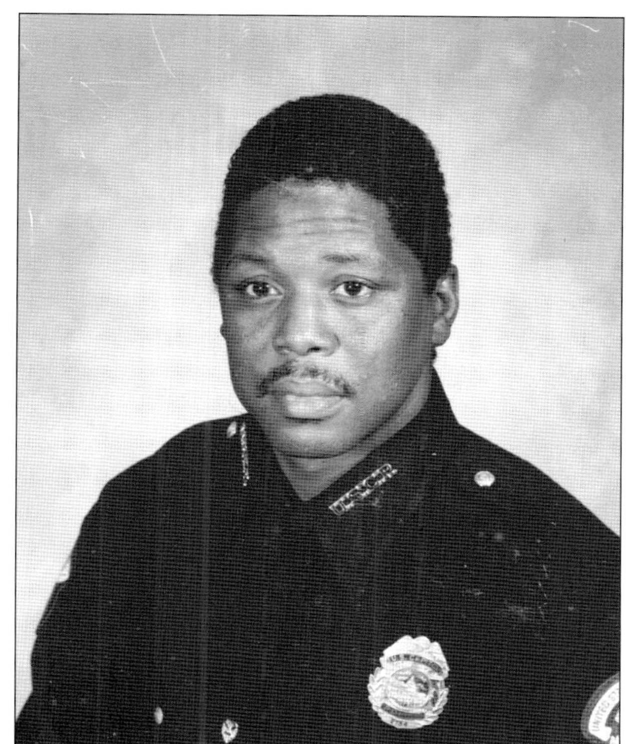

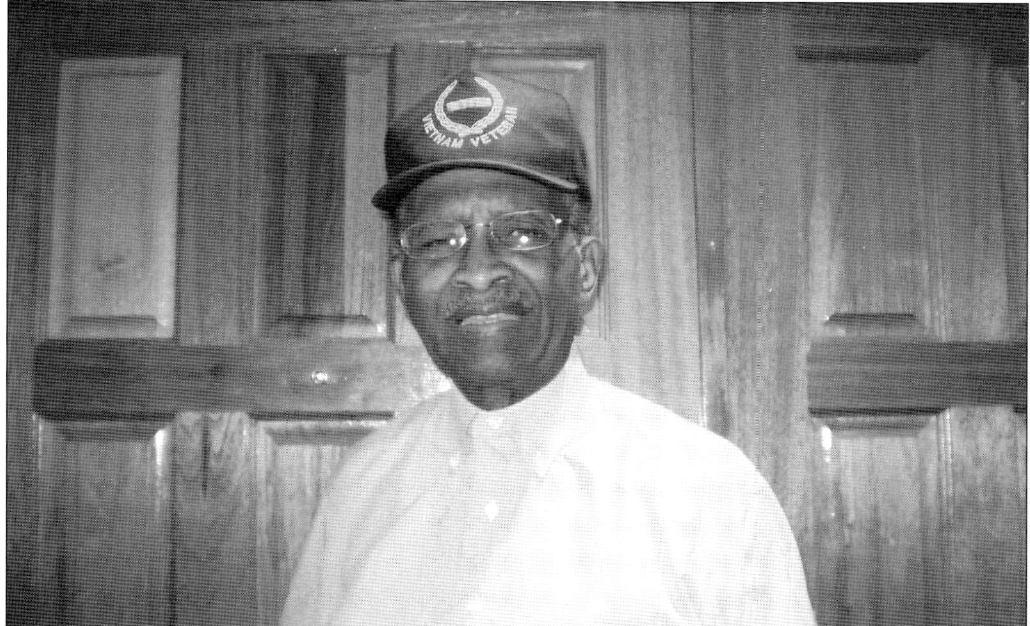

Community activist James Marshall served the United States during World War II while stationed in Germany and earned a Purple Heart. He began his undergraduate studies while in Germany and finished at Florida A&M University. In addition, he obtained his master's degree from Florida International University in its first graduating class. (Courtesy of the Marshall family.)

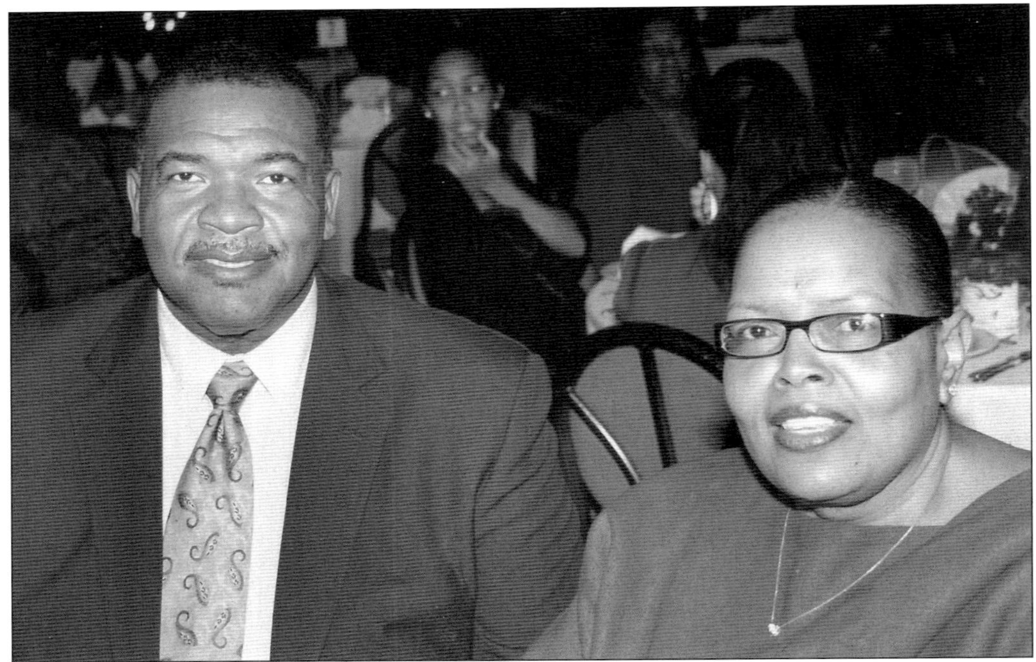

Barry Huff, who grew up on Pierce Street, is a renowned jewel in the community. His studies at the University of Iowa's Henry B. Tippie College of Business and corporate savvy led him to become the president of Glory Foods in 2002. Glory Foods' products are the No. 1 brand of choice by blacks for preseasoned, canned Southern-style food. Pictured are siblings Barry Huff (left) and Gisele Huff Riley (right).

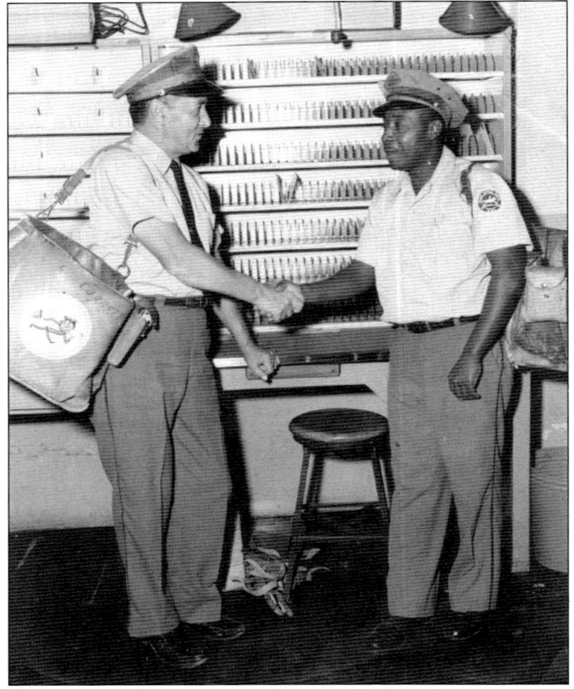

Captain Martin worked to get a post office in the community for mail delivery since residents were refused home mail delivery. The post office was located at the dead end of Pinkston Drive and Polk Street. This ultimately created an opportunity for Florida's first black postmaster and the first black postmen in Miami-Dade County. On May 15, 1949, the City of Miami integrated the Miami Post Office with two black men. The National Alliance of Postal Employees was able to take that number to 31 carriers. Three of those men were residents of Richmond Heights, postmaster Anthony Palmore, Willie Redding, and Roy Bentley. Pictured are an unidentified man (left) and Willie Redding (right). (Courtesy of the Redding family.)

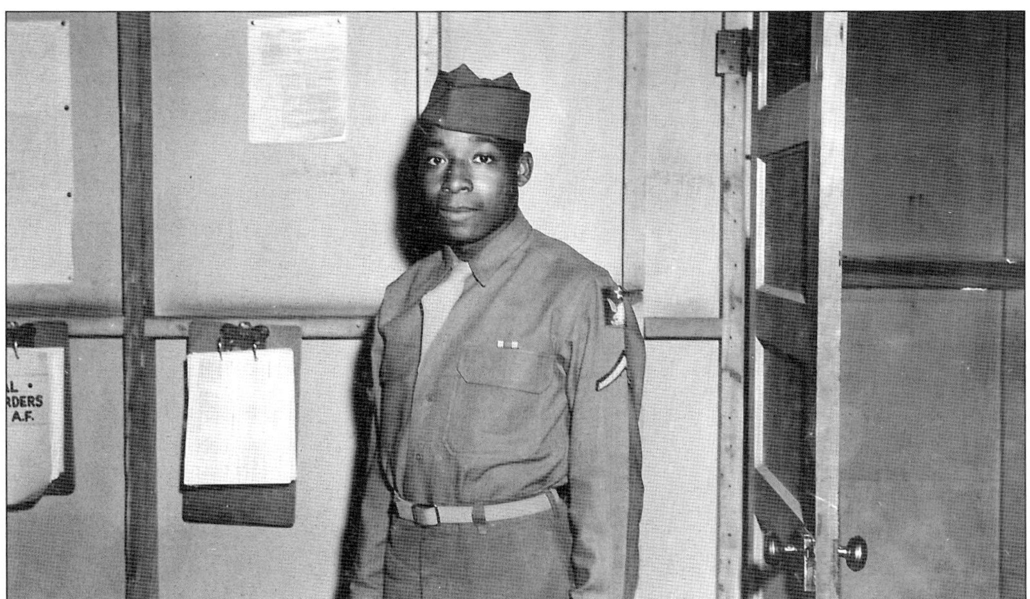

World War II veteran Willie Redding and his wife, Eddie, purchased their home on May 17, 1950. Willie's tour of duty was from 1943 to 1946 in the Army Air Force. He was awarded the Victory Medal of Honor for his service to the United States. (Courtesy of the Redding family.)

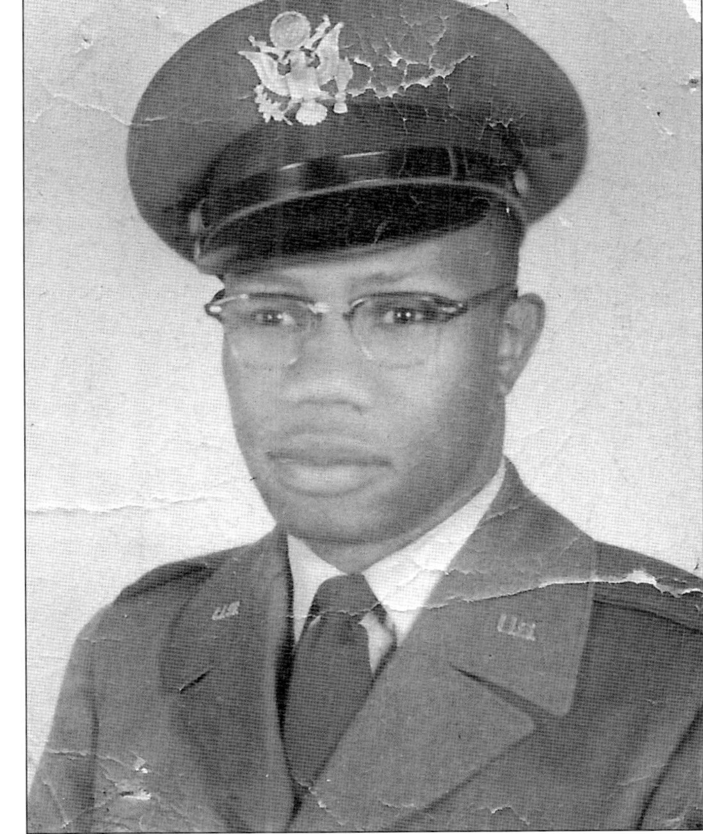

Lt. Taylor Jackson entered the US Air Force after participating in the ROTC at Tuskegee Institute. His tour of duty was in Japan. After moving to Richmond Heights, he was a steward and sang in the choir at Martin Memorial AME Church. (Courtesy of the Jackson family.)

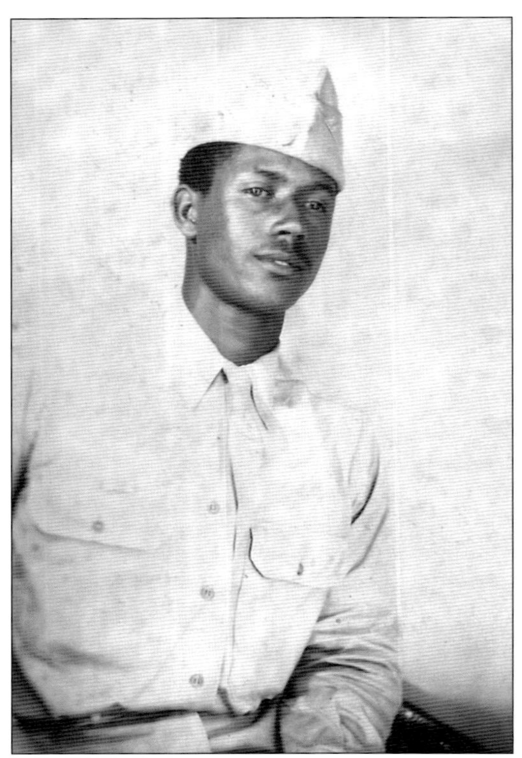

Capt. Samuel Armstrong, of the United States Army, moved to Richmond Heights in 1950. That same year, he became a tracker trailer operator with the United States Postal Service. For 18 years, Armstrong was the president of the Alliance of Postal & Federal Employees with the post office. In 1982, Armstrong retired with 32 years of service from the United States Postal Service. (Courtesy of the Armstrong family.)

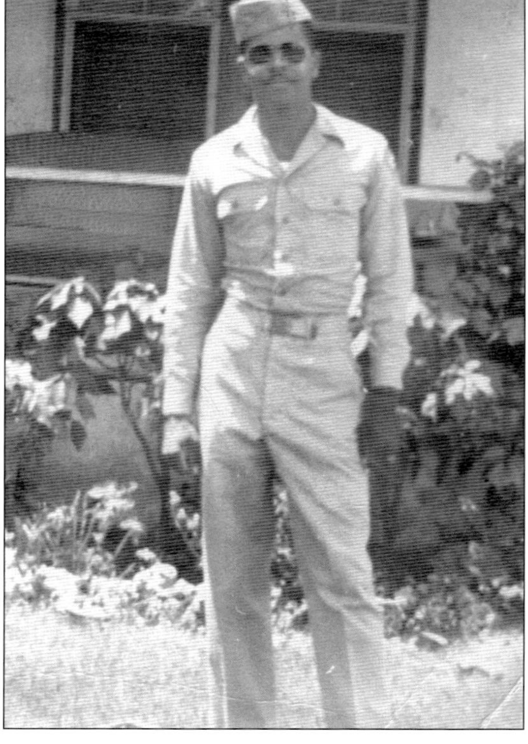

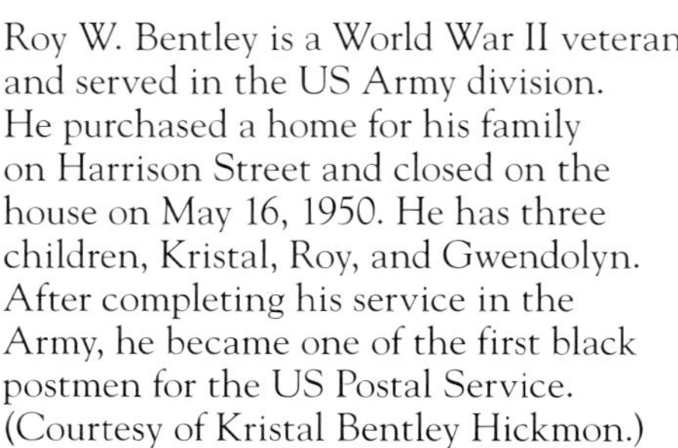

Roy W. Bentley is a World War II veteran and served in the US Army division. He purchased a home for his family on Harrison Street and closed on the house on May 16, 1950. He has three children, Kristal, Roy, and Gwendolyn. After completing his service in the Army, he became one of the first black postmen for the US Postal Service. (Courtesy of Kristal Bentley Hickmon.)

Eugene Williams served in the US Army, and his tour of duty was in Germany. He and wife, Mary, moved to Richmond Heights in 1961. They had three children and were charter members of Second Baptist Church. In 1981, he received the TAC Commander Award and the Transportation Professional of the Year for the 31st Transportation Squadron. (Courtesy of Eugene Williams.)

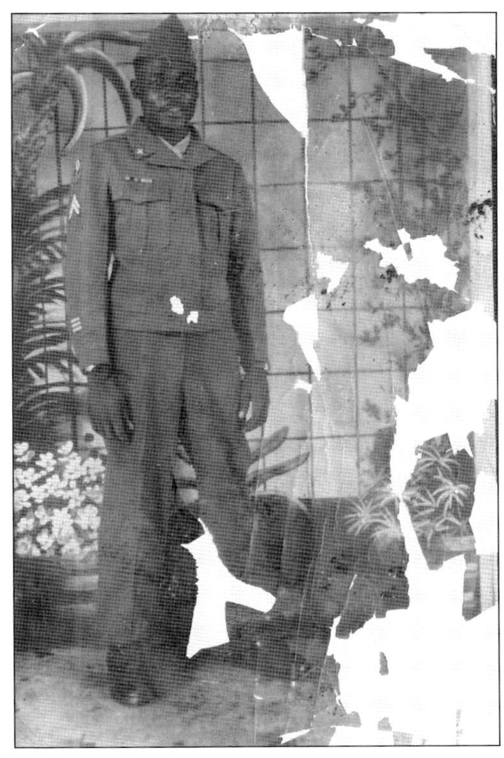

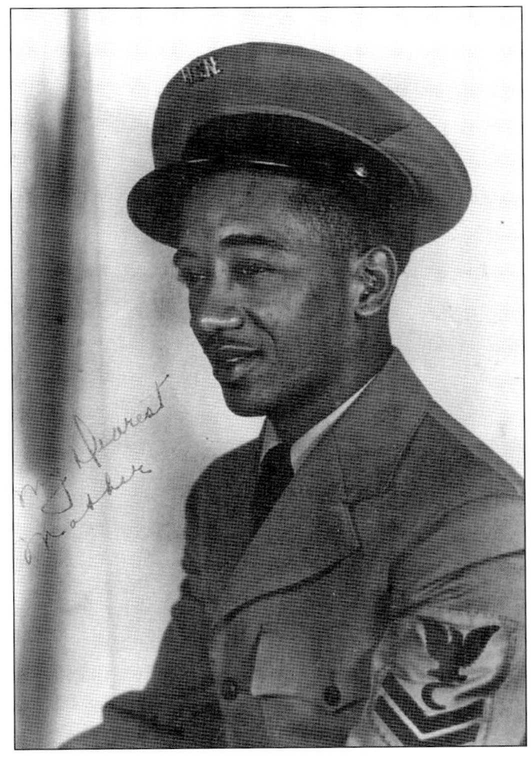

Archibald Pinder is photographed in his US Navy uniform. He purchased a home for his family in Richmond Heights on August 17, 1950, at 14821 Fillmore Street. He married Beulah in Key West, and they had five children, Archibald, Pam, Ferrecita, Stephanie, and Terrance. He owned a printing company on NW Sixty-fourth Street in Liberty City and also was a journalist for the *Miami Times*. (Courtesy of the Pinder family.)

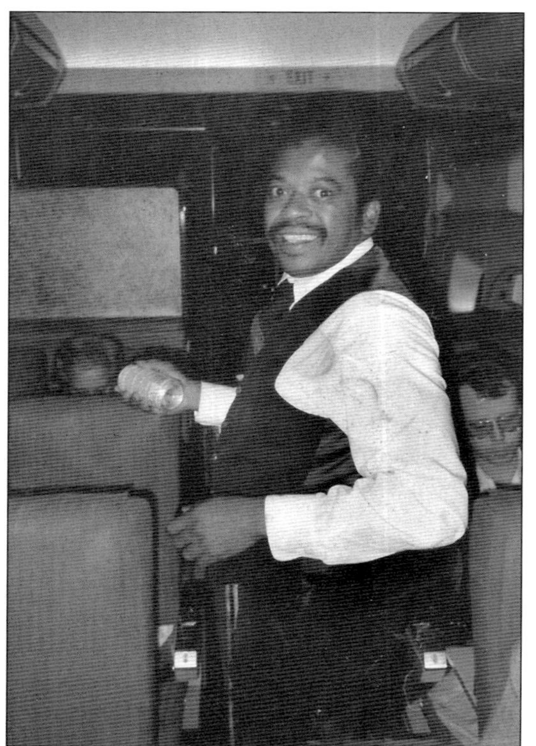

Larry Harper grew up on Monroe Street in Richmond Heights. He was the son of Charlie and Bobbie Harper. His love for life led to him pursuing careers in the hospitality field. He traveled the world internationally as a flight attendant for National Airlines and Pan Am Airlines before they went out of business. He later went on to work for Amtrak as a steward.

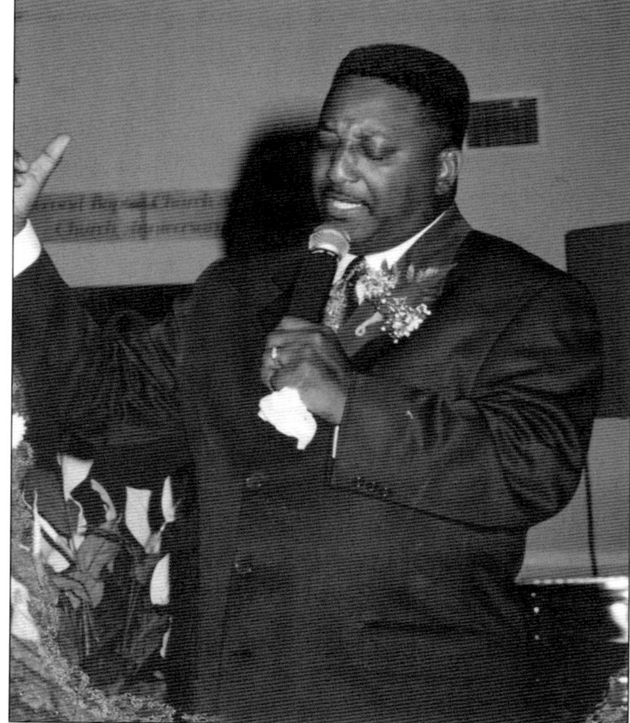

After 31 years, Ronald Smith retired from Dade County Aviation Department as the division director of airside operations. He also spent 29 years as the associate minister for Glendale Baptist Church. He is now the pastor and founder for Community Bible Baptist Church. (Courtesy of the Smith family.)

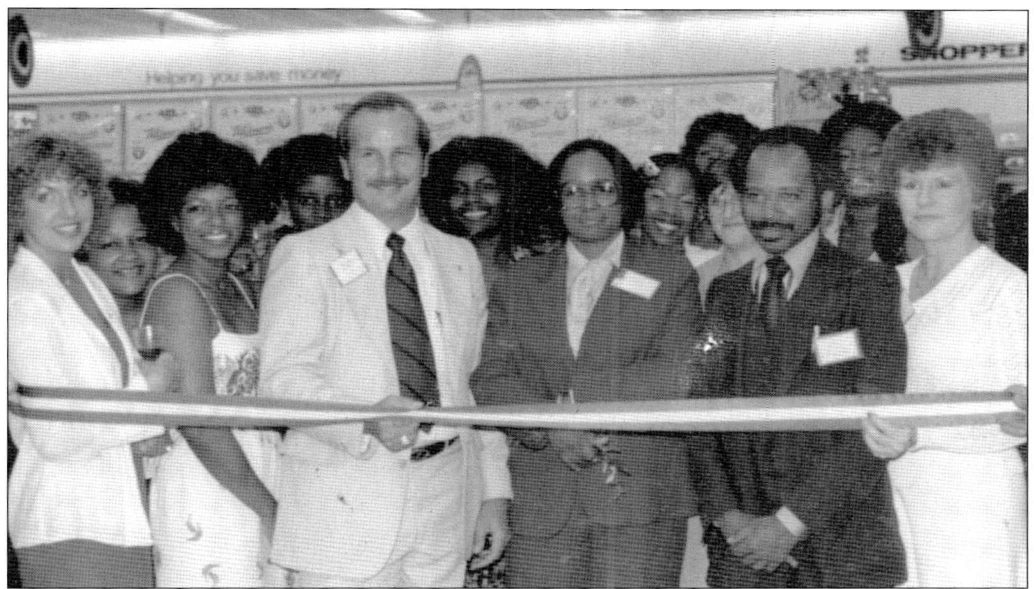

Shoppers Drug Mart opened to the community in 1980 on the northwest corner of Lincoln Boulevard and SW 152nd Street. Residents enjoyed the convenience of another retail store in the community. Richmond Heights resident Archibal Pinder was the owner as well as the store's pharmacist. Pinder (first row, second from right) is seen at the store's grand opening. (Courtesy of Archibald Pinder.)

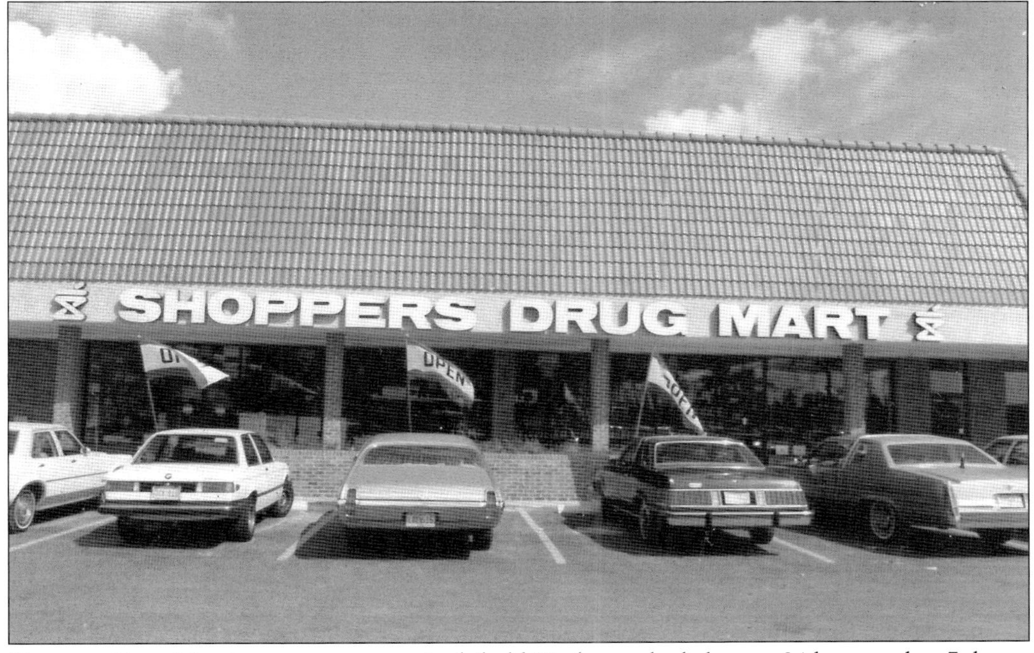

Shoppers Drug Mart's owner-operator Archibald Pinder worked close to 24 hours a day, 7 days a week. He served as the operations manager as well as the pharmacist. Archibald is still serving the community of Richmond Heights as a pharmacist for CVS in the same location. He works two days a month. (Courtesy of Archibald Pinder.)

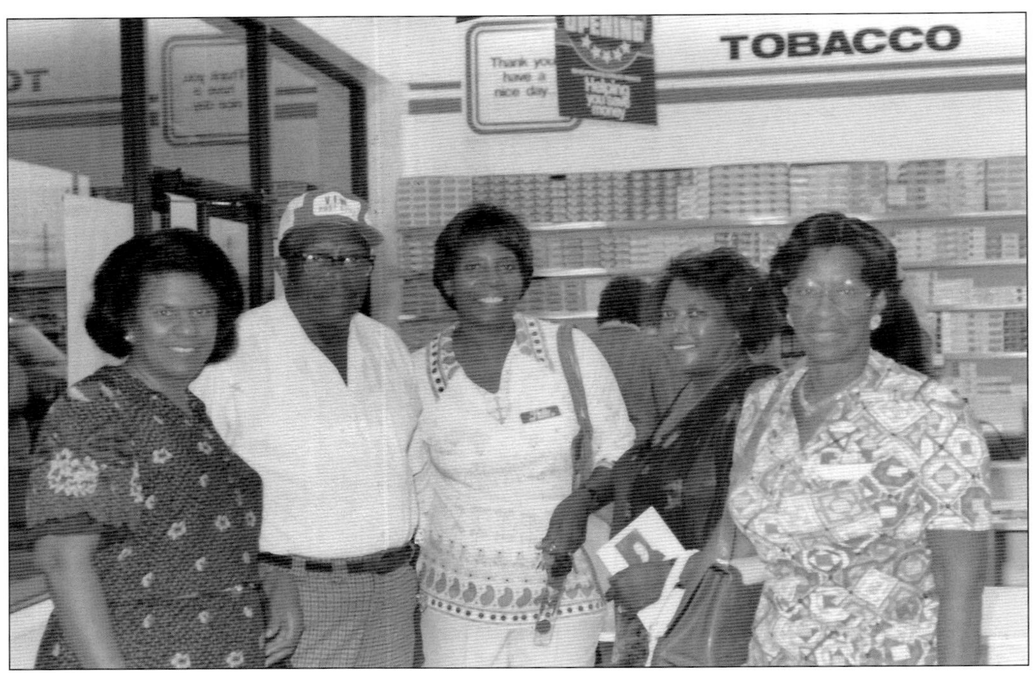

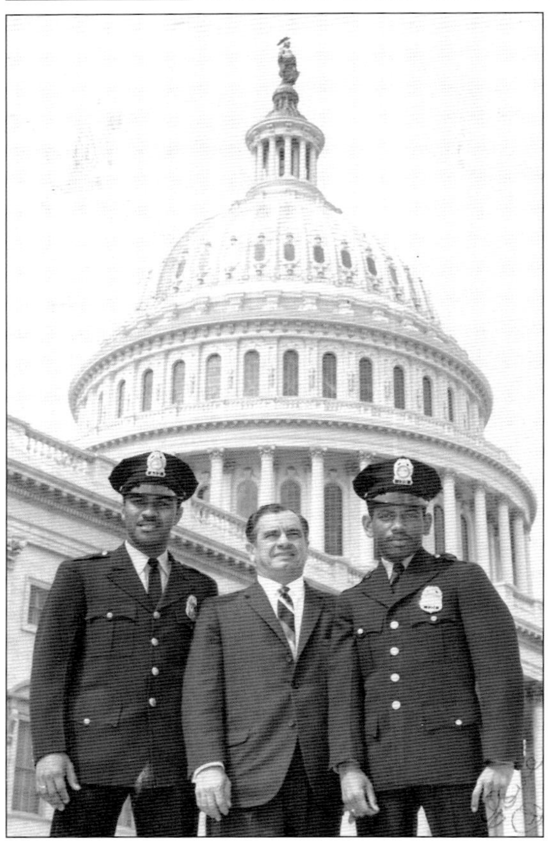

Shoppers Drug Mart was the answer to the big-box retailers moving into the community. It went through several name and ownership changes over the years. After Shoppers Drug Mart, it became Grey's Drugs, Rite Aid, Eckerd Drug, and, today, CVS. Pictured are residents who came to shop and support the grand opening. From left to right are Mariquita Gibson, Herbert A. Ammons, a Mrs. Ammons, unidentified, and Myrtle Bethel. Miami-Dade County Public Schools named a middle school in honor of Herbert A. Ammons for his untiring community service and dedication to the youth. (Courtesy of Archibald Pinder.)

US congressman Dante Fascell was a proponent for the community of Richmond Heights. He was instrumental in the hiring of five young men from the community to work on Capitol Hill. The first was Archibald C. Pinder and then came Abraham Turner, Clarence Martin, Randy Rudolph, and Charles Anderson. Pictured are, from left to right, Abraham Turner, Congressman Dante Fascell, and Archibald C. Pinder. (Courtesy of Archibald Pinder.)

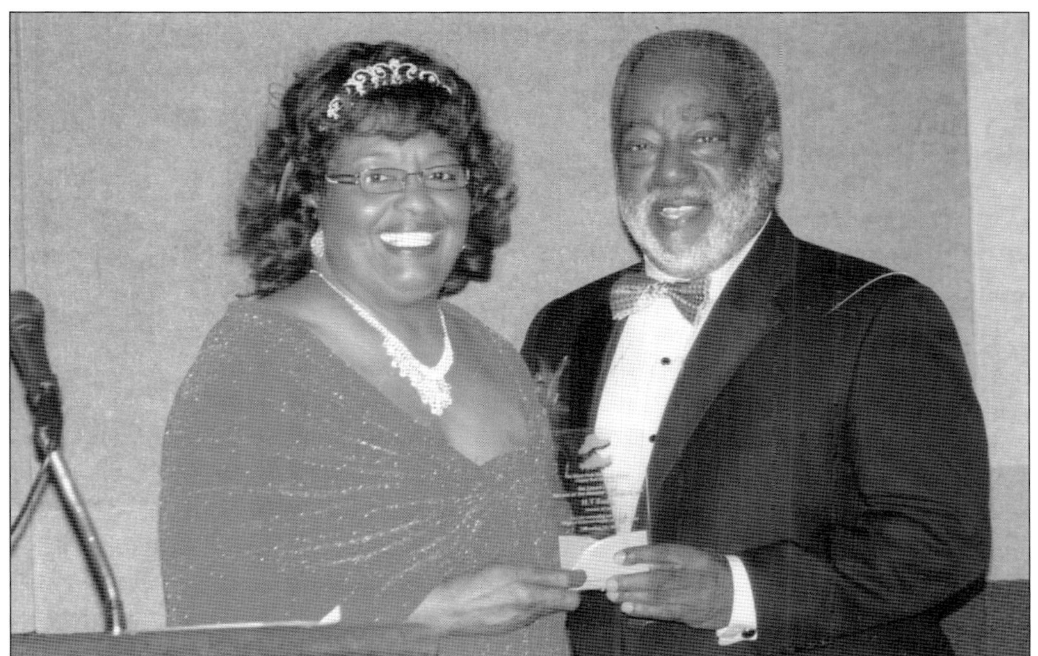

H.T. Smith was raised in Richmond Heights and created many opportunities for future lawyers. He was Dade County's first black assistant public defender as well as the first black assistant county attorney. He went on to be the founding president for the Black Lawyers Association of Dade County. This photograph shows H.T. Smith receiving an award at Richmond Heights' 60th anniversary celebration from Red Hat queen Patricia Garrett.

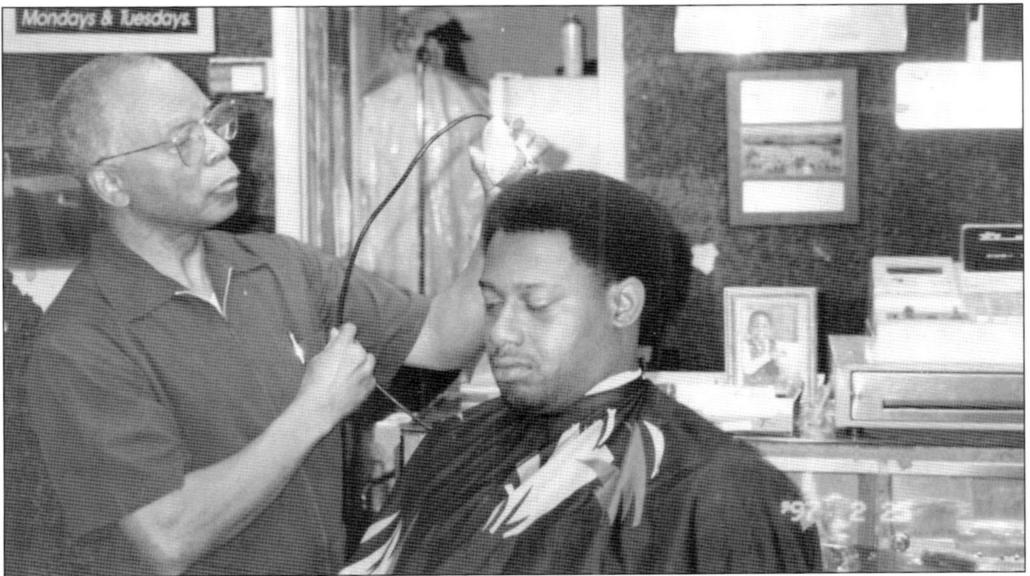

The Richmond Heights Barbershop opened its doors to the community in 1961. Robert "Bob" Linton knew his idea was a great business venture for the community. The barbershop is fitted with old-fashioned chairs. Robert Linton passed his barbershop down to his nephew Clinton Hines. Pictured are Robert Linton (left) and Clinton Hines (right). (Courtesy of the Linton family.)

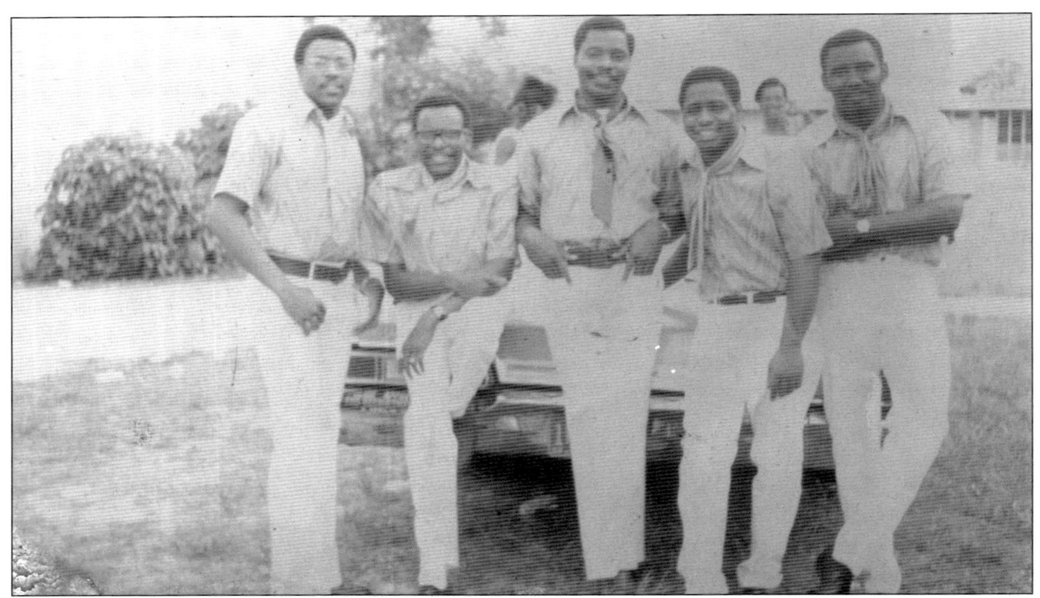

This 1970s photograph is of the Fabulous Five Club, which was an investment company. Its mission was to generate funding. The men were all Richmond Heights residents but met while teaching at R.R. Moton Elementary and decided to create a company together. Members are, from left to right, Willie Garrett, Rudolph Adams, General White, Walter Frierson, and Moses Poole.

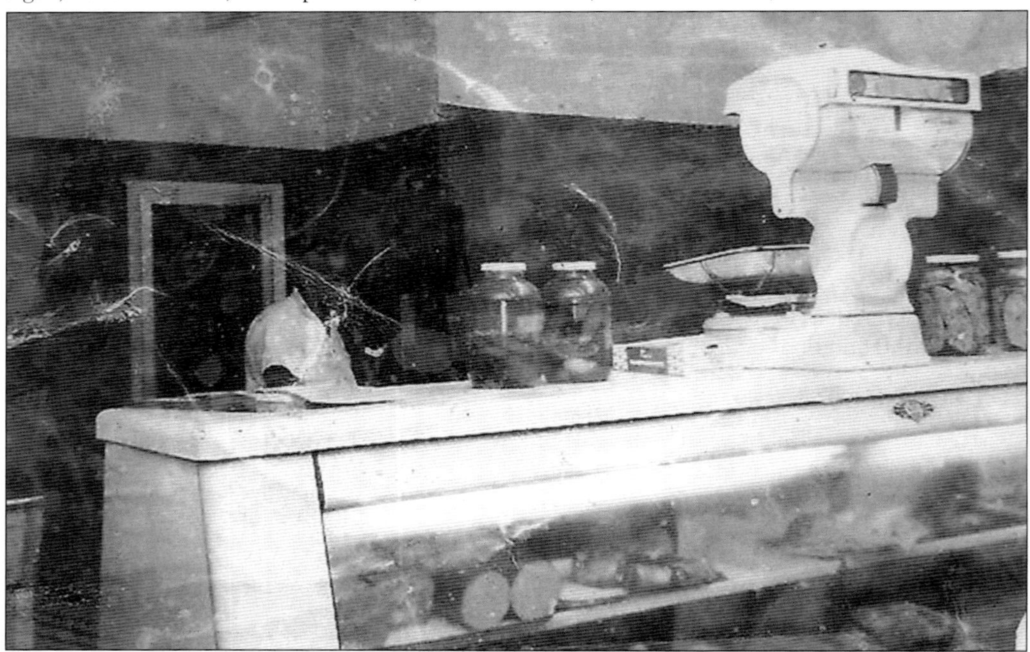

Anderson Fairdeal Grocery, also known as "the meat market," was located off Bethune Drive and Lincoln Boulevard across the street from the Ms. Ross Day Care. The grocer was Charles Arthur Anderson. He and his family opened Anderson Fairdeal Grocery in 1961 and served the community on and off until 1987. For years, locals would meet up at all hours just to "shoot the breeze" under the tree at the meat market. (Courtesy of the Anderson family.)

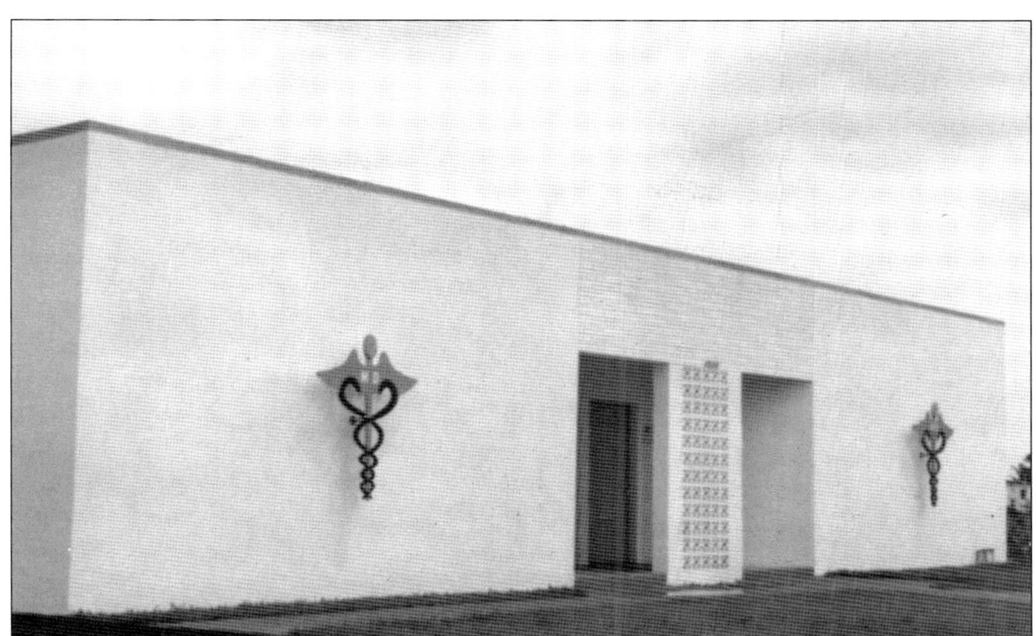

Dr. Herbert Greene practiced medicine for some 35 years. During this time, he was an active member of DCMA, Florida Medical Association (FMA), American Medical Association (AMA), American College of Emergency Physicians (ACEP), and National Medical Association (NMA) and was the founding president of the local chapter of the NMA. Dr. Greene now serves on the Baptist Health South Florida Board of Trustees. Pictured above is Dr. Greene's third and final office in Richmond Heights on Dunbar Drive. He did obstetrics and delivered many Richmond Heights babies. (Courtesy of Dr. Herbert Greene.)

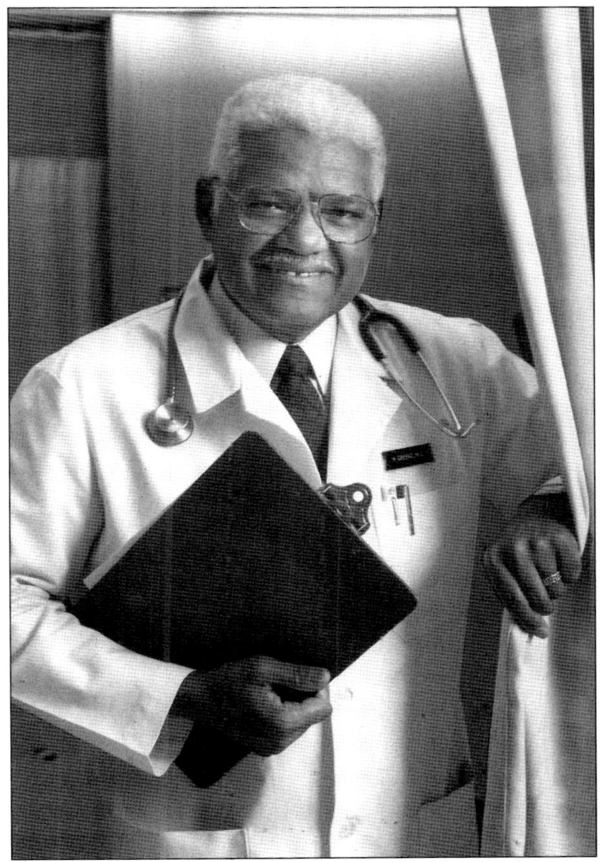

Dr. Herbert Greene had several medical practices in Richmond Heights. He became a charter member of the American College of Emergency Physicians (ACEP). He practiced in the emergency department at Baptist Hospital of Miami until he retired in September 1998. (Courtesy of Dr. Herbert Greene.)

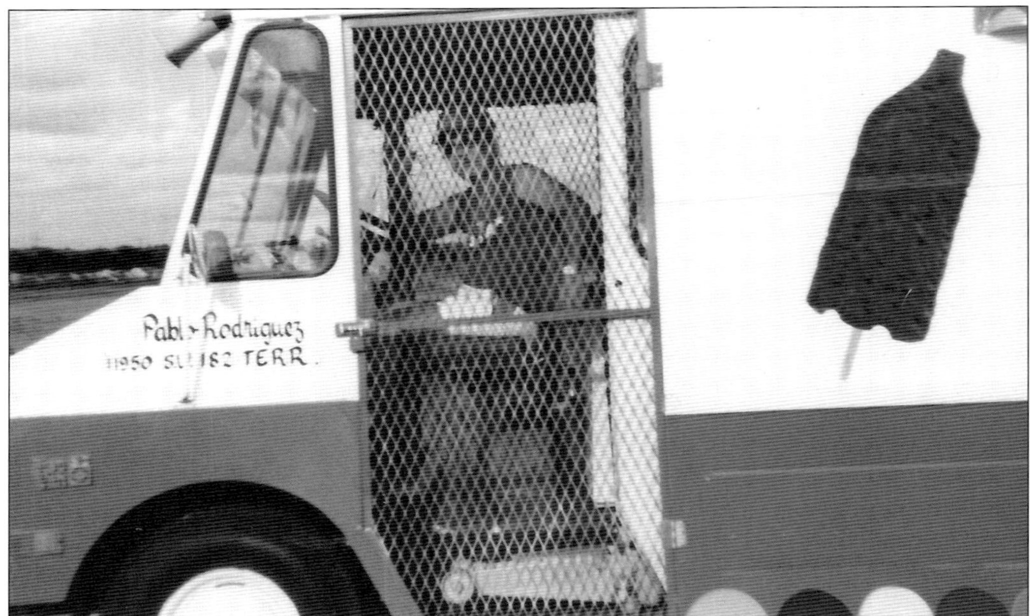

Pablo Rodriguez, the ice cream man, is a continued staple in the Richmond Heights neighborhood. Pablo rides at speeds of five miles per hour, up and down each street in the neighborhood, while playing catchy tunes loud enough to hear from inside one's home. To get his attention to stop, children run outside and yell, "Hold!" (Courtesy of the Rodriguez family.)

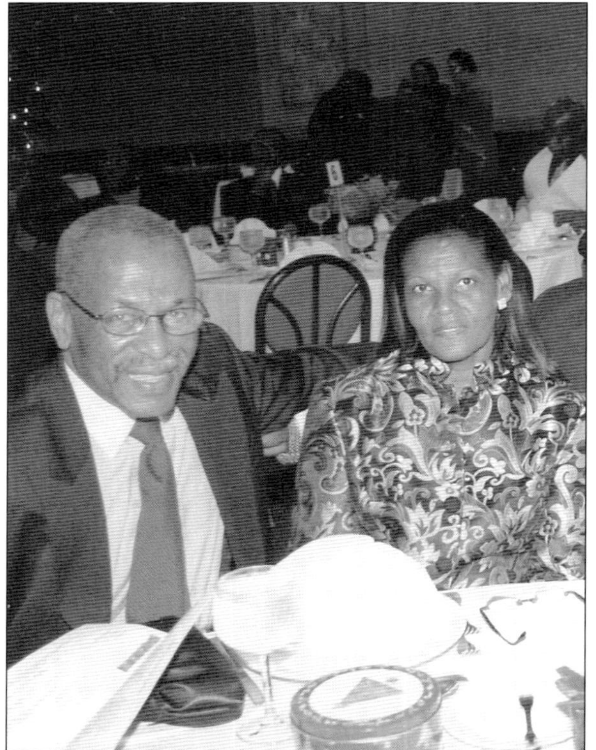

Dr. George Battle has truly been able to provide support to the women of Richmond Heights and beyond by serving as an OB/GYN for over 35 years. With an office located in the community, he has been credited with delivering hundreds of babies in the area. This photograph captures Dr and Mrs. George Battle when he was recognized for his work in the community at Richmond Heights' 60th anniversary gala.

Six

Organizational Life

Organizations are the collection of like minds for a common desired purpose or goal. The residents of Richmond Heights knew this, and as the community was being built, so were organizations. There were civic, religious, political, youth, and fraternal organizations that outfitted this area.

Richmond Heights was built on the backs of war veterans, so it is only befitting that the first organizations established were the American Legion Richmond Heights Post No. 281 and the Veterans of Foreign Wars Post No. 8197 in the 1950s. Their shared mission is to promote assistance to US veterans. Their office is still located in the same place, 14640 Lincoln Boulevard.

There were also organizations founded in Richmond Heights that were just for women. For several months in 1954, Anita Gray went from door to door in Richmond Heights to speak with the lady of the house. She spoke about her interest to promote the welfare of the community residents by initiating and following through on civic, educational, and social projects. On May 2, 1954, she held her initial meeting with 31 interested women at her home. All of the women decided that as a unified group, they would be able to make a significant difference with every goal they set to accomplish.

The Richmond Perrine Optimist Club is another example of like minds uniting for a common goal. This organization was incorporated in 1971 by 84 men to provide a multitude of social services, from youth enrichment activities like football, cheerleading, and tutoring to elderly assistance for homes, food drives, and community gardening. The organization began because of a lack of organized youth sports and has led to an endless amount of solutions.

In 1992, the Richmond Heights United Pastors Foundation was founded under the vision of Apostle Carlos Malone, who is pastor of the Bethel Church. Apostle Carlos Malone shared his vision with Second Baptist pastor and founder Rev. John Ferguson and Macedonia Church of God in Christ pastor and founder Elder Paul Golatt Sr. It was created to serve as the governing umbrella for all of the community groups and to focus on economic development and community revitalization. It is now known as the Richmond Heights Community Development Corporation.

Richmond Heights Alliance, Inc., a nonprofit organization, began in 2009. It is comprised of all the ministers and organizations that are based in Richmond Heights. Once a month, they meet at Second Baptist Church to discuss matters that affect the community.

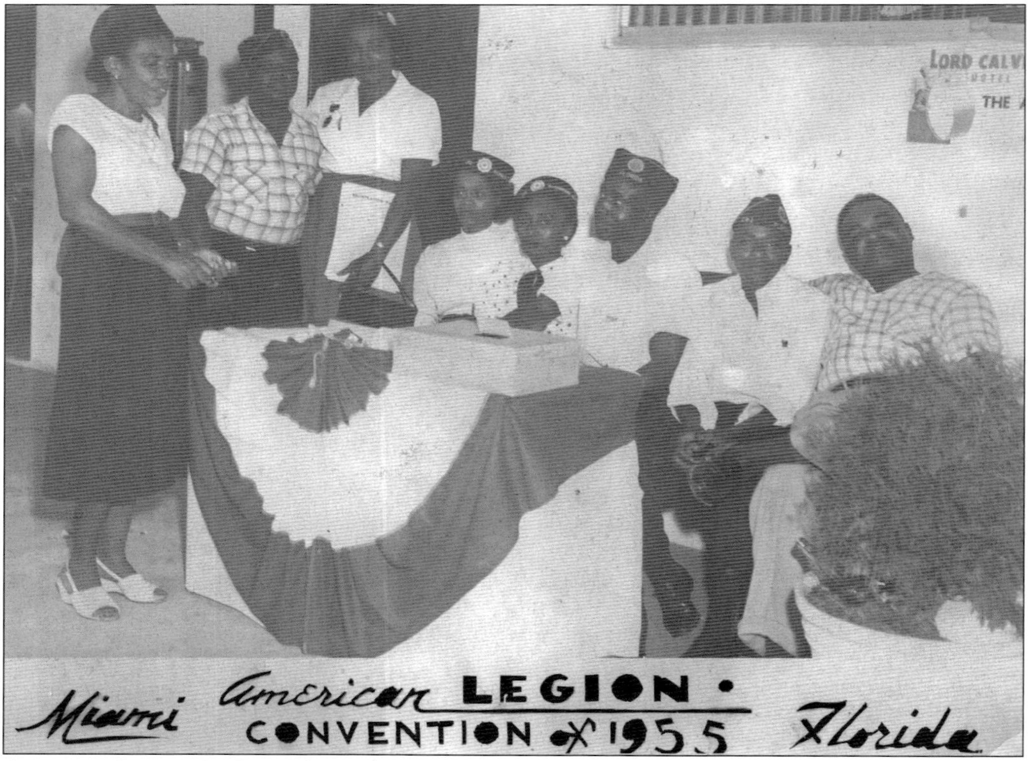

American Legion Richmond Heights Post No. 281 has evolved into one of the most influential nonprofit groups in the United States. Over the years, the American Legion has encouraged considerable social change in America, won hundreds of benefits for veterans, and produced many important programs for children and youth. This is a photograph of the American Legion Miami Convention of 1955. (Courtesy of the Redding family.)

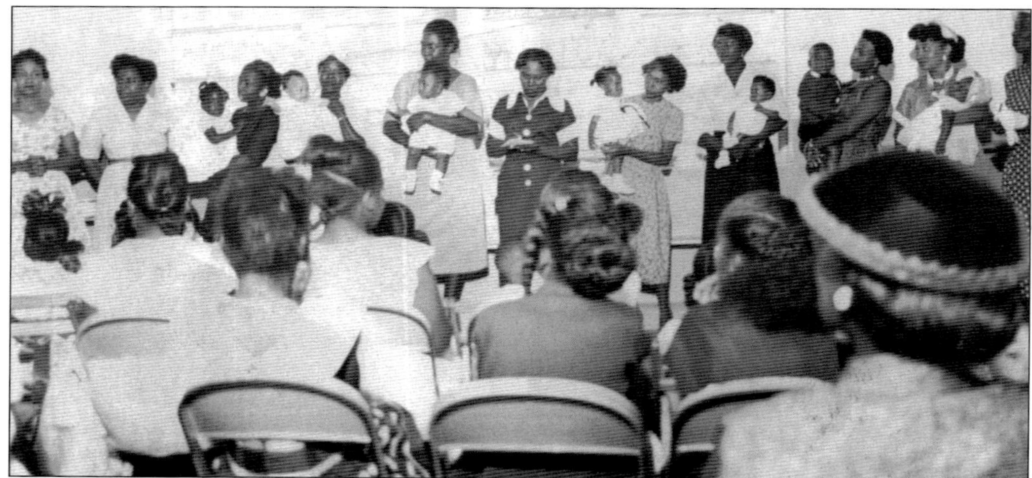

This photograph captures an early meeting of the Woman's Club, which was founded in 1954 by Anita P. Gray. She was looking for women who wanted to work together to enhance the best interest of Richmond Heights. The group was responsible for making early strides on the community to empower the residents. (Courtesy of the Woman's Club.)

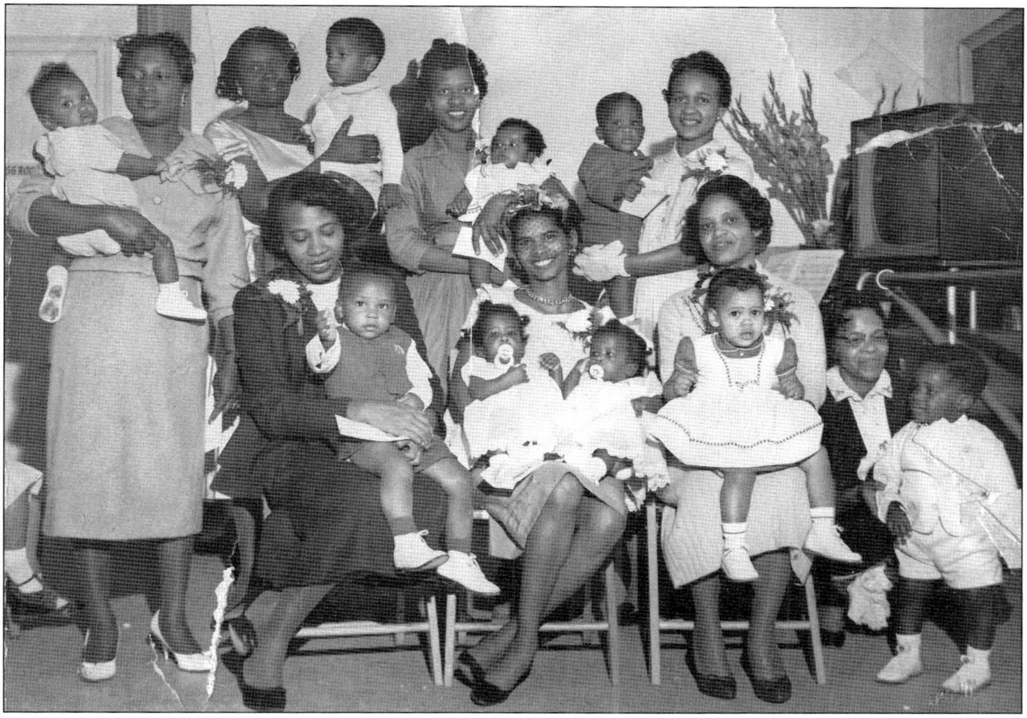

The Woman's Club of Richmond Heights is a staple in the community. They sponsor countless community events in an effort to educate. This event was a baby contest in 1960. The women photographed are, from left to right, (first row) Glenda Harris, Shirley Ross, Bessie Holloway, and Myrtle Benbow; (second row) France Stevens, Earnestine Dorsey, Geraldine Benbow, and Evelyn Troup. (Courtesy of Margaret Holloway.)

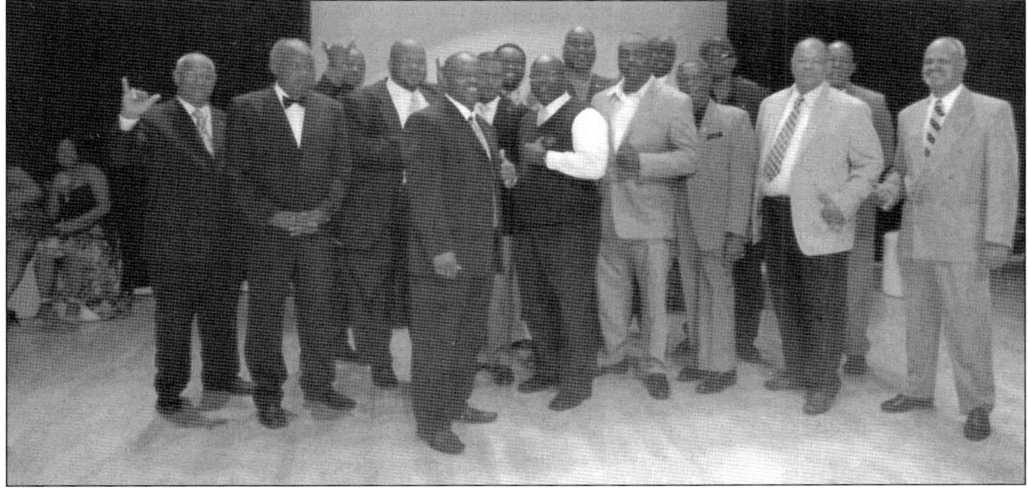

Iota Pi Lambda Chapter of Alpha Phi Alpha Fraternity, Inc., was founded in 1968 at the home of Tom Anderson in Richmond Heights. Eight distinguish men were in attendance and became the founders of this group. They are Tom Anderson, Linkston Cryer, Clarence Cryer, Earl Dinkson, Emanuel Fryar, Paul Joseph, John Pittman, and Lee Perry. (Courtesy of the Iota Pi Lambda of Alpha Phi Alpha.)

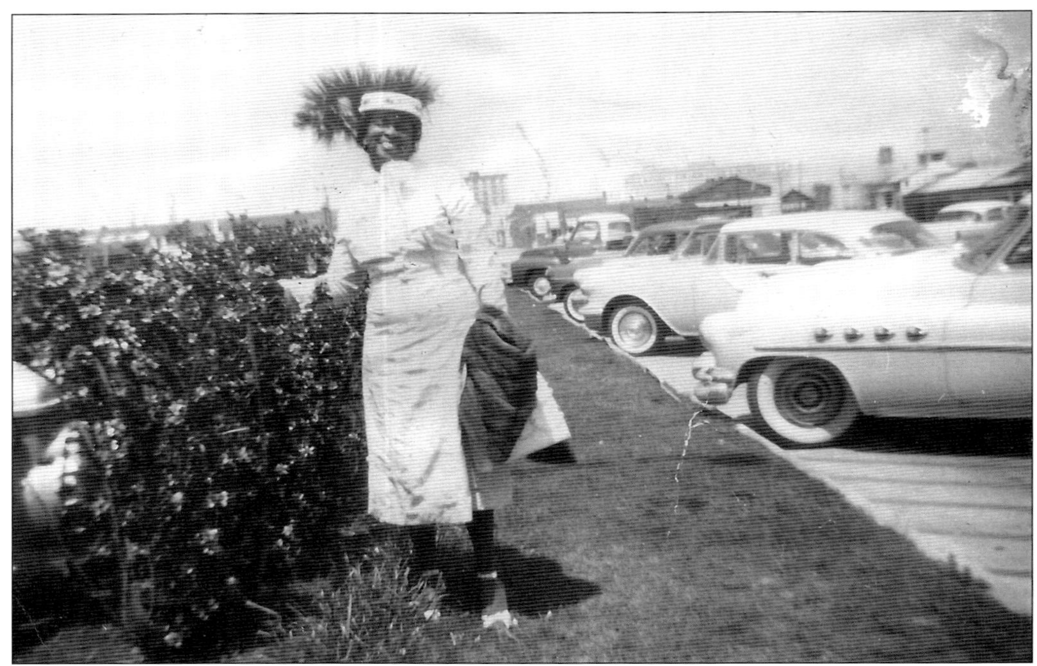

Here, Mallie Hunter, dressed to the nines, heads out to a Sigma Gamma Rho meeting. Mallie was a 1955 charter member for the South Florida Gamma Delta Chapter of Sigma Gamma Rho Sorority, Inc.

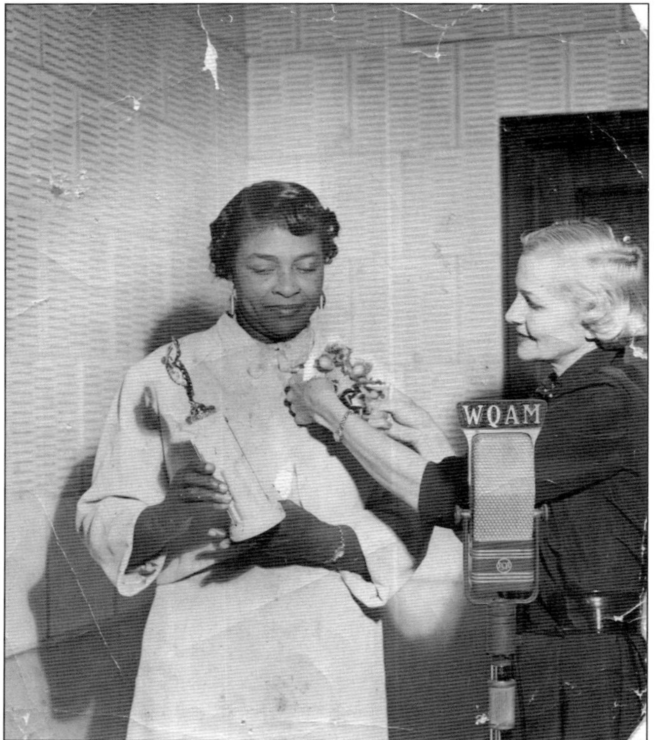

Always ambitious, Mallie Hunter is seen at left receiving a trophy given by the Junior Woman's Club of Miami as the Most Distinguished Woman of 1953 for civic and community work. She retired from the Dade County Board of Public Instruction.

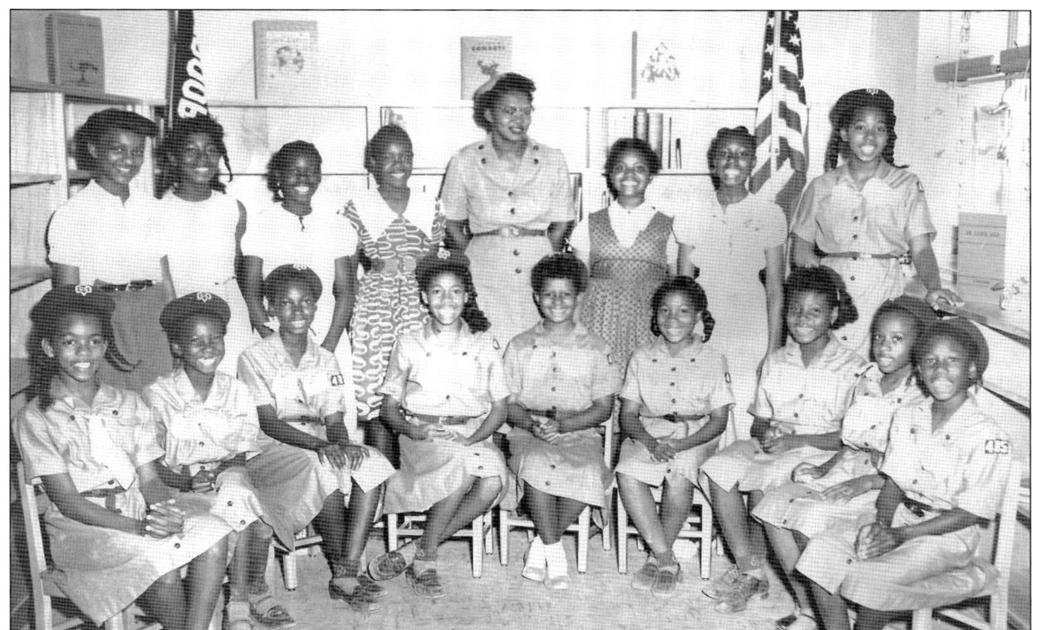

This is a picture of Frank C. Martin Elementary School's Girl Scout Troop No. 405. Civic participation was once a requirement in rearing. Girl Scouts were taught how to sew, bake, and create a future home for their families. Eddie Redding and A.L. Crawford were troop sponsors. (Courtesy of Eddie Redding.)

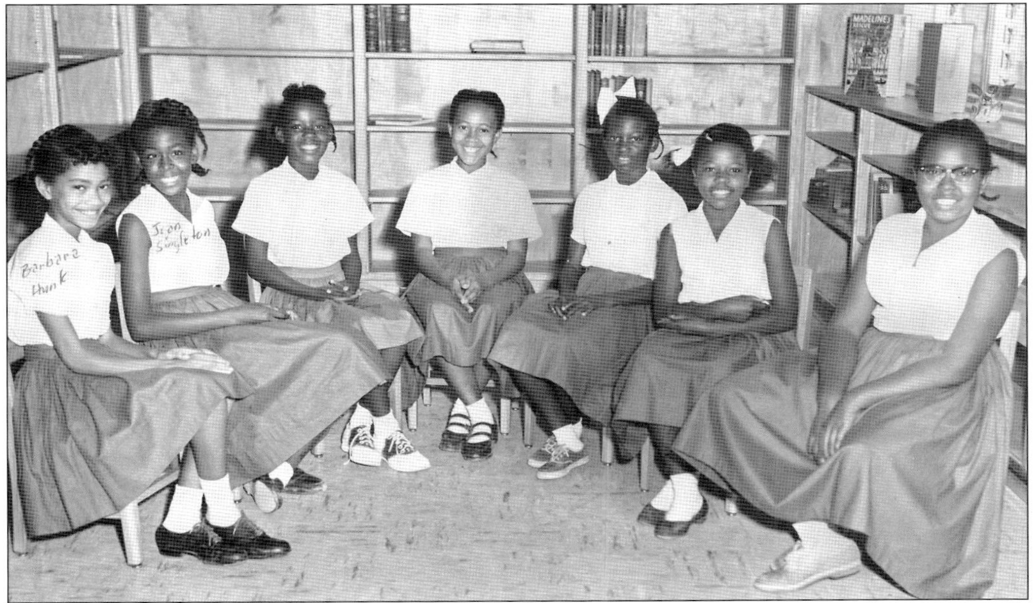

The picture above is of the Frank C. Martin Elementary 4-H Club in April 1957. Hazel D. Aiken and Bernice W. Thompson sponsored the club. From left to right are Barbara Hunk, Jean Singleton, unidentified, Lessie Haynes, two unidentified, and Barbara Hankerson. The mission of the 4-H Club is to provide youth with hands-on real-world experiences in preparation to be leaders. (Courtesy of the Armstrong family.)

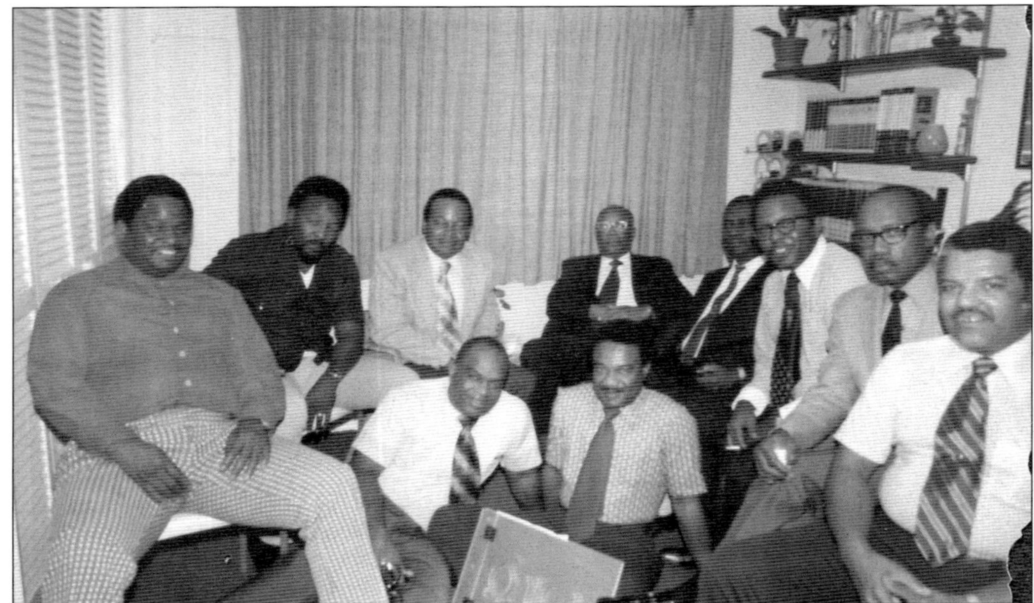

The Pi Nu Chapter of Omega Psi Phi was brought into fruition on February 17, 1971. Charter members included Ronald Baskins, Abraham Bassie, Will Blount, Johnnie Brown, Larry Clements, George Demeritte, Dr. Herbert Greene, Harold Martin, Bernard Pennington, Alfred Shootes, Bertrum Smith, Hubert Thompson, Rufus Tribble, and Lt. Charles Walker. Harold Martin served as the charter basileus. This is a photograph of the Pi Nu Chapter of Omega Psi Phi in the 1970s. (Courtesy of Dr. Herbert Greene.)

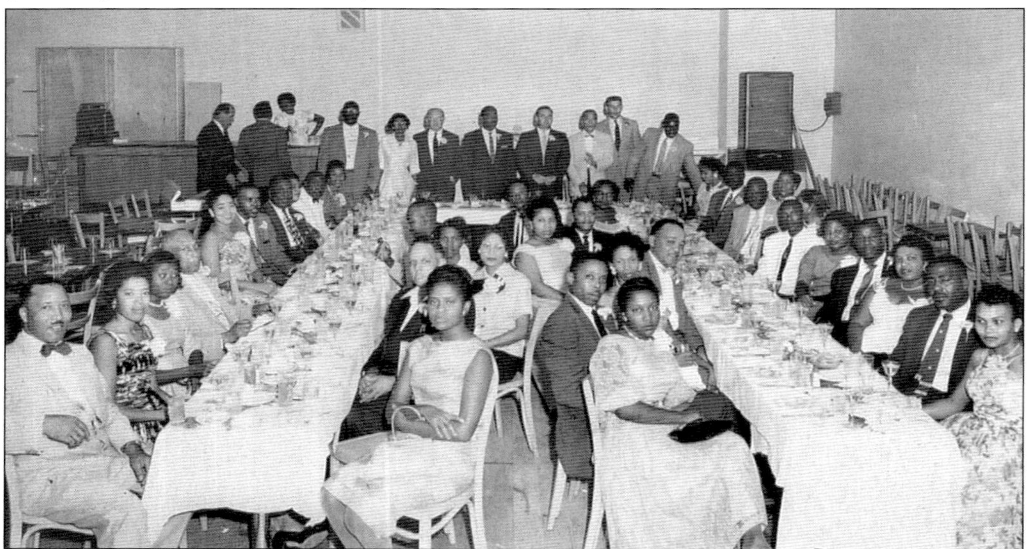

The gentlemen pictured are members of the AFL-CIO Transportation Coalition and worked as skycaps for Miami International Airport. They were instrumental in urging Capt. Frank C. Martin to develop the community of Richmond Heights. Here, the union members are at Dinner Key Auditorium in Coconut Grove at the AFL-CIO's annual dance. Dinner Key Auditorium was located in one of Pan American World Airways' original four hangars for seaplanes. (Courtesy of Mona Jackson)

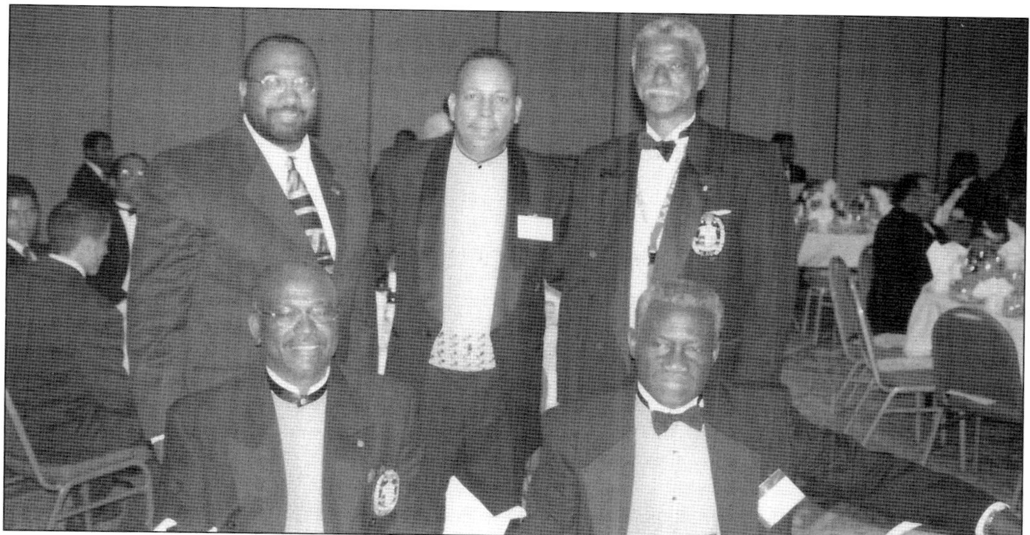

The Richmond-Perrine Chapter of Kappa Alpha Psi Fraternity was chartered in the fall of 1997. After many meetings, active and inactive fraternity members were united to serve as a tool for change in the lives of young men in southern Miami-Dade County. Included in this picture are several of the 31 charter members; they are, from left to right, (first row) Ervie Wright and Ransom Hill Sr.; (second row) Pearley Richardson Jr., Randy Spann, and Donald Hollis Sr. (Courtesy of Donald Hollis.)

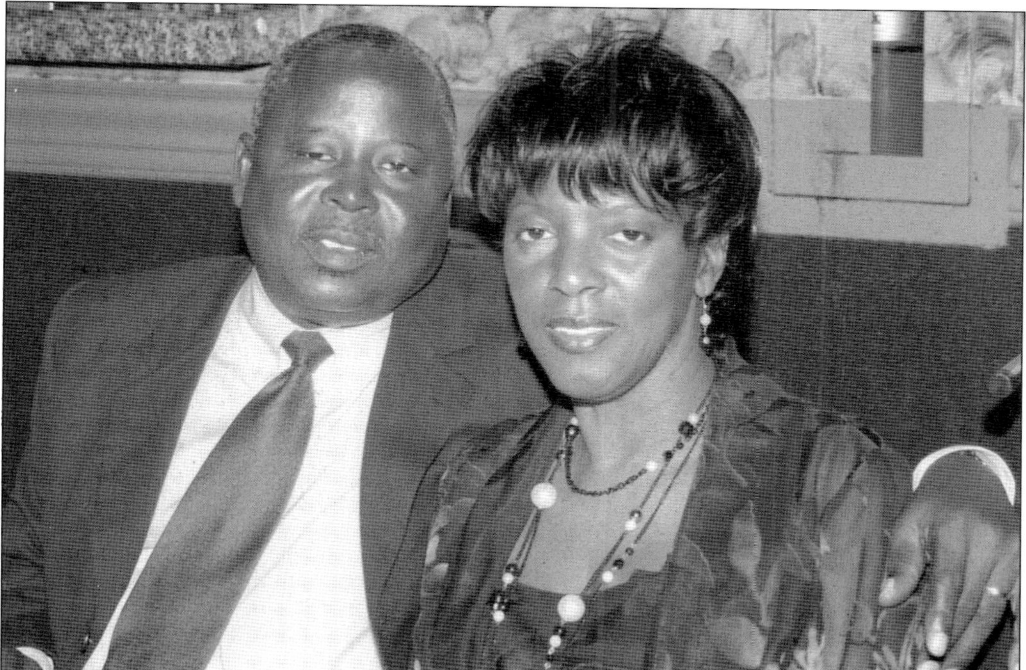

Alvin Patterson is one of the founding members for the Concerned & Committed Brothers of the Community, Inc. The organization was established to give back to the community and residents of Richmond Heights. Some activities of the group include mentoring youth, helping the elderly, and feeding the hungry. Pictured are, from left to right, Alvin and Mable Patterson.

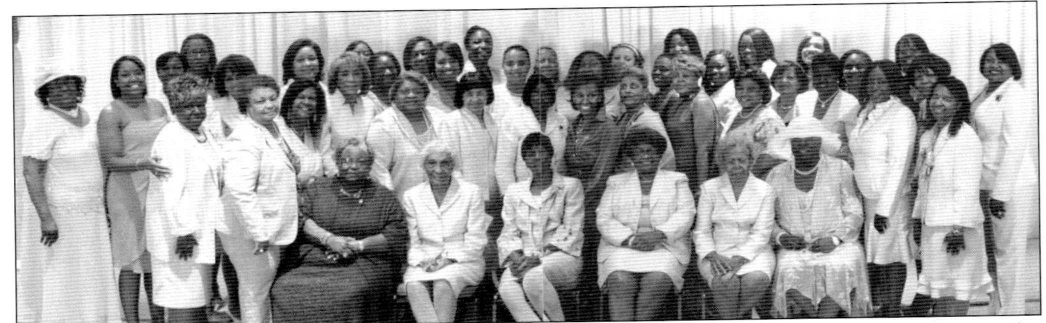

A group of inactive Alpha Kappa Alpha Sorority members decided to establish a new chapter, the Pi Delta Omega Chapter of Alpha Kappa Alpha Sorority, Inc. By the end of July, activities were well under way to not only demonstrate a need for a second chapter in the Greater Miami area, but also to comply with requirements for chartering. On February 8, 1986, the new chapter was chartered at the Kings Bay Yacht and Country Club. The charter members are Virginia Adger, Gloria Alexander, Addie Anderson, Sue Baety, Shirley Barbee, Barbara Benton, Valarie Carter, Eleanor Wheeler Chamberlain, Eva Cofield, Laura Collier, Elizabeth Collins, Priscilla Dames, Carmelita Davis, Mary Floyd, Alethea Fryar, Alexandria Holloway, PhD, Lafrieda Hudson-Grandberry, Rosbin Ivery, Shirley James, Roslyn Jennings, Bettye Mears, Jacqueline McCollum, Ruthie Pittman, Margaret Polite, and Joan Timmons. Pictured are members attending the 2011 Little Miss Fashionetta Pageant.

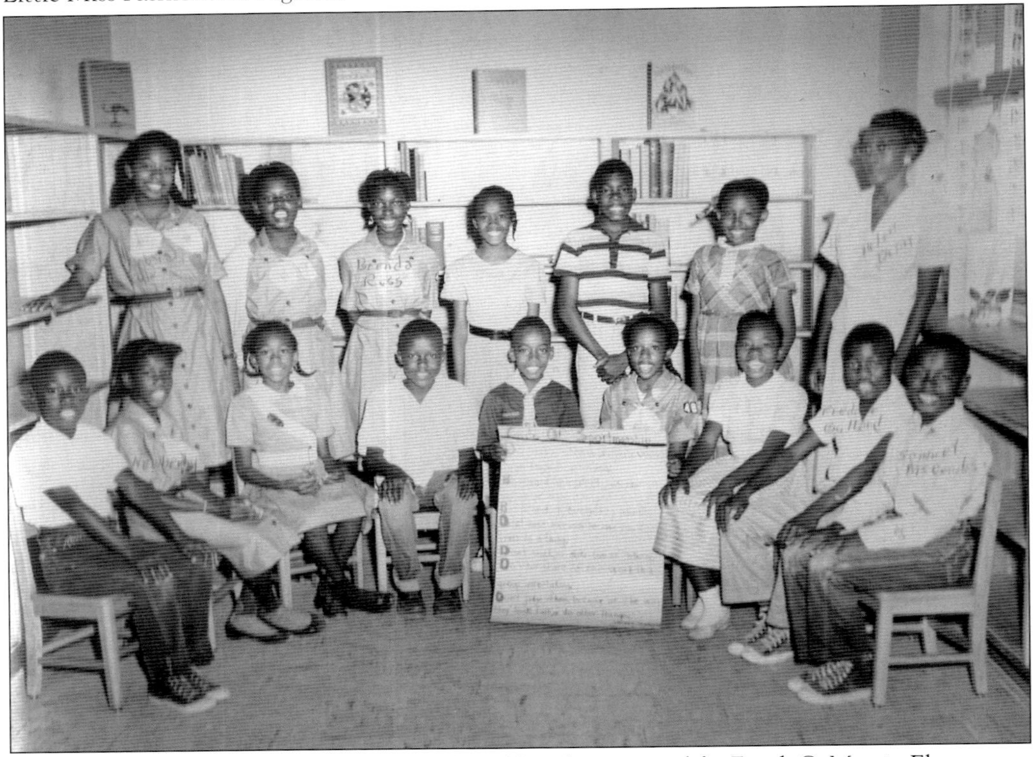

Helen P. Dean was the sponsor for the 1955–1956 student council for Frank C. Martin Elementary School. The council represented structure through which students could become involved in the affairs of the school, while working with the school's management, staff, and parents for the benefit of the school and the students. (Courtesy of Armstrong family.)

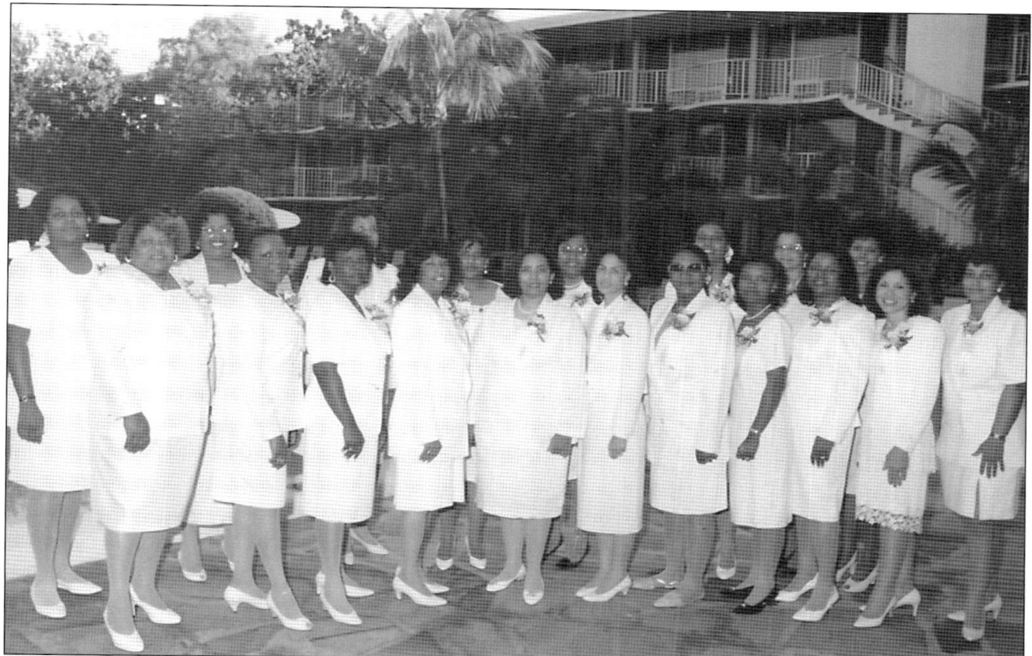

The South Miami Chapter of Jack and Jill of America, Inc., became a chapter at the July 1988 National Convention in San Francisco, California. On September 14, 1988, a total of 22 ladies were inducted as members. The president-elect for the chapter was Rene Beal.

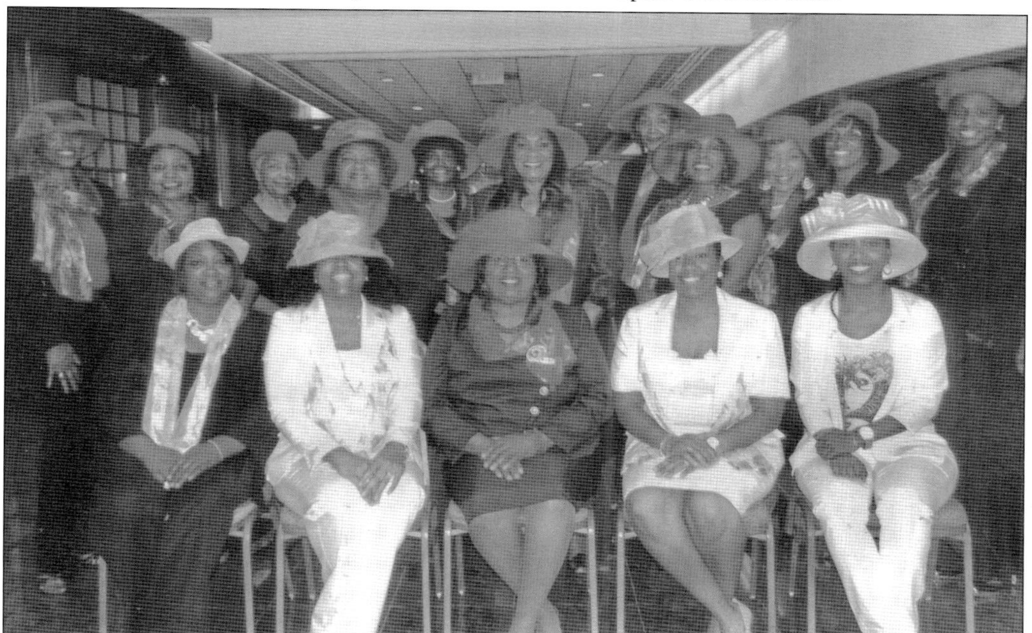

Miami-Dade Richmond Heights Chapter of the Red Hat Society, Sophisticated Sables, was chartered on April 20, 2005. This women's society of 50-plus members has sponsored a Christmas gala at Signature Gardens for the Richmond Heights residents since 2005. In 2009, they celebrated Richmond Heights' 60th anniversary at the gala. Patricia Harper Garrett is the queen.

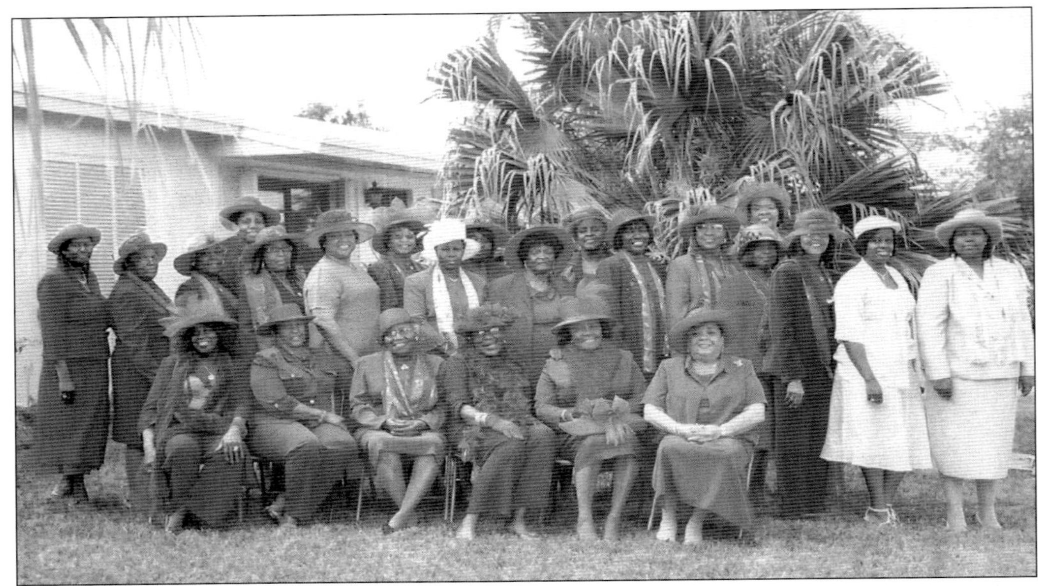

The Silver Foxes of Richmond Heights was chartered on April 26, 2006. The charter members were Margaret Cruz, Rosetta Harris, Mary McCray, Frances Moore, Dorothy Passmoore, Martha Price, Frances Stevens, Jessie Tanner, and Rosa Washington. Margaret Cruz was elected as the first queen. (Courtesy of Helen McCray.)

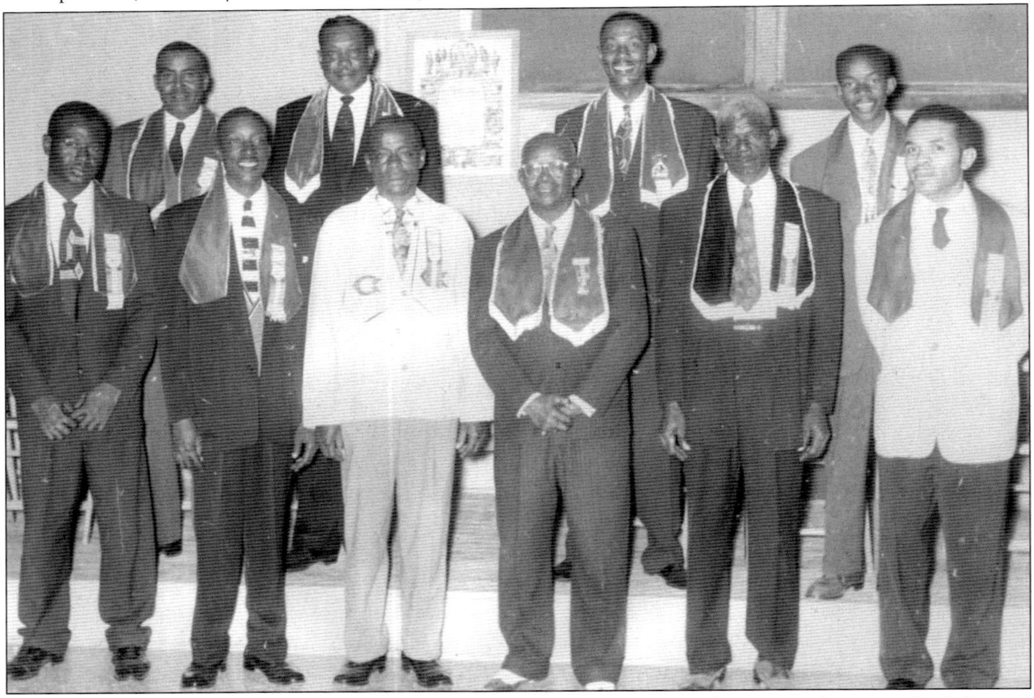

This is a 1950s photograph of the Knights of Pythias organization. They were photographed during a meeting being held at Walter Bell's home on Grave Drive. From left to right are (first row) Ulysses Turner, Chester Fair Sr., Earnest White, two unidentified, and Murray James; (second row) Willie Smith, Robert Glover, Walter Bell (president), and Don Bell. (Courtesy of the Fair family)

Seven

Family Life

Richmond Heights was famous for its nurturing environment. Picture a place deliberately segregated, which may sound a bit odd, but for the 1950s, it was perfect. There was a sense of community pride that exuded in the air. It has been said that even when undesirables would come into the neighborhood, they would reform to picture-perfect behavior. The spirit of excellence was infectious and spread through every home.

In fact, in 1963, *Jet* magazine noticed that same family quality in Richmond Heights and crowned the community as one of the safest black neighborhoods in Florida after Metro-Dade County public safety director R.A. Buchanan reported the facts. With self-imposed sanctions on nightlife and alcohol sales, Richmond Heights did not even have crime. In fact, people did not lock their doors. Parents did not fret over their children playing outside. It was approximately 10 years after the inception of Richmond Heights that streetlights were erected. In order for the streetlights to be erected, a special assessment tax for homeowners had to be in place to provide funding for the installment.

The first family to select their home and to put a contract down was that of Johnnie Henderson. On December 13, 1949, he selected block No. 22, lot no. 8 at 14961 Monroe Street. This was the first street to be built, and the residents took so much pleasure in their newfound homesteads that the families would gather weekly for fellowship. In a rotation style, different families would host these gatherings. For example, one week, it was at the McKays' house to watch the Wednesday night fight. The next week, it was to play cards at the Taylors' home. And then onto the Williamses' house the following week and so on.

The first 25 residents of Richmond Heights signed their contracts in 1949. Those original residents are as follows and are listed in chronological order of signing their contracts: Johnnie Henderson, Earnest White Sr., Livingston James, Warric Ferguson, George Swain, Buchie McCray, Willie Johnson, Barfield Burch, James Holmes, Dewey Keyes, John Byrd, Richard Bullard, Spencer Murray, Willie Pearson, Lee Burton, William Phillips Jr., Grady Holloway, Henry Prince, Luther Wallace, Samuel Hutchinson, James Wanza, Albert Sample, Walter Bethel, Gladston Taylor, Stephen Worthy, and Oliver Page.

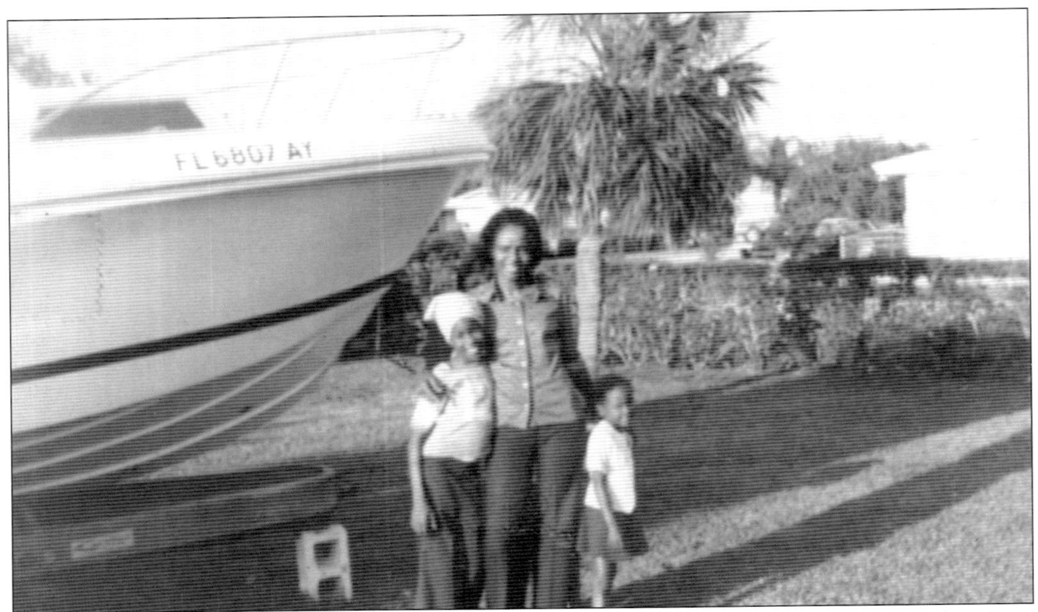

The Dorseys are pictured at home on this relaxing Sunday afternoon after going to church at Martin Memorial AME Church. It is spring break of 1973, and Earnestine Dorsey is enjoying time with her family during her school break. Her teaching career began at Frank C. Martin Elementary School. From left to right are 11-year-old Wanda Dorsey, mom Earnestine Dorsey, and 6-year-old Marci Dorsey. (Courtesy of the Dorsey family.)

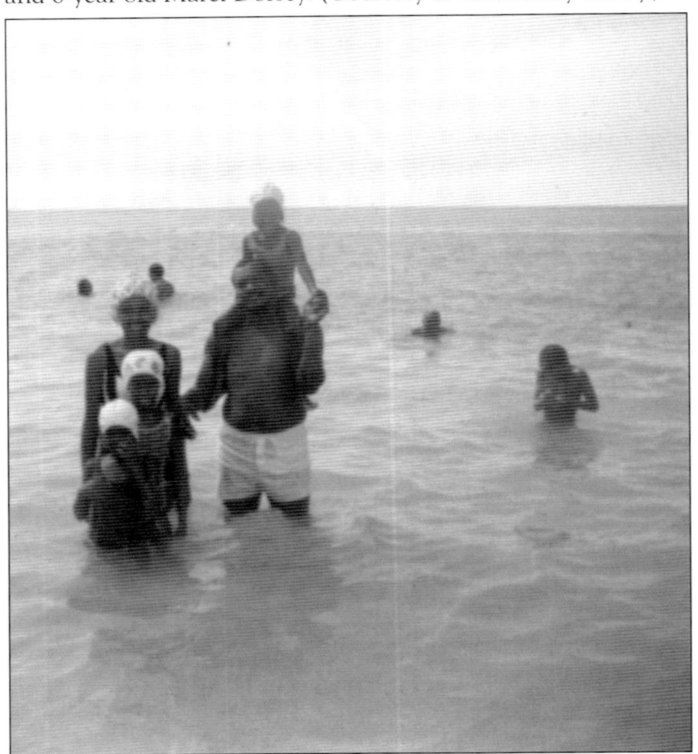

Earnestine and Mantley Dorsey met and fell in love in Richmond Heights; the couple first saw each other while walking on the path from the park to the strip shopping center. After 30 years, Mantley Dorsey retired as a microbiologist for the University of Miami School of Medicine. On this day at the beach, the Dorseys enjoy the sun and family time. Shown from left to right are Kathy, Wanda, Earnestine, Mantley, and Marci (on Mantley's shoulders. (Courtesy of the Dorsey family.)

Mary and Eugene Williams Sr. had three children and were charter members of Second Baptist Church. They moved to 14825 SW 104th Place in Richmond Heights in 1961. This is a photograph of the family at an outing. Pictured are, from left to right, Mary Ann Williams, Eugene Williams Jr., and Mary Williams. (Courtesy of the Williams family.)

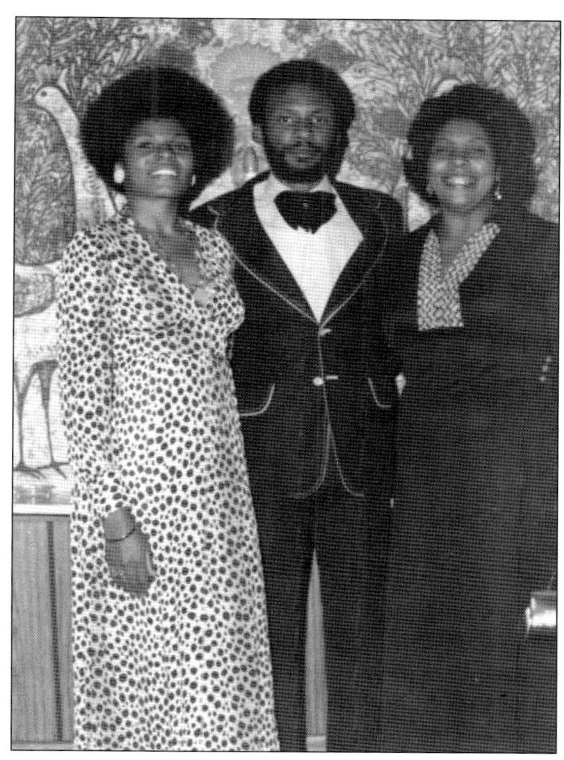

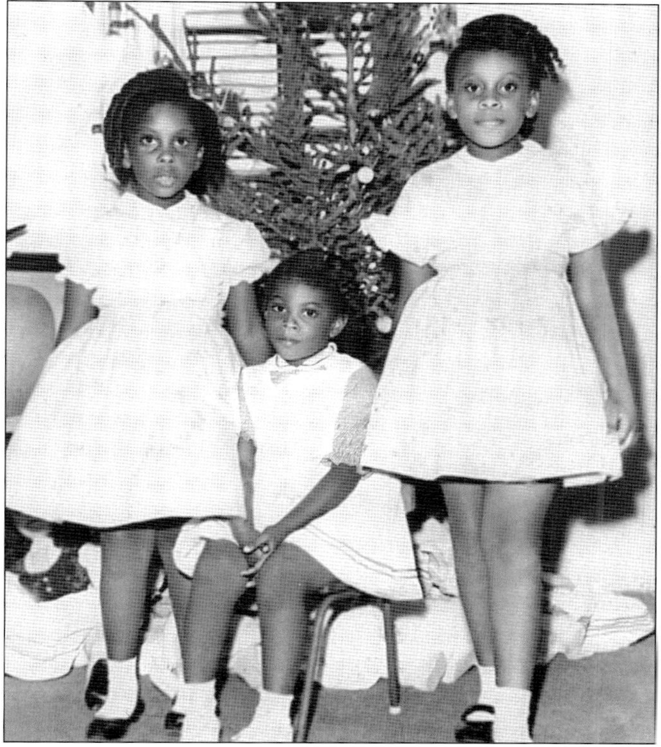

The Cambridge girls pose for a picture at Christmastime in 1962 in front of their Christmas tree. They lived on Jackson Street. Pictured from left to right are six-year-old Vivian Cambridge, four-year-old Audrey Cambridge, and eight-year-old Vanessa Cambridge. (Courtesy of the Cambridge family.)

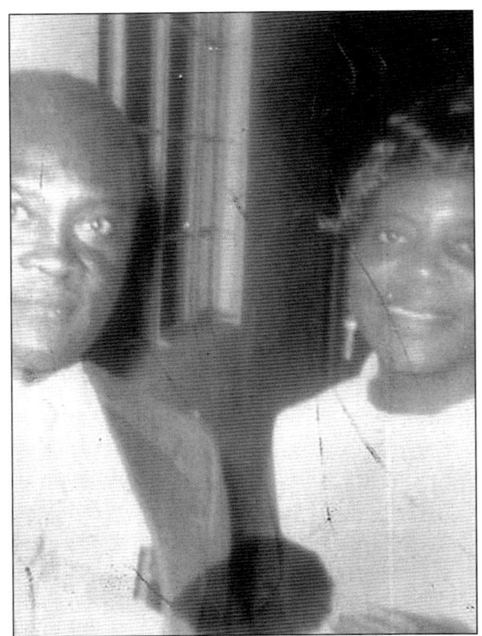

Alfred S. Cambridge and Mary Lynn Payne were married on January 31, 1945, in Coconut Grove by Reverend Tanner, pastor of St. Mary's Baptist Church. They closed on their Jackson Street property on March 10, 1950. Mary was a community organizer for the Economic Opportunity Program, Inc. (EOPI), and retired as a social worker for the State of Florida. Alfred retired from Homestead Air Force Base. They have four daughters, Mary Jacquelyn, Vanessa, Vivian, and Audrey. (Courtesy of the Cambridge family.)

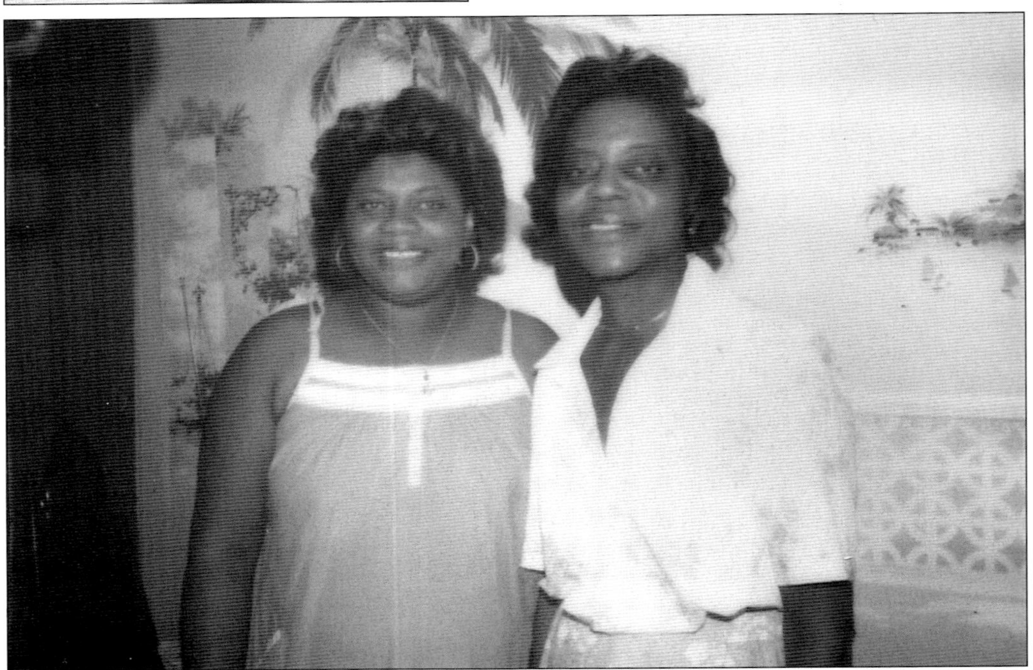

In 1950, the community of Richmond Heights was so connected that neighbors knew everything about each other even before they moved into their houses. Jacqueline Porter was a little kid when she would visit the Richmond Heights sales office with her parents. One wall had a board with many little key rings that named the purchaser of that property. The office was also full of big layouts that illustrated the plans for the community. Pictured are Mary Jacqueline Cambridge (left) and her mother, Mary Cambridge. Both are named Mary because they were both born on Christmas Day. (Courtesy of the Cambridge family.)

Essie Mae Major is pictured in her Van Buren Street home in the late 1950s. She was a homemaker and is shown in her kitchen. She was such a fabulous cook that she eventually sold cakes for 75¢. Her biggest sellers were her sweet potato pie and carrot cake. Her husband was Nathaniel Major Sr., and his favorite dish that she would make was a leg of lamb. (Courtesy of the Sadie Miller family.)

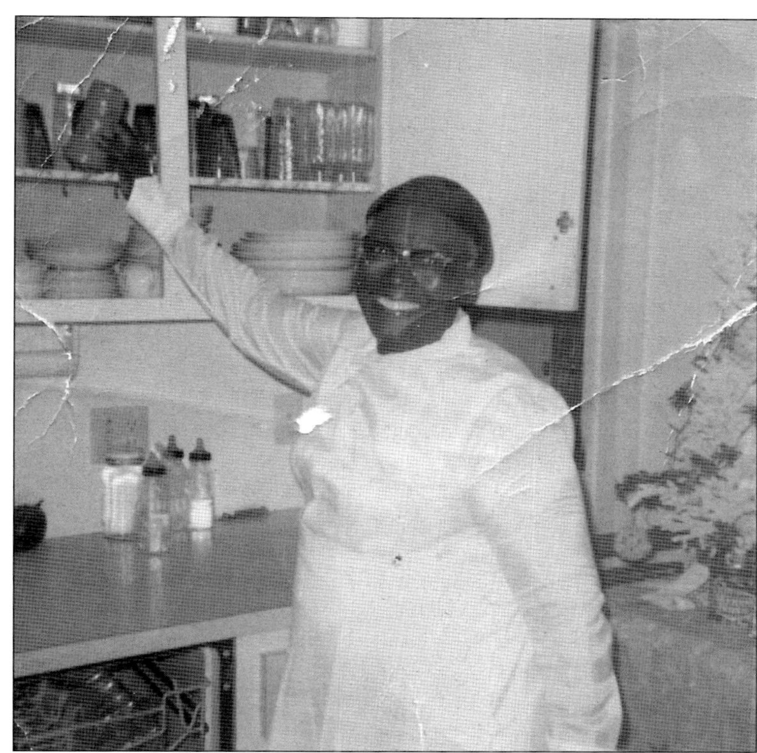

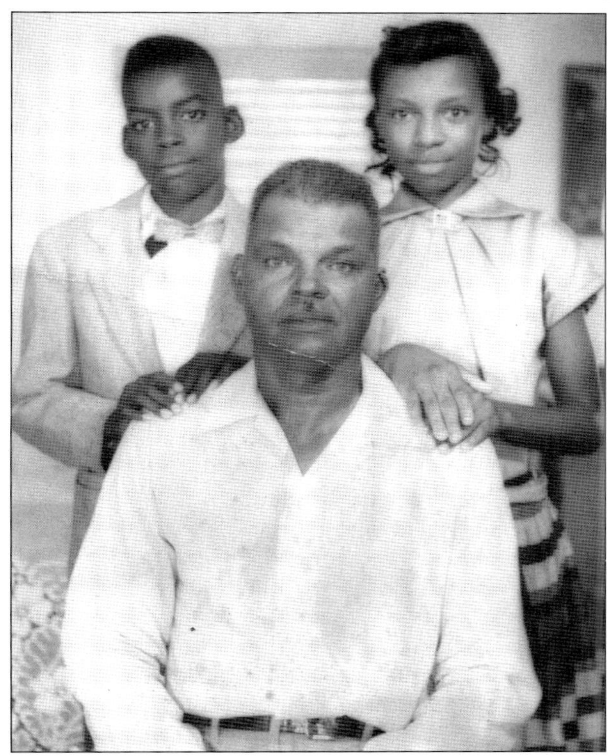

Nathaniel Major Sr. and his wife, Essie Mae Major, moved into their home at 14045 Van Buren Street in 1951 with their children Sadie, Nathaniel, and James. Nathaniel Sr. is pictured with two of his children, Nathaniel Major Jr. (back left) and Sadie Major (back right). This picture was taken in the living room of their Van Buren Street home, which, in 1951, cost $8,030. The couple made a down payment of $29.95 and had monthly payments of $45. (Courtesy of the Sadie Miller family.)

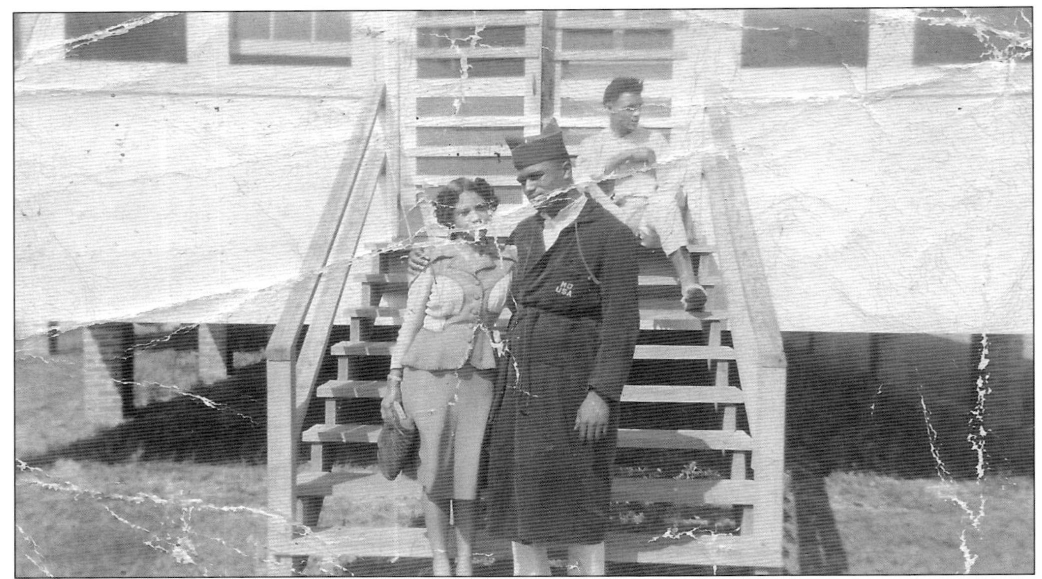

Grady and Bessie Holloway met in Thomasville, Georgia, while Grady was a patient at the VA Hospital recovering from injuries he received serving in the Asiatic-Pacific theater. He served in the US Army in India-Burma from 1942 to 1945. Grady and Bessie married in 1945 and relocated from Georgia to Miami, ultimately settling in Richmond Heights. They had one daughter, Margaret Holloway. (Courtesy of the Holloway family.)

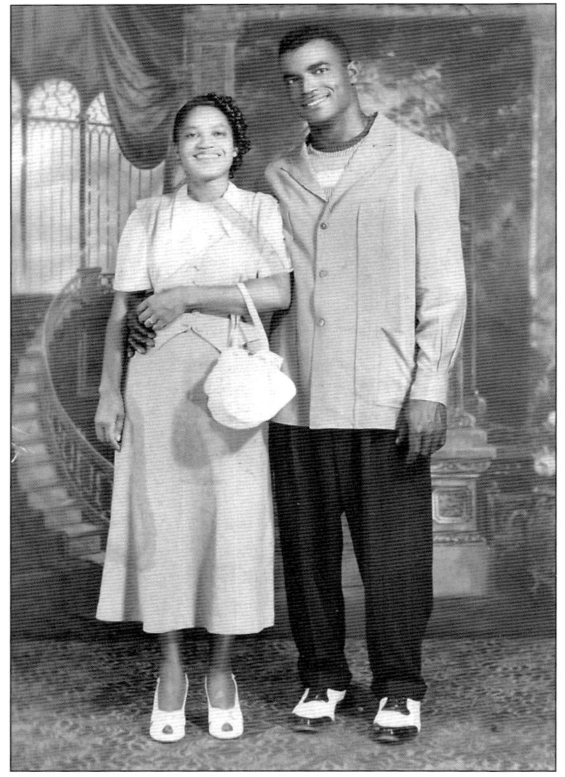

In 1949, the Holloways lived in a community of Coconut Grove called Golden Gates. News was spreading through the neighborhood of a new housing community, named Richmond Heights, being built for black soldiers. Bessie was happy and excited to fill out the papers and sign the actual contract in Captain Martin's office on December 12, 1949. Grady would later start his own lawn service company, and Bessie worked as a beautician. (Courtesy of the Holloway family.)

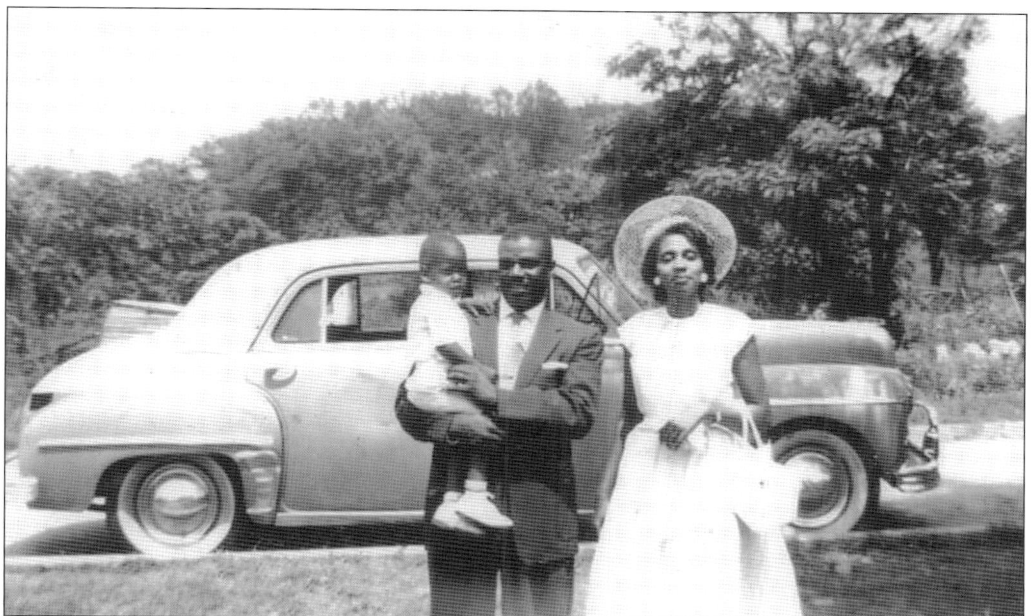

The Greene family is pictured here in the early 1950s in Anniston, Alabama, before settling in Richmond Heights. It is an early Sunday morning, and the family is headed to church. Pictured are, from left to right, Doug Greene, Andrew Jackson Greene II, and Valerie. (Courtesy of the Greene family.)

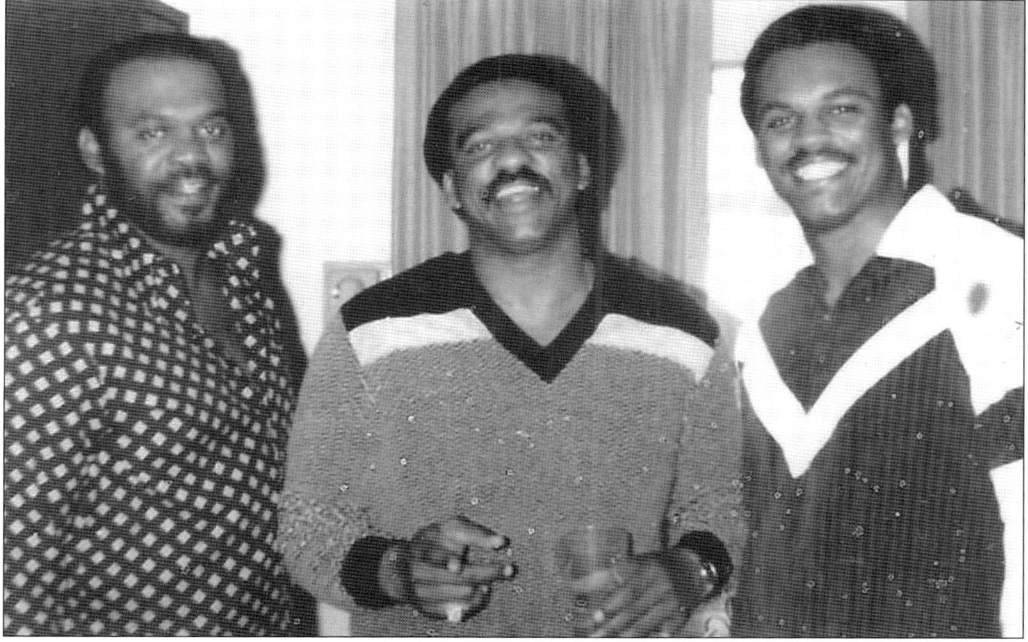

The sons of Andrew and Valerie Greene are photographed here inside of their Jackson Street home in the 1970s. The Greene family migrated from Alabama to Richmond Heights in the late 1950s. Pictured are, from left to right, Doug "Bommer," Andy "Prime," and David "Big D." (Courtesy of the Greene family.)

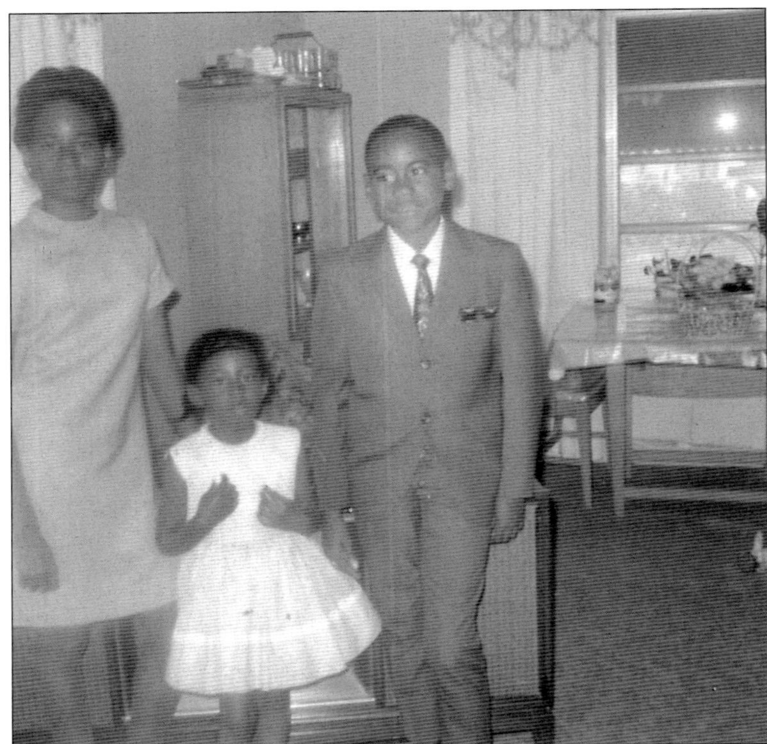

Emanuel Fryar was a longtime resident of South Miami. Fryar served in the US Army. Thanks to his GI Bill, he was afforded the opportunity to go to college, and it was there that he met and fell in love with Alethea Hawkins. After graduation, they married on August 10, 1952, and moved to Richmond Heights. This photograph is of their children on their way to church; they are, from left to right, Renita, Lisa, and Eric. (Courtesy of the Fryar family.)

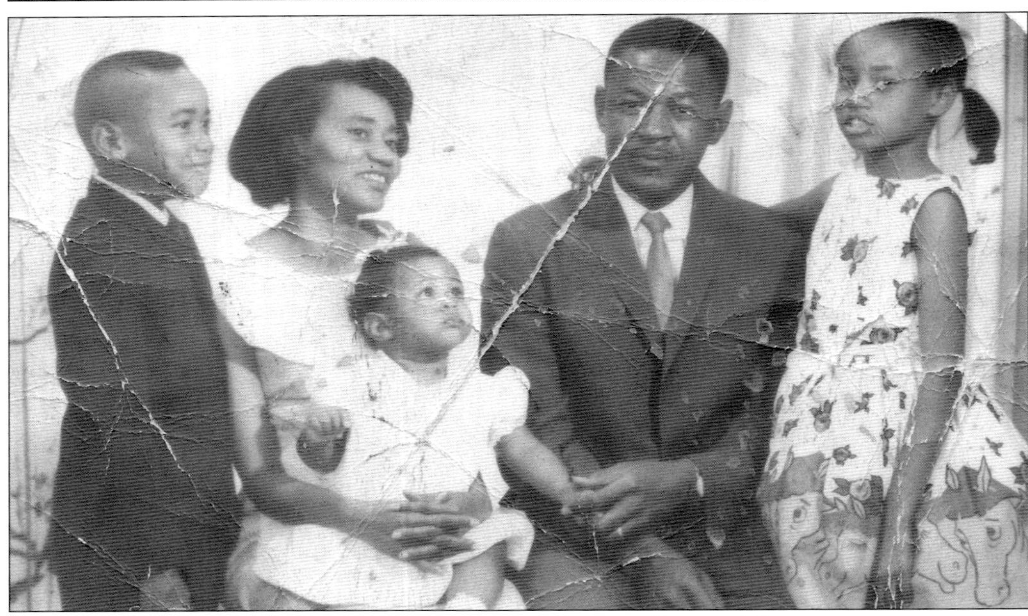

This is a fall picture of the Fryar family in their Sunday best. Emanuel Fryar was an entrepreneur and opened and operated a funeral home business for 20 years in Richmond Heights. The name of the business was Barrett-Fryar-Thompson Funeral Home. It later became Paradise Memorial Funeral Home. In this photograph, Emanuel is joined by, from left to right, his son Eric; wife Alethea, who is holding their daughter Lisa; and Renita. (Courtesy of the Fryar family.)

The Raulerson family moved to Richmond Heights in 1959. They are pictured at right sitting in their front room on Jackson Street. Pictured are, from left to right, Evelyn Raulerson, William Raulerson, and Warren Raulerson. Evelyn retired from Miami-Dade County Public Schools, and William was a Korean War veteran and later retired from the United States Postal Service. Son Warren was in the banking industry. (Courtesy of the Raulerson family.)

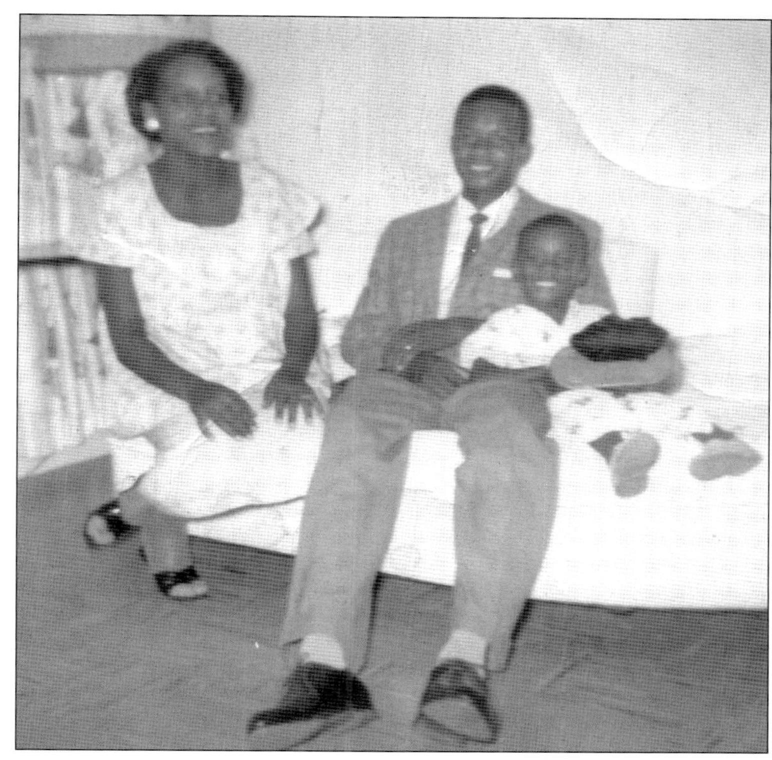

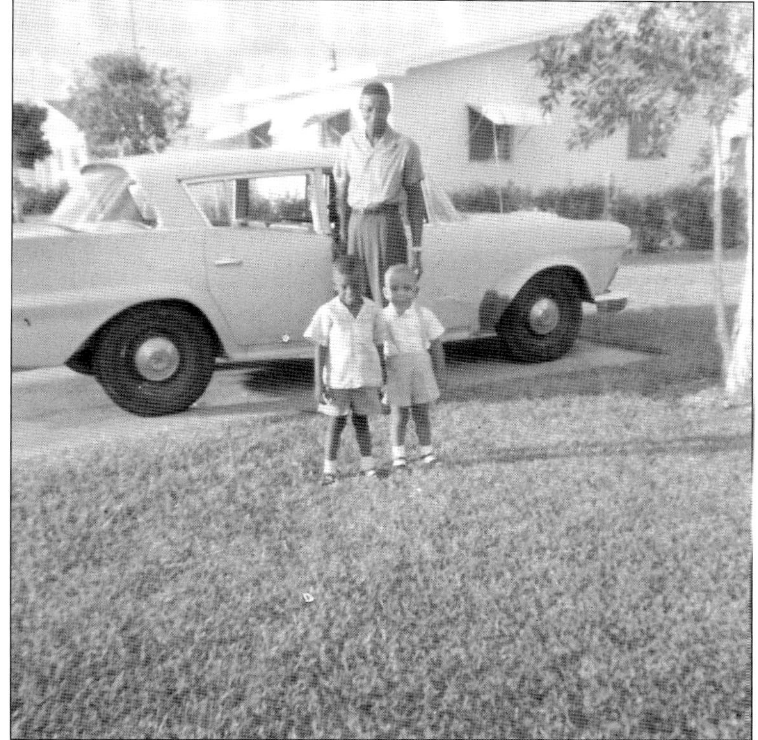

This is a beautiful August day in 1961 in Richmond Heights, and the Raulersons are standing in front of their home on Jackson Street with a perfectly manicured lawn and cherry bushes. The children pictured are, from left to right, Warren Raulerson and neighbor Chris Westfield. Standing behind them is William "Herbert" Raulerson in front of his American Motors' Rambler car. (Courtesy of the Raulerson family.)

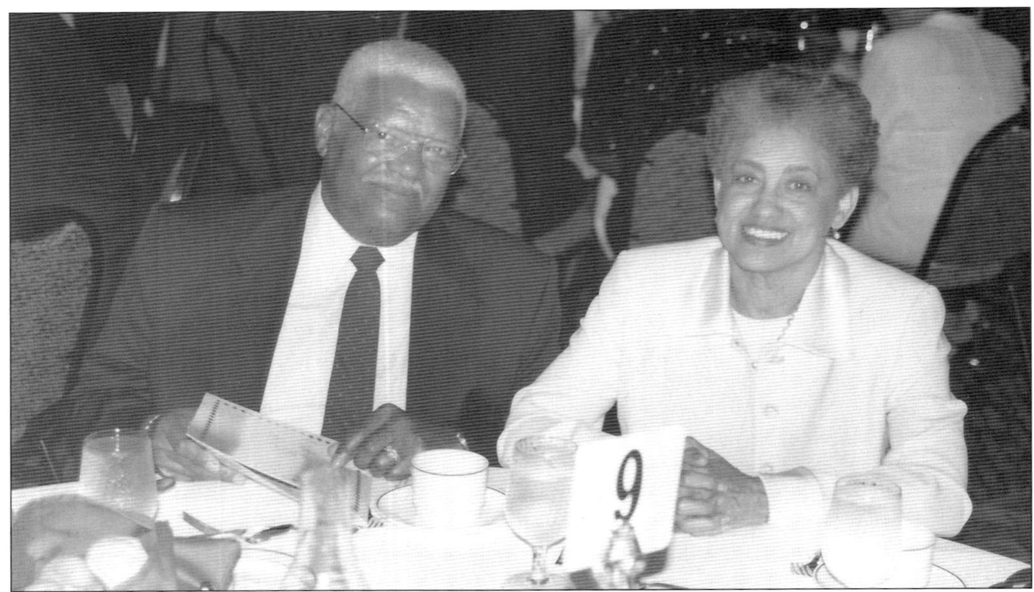

Dr. Herbert Greene met a beautiful woman named Vivian Buggs in his senior year of medical school at Howard University in Washington, DC. Shortly after meeting, they married and were blessed with three sons, Herbert Jr., Jeffery, and Howard. The couple had their home built on Booker T. Washington Boulevard. (Courtesy of the Greene family.)

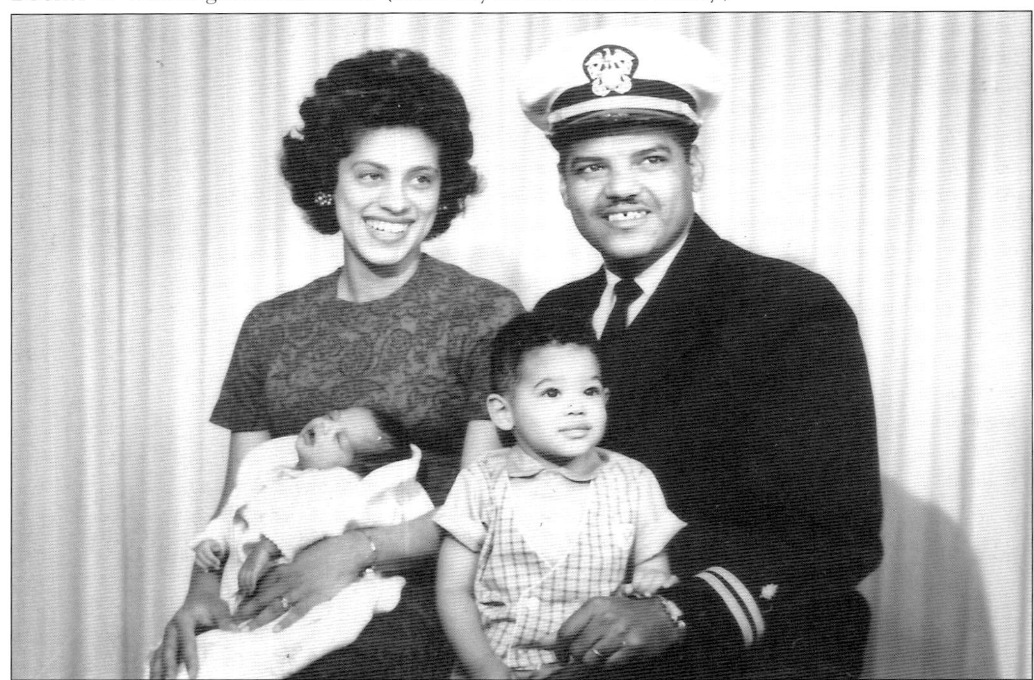

The Greenes are pictured in 1961 in Great Lakes, Illinois. At this time, Dr. Herbert Greene served as a medical officer in the US Navy. Pictured are, from left to right, Vivian holding baby Jeffery and Herbert Sr. holding Herbert Jr. Jeffery is currently a computer analysis, and Herbert Jr. is an airline pilot. (Courtesy of the Greene family.)

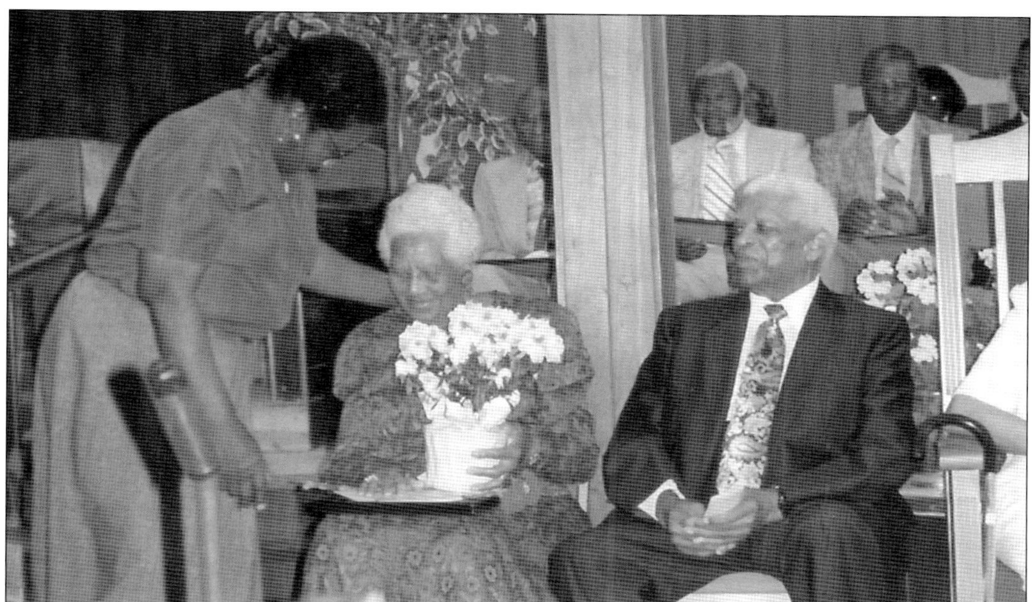

Elnora and Daniel Green (sitting) had three children, one son and two daughters. They were originally from Roanoke, Alabama, where they met at church. They got married on February 12, 1932. They purchased a home on Jackson Street and were long-standing members of Second Baptist Church. This picture was taken as they were being honored at Second Baptist Church. (Courtesy of Second Baptist Church.)

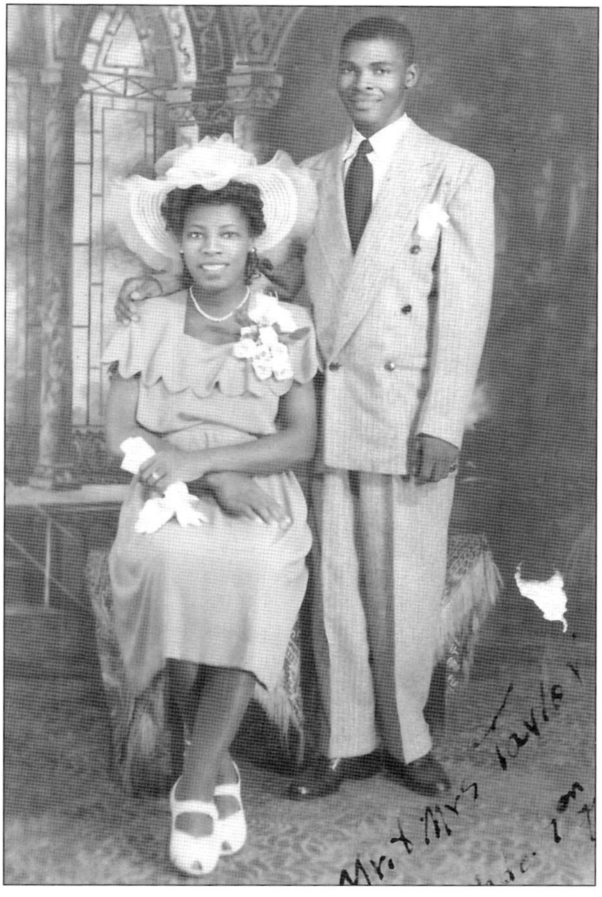

Gladston and Ruth Taylor met and married in Miami, Florida. The Taylors were one of the first families to move to Richmond Heights in February 1950. Gladston served in World War II as an Army sergeant. This picture was taken of the couple in August 1947 in a photography studio. (Courtesy of the Taylor family.)

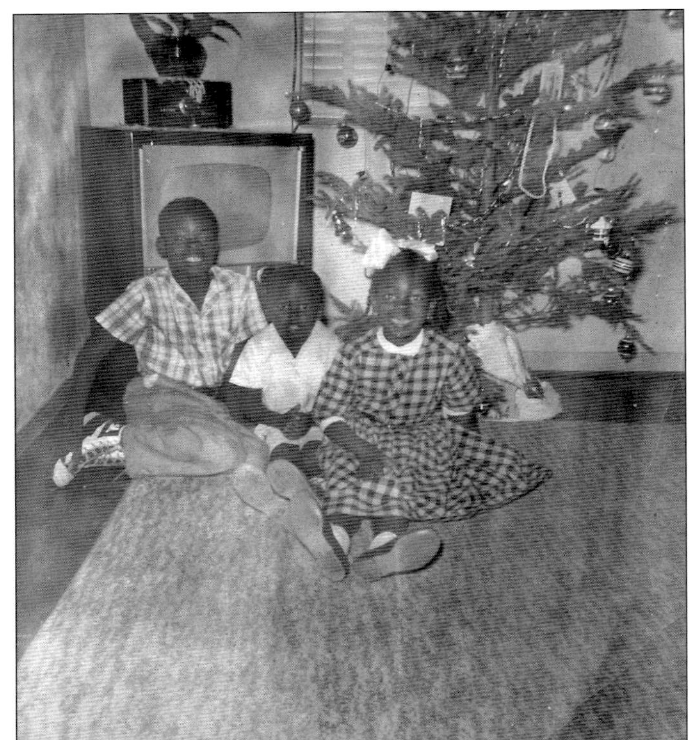

It is Christmastime at the Taylors' house in 1958. Monroe Street was full of holiday cheer as one of Richmond Heights' first families celebrates God and family. From left to right are Robert Taylor, Gladston Taylor Jr., and Ruthie Taylor. Robert resides in Atlanta, Georgia; Gladston resides in Houston, Texas; and Ruthie resides in Richmond Heights. (Courtesy of the Taylor family.)

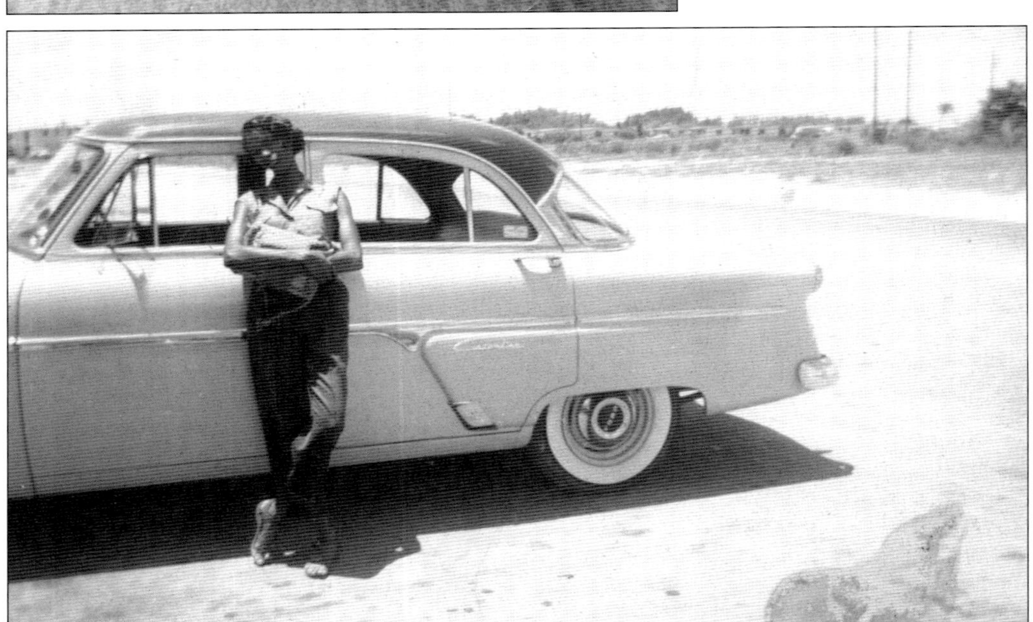

Olga Goodman Bethel posed in front of her home on Buchanan Street. She and her Carver High School sweetheart, Charles Edwards Bethel, married in 1941 and moved into their new home in the early 1950s. This 1951 photograph was taken before the completion of homes off Buchanan Street, which is now Walter White Park. She and her husband would take their daughters, Ellen and Mona, for Sunday evening drives on Old Cutler Road. (Courtesy of Mona Bethel Jackson.)

Mary and Johnnie B. Hinson met in South Miami and were married in 1953. Shortly after marrying, they knew that the newly built community of Richmond Heights was going to be their home. They looked over the available homes in Richmond Heights and moved into their new house on Polk Street in 1956. (Courtesy of the Hinson family.)

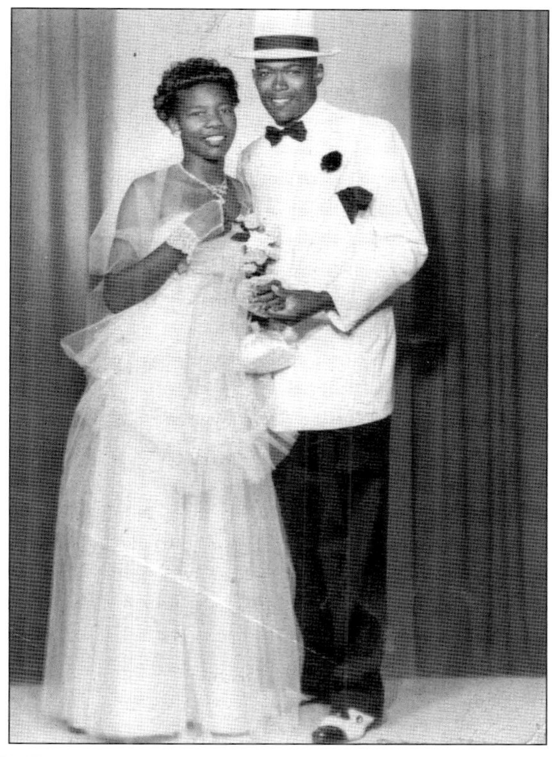

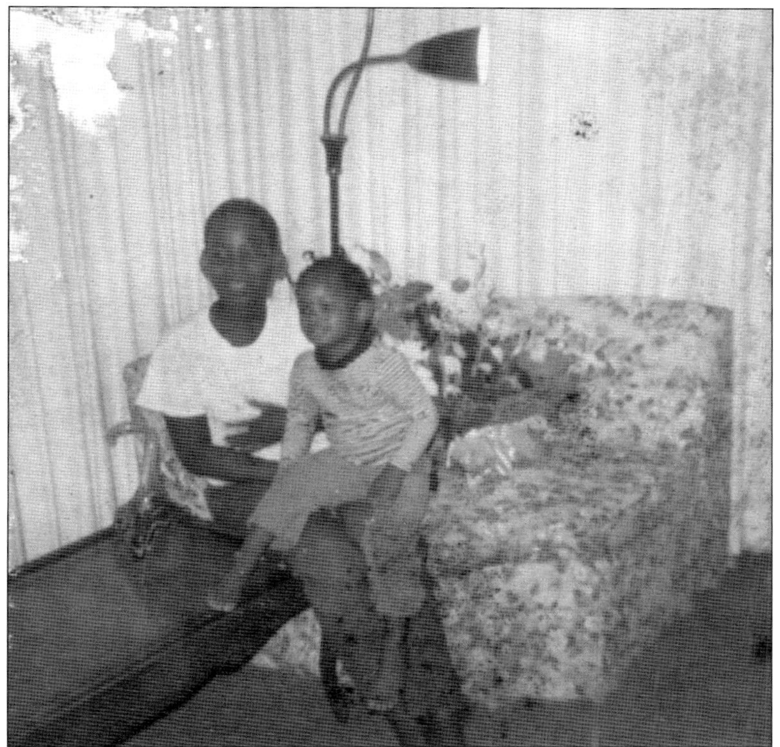

Marcine Hinson and John Hinson are the beautiful children of Mary and Johnnie Hinson. Their memories of Richmond Heights are summarized in the following African proverb: "It takes a village to raise a child." Essentially, the community was one big family. (Courtesy of the Hinson family.)

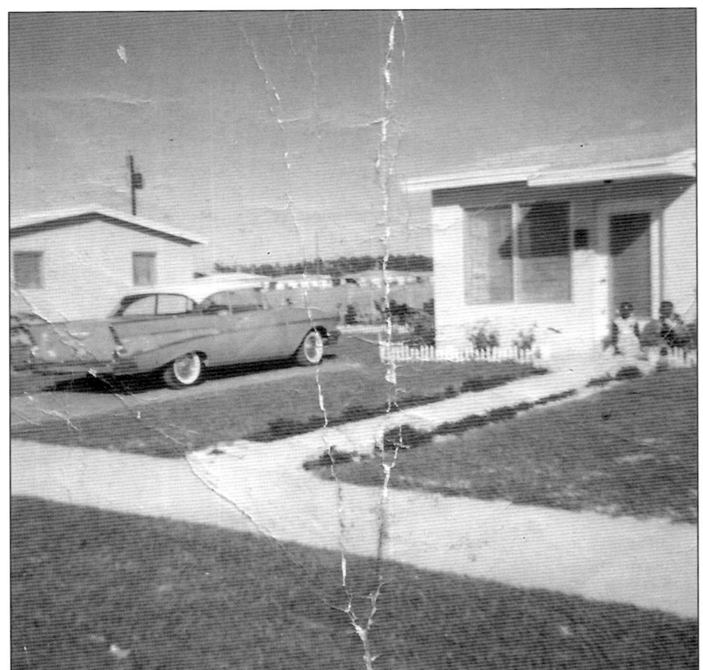

It is a leisurely Sunday afternoon on May 10, 1959. Pictured are the early homes of Richmond Heights along with a Chevrolet Impala. It was not rare to find children enjoying the outdoor air. This is a picture of Twila Hargrove and brother Issac Hargrove sitting on the front porch of their home on Polk Street. (Courtesy of the Jackson family.)

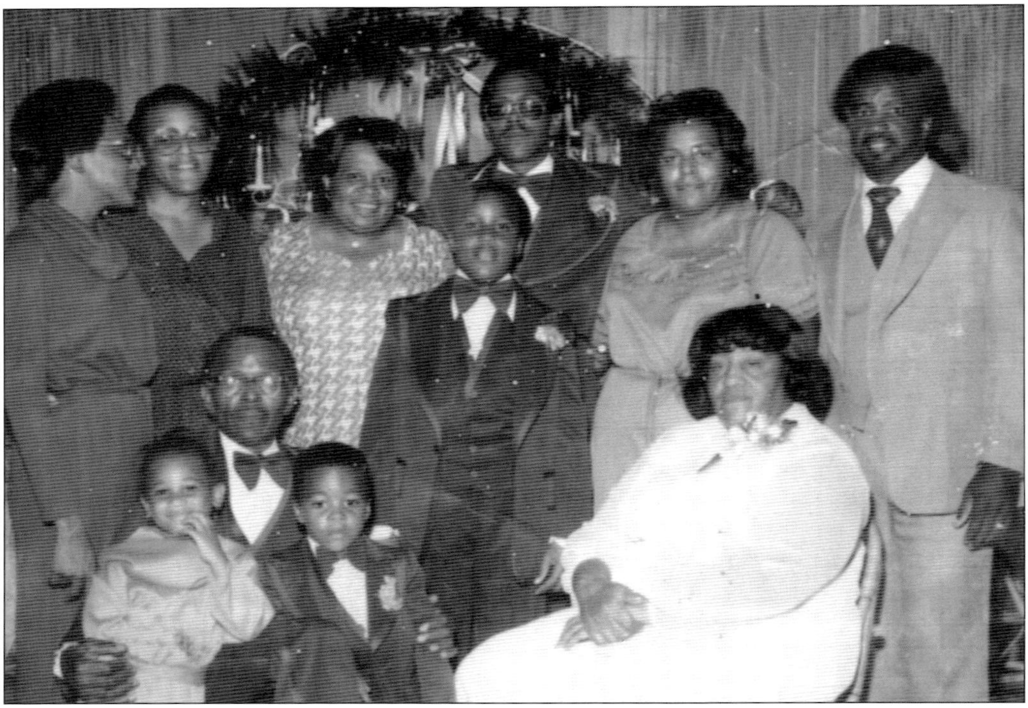

Osa and Ethel Nickerson and their two children moved from Overtown to Richmond Heights in 1950, after Nickerson completed his term in the Navy. Osa Nickerson ran a dry cleaners in Overtown. Ethel Nickerson was a homemaker and also ran a day care. Their children were Barbara, Sandra, Stanley, Vanessa, and Pamala.

This 1980 photograph captures Anita and Charles Gray, who have been so instrumental in the development of Richmond Heights. Charles Gray is a World War II veteran and used his GI Bill to attend Tuskegee Institute. During his studies, he met the love of his life, Anita, and also encountered time with inventor George Washington Carver. They moved to Richmond Heights in 1952. Charles was an assistant principal for administration and retired from Miami-Dade County Public Schools. He is a life member of the NAACP and Omega Psi Phi Fraternity. Anita Gray is the founder of the Richmond Heights Woman's Club. (Courtesy of the Gray family.)

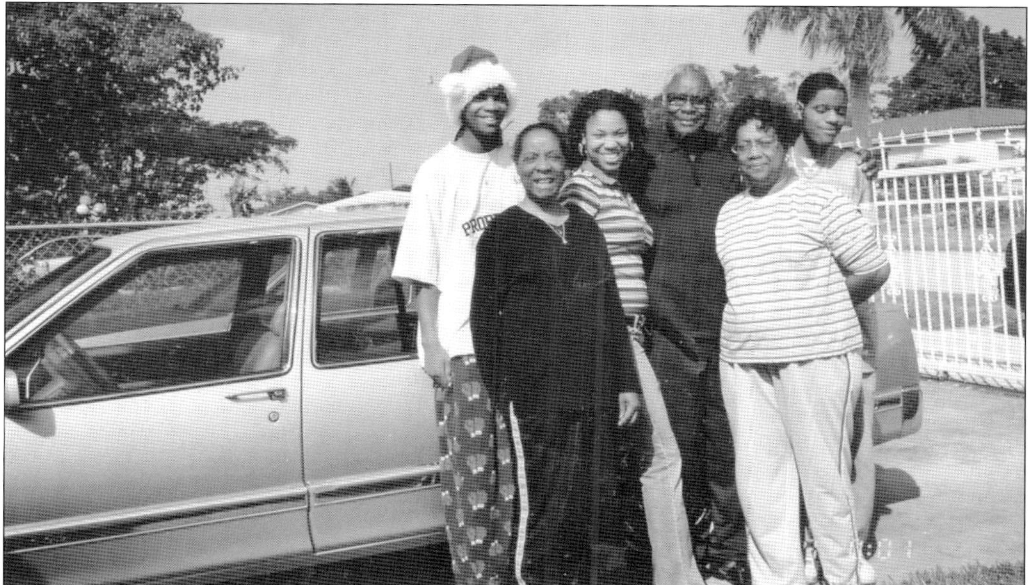

Since May 1950, the Redding family has grown. Pictured are the Redding girls and their families during the Christmas holiday. From left to right are (first row) Sylvia Redding Fosha and Priscilla Redding McKinnon; (second row) Stephen Redding Fosha, , Lenae McKinnon, Leonard McKinnon, and Zachary Redding Fosha. (Courtesy of the Redding family.)

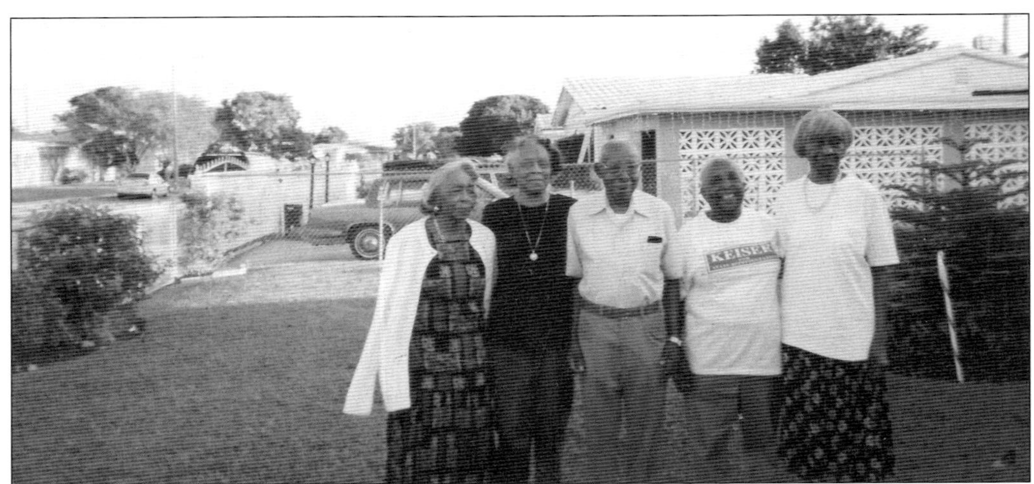

Polk Street is known as the home of the legendary "little mayor of Richmond Heights," Willie Redding. Willie was instrumental in school and park development, community business development, and the community crime watch organization. Pictured are, from left to right, Millie Taylor, Eddie Redding, Willie Redding, Gladys Brown, and a Ms. Whitehead as they talk over plans in front of the Reddings' home. (Courtesy of the Redding family.)

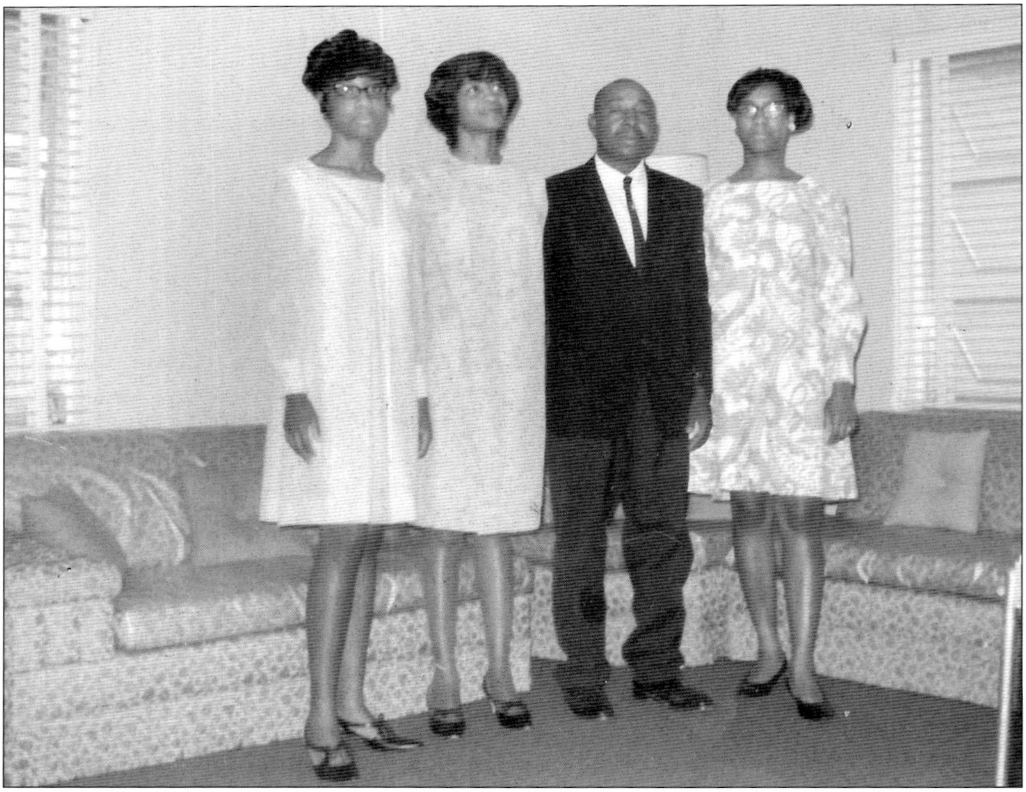

The Redding family is shown dressed for the day. It is April 1967, and pictured are, from left to right, Sylvia, Eddie, Willie, and Priscilla. Willie was featured in a *Jet* magazine article (August 15, 1963) about crime-free Richmond Heights. (Courtesy of the Redding family.)

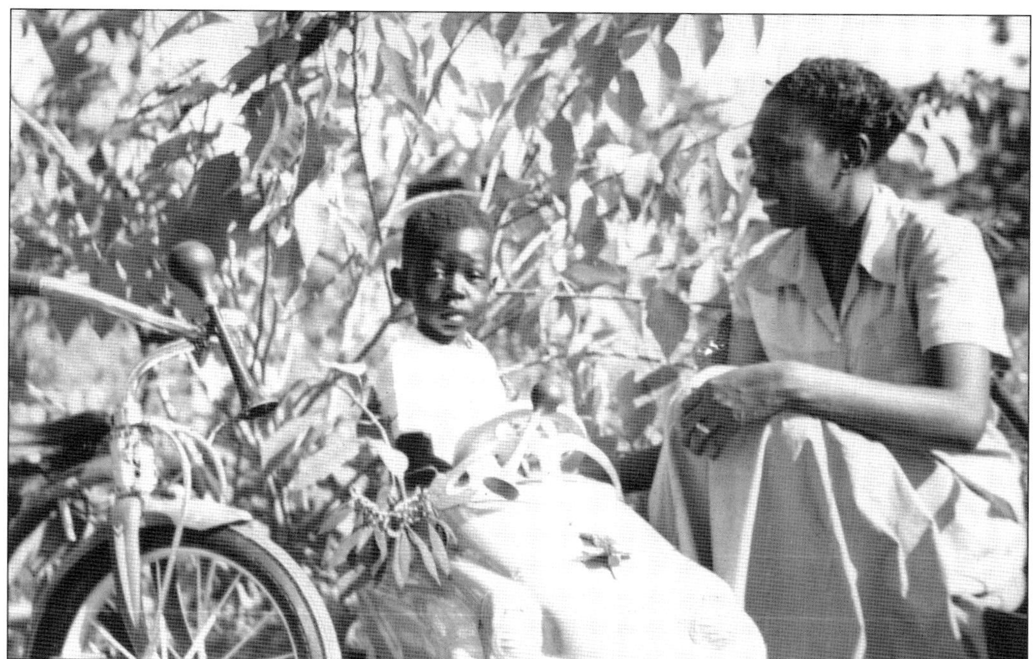

Doran Porter is photographed with his mother, Ruth Porter, who was a nurse, in front of their Fillmore Street home. Doran worked for Miami-Dade County Corrections until April 25, 2003, when he retired. His love for music mimics the record collection of his father, Warren, and the songs DJ Butterball played on WMBM. (Courtesy of the Porter family.)

Bobbie Harper, a graduate of Bethune Cookman College, was an elementary teacher at Frank C. Martin Elementary School. In 1968, integration was implemented in Dade County Public Schools, and as a result, the most influential black instructors were move to white schools. She was moved to Banyan Elementary and, after working 34 years for Dade County Public Schools, retired in 1989.

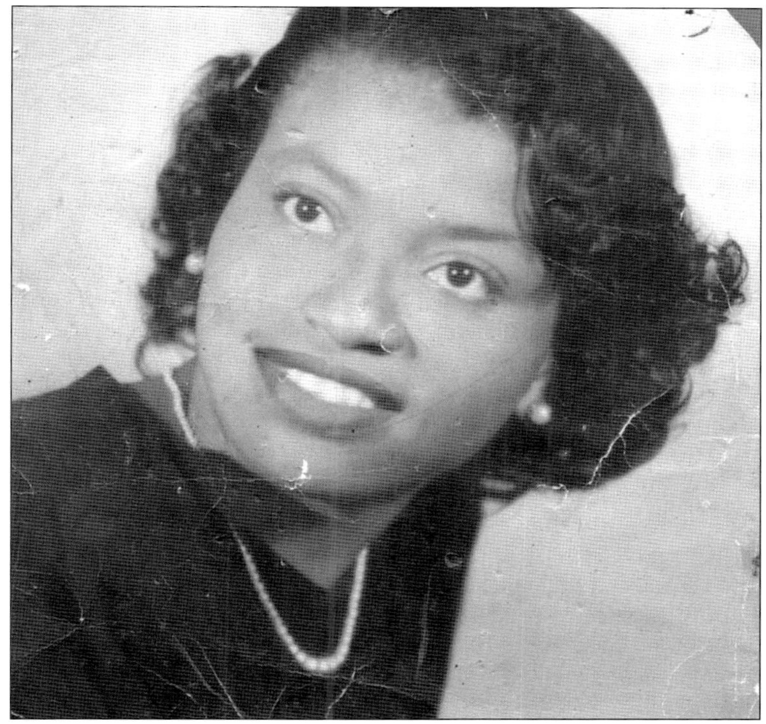

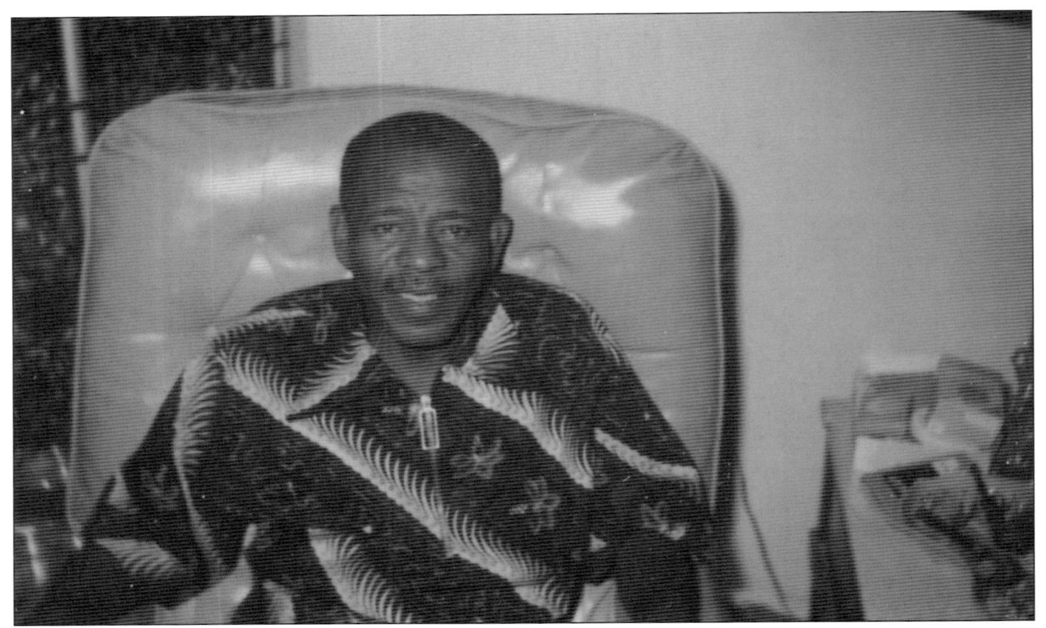

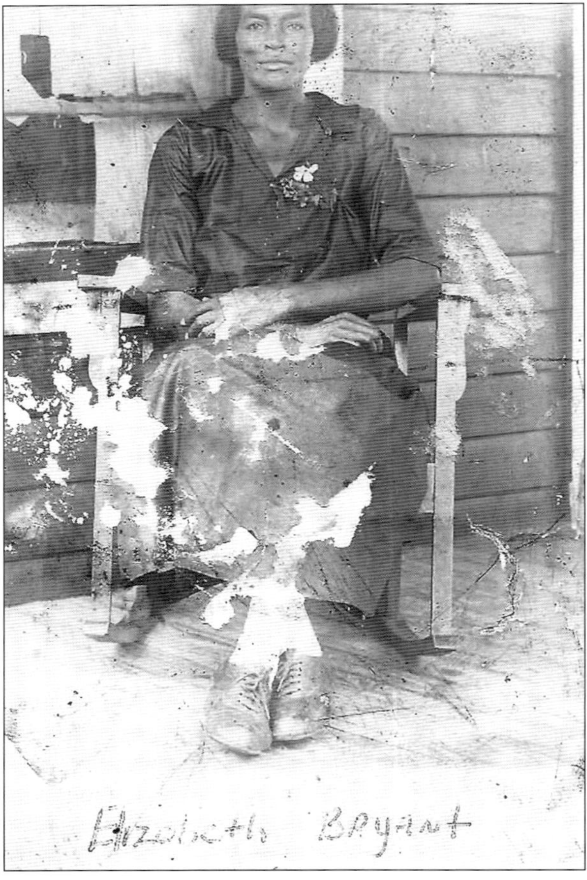

Charlie Harper was born August 17, 1923, in Jacksonville, Florida, to Hattie and Charlie Harper Sr. He was the second of eight children to this union. After he was discharged from serving the US Army, he went on to work for National Airlines. He and wife, Bobbie, enjoyed watching football, baseball, and boxing on television.

Elizabeth Blake was born in Valdosta, Georgia, on December 2, 1875. In her prime, she taught in a one-room schoolhouse, which was also in Valdosta. At the urging of her granddaughter Bobbie Harper, she moved to Richmond Heights in 1956 to live with Bobbie and her husband, Charlie, to help raise their children, Larry and Patricia. She lived a full life and passed at the age of 91 in 1967.

At three years old, Ronald Smith and his family moved from a small area outside of Coconut Grove called Sweetening Town to Richmond Heights. Smith's uncle Hatcher, a veteran, purchased the home for his sister Ruby Smith and his mother, Annie Mae Smith. Pictured are, from left to right, Ronald Smith, Marilyn Smith, and Ruby Smith in 1959. (Courtesy of the Smith family.)

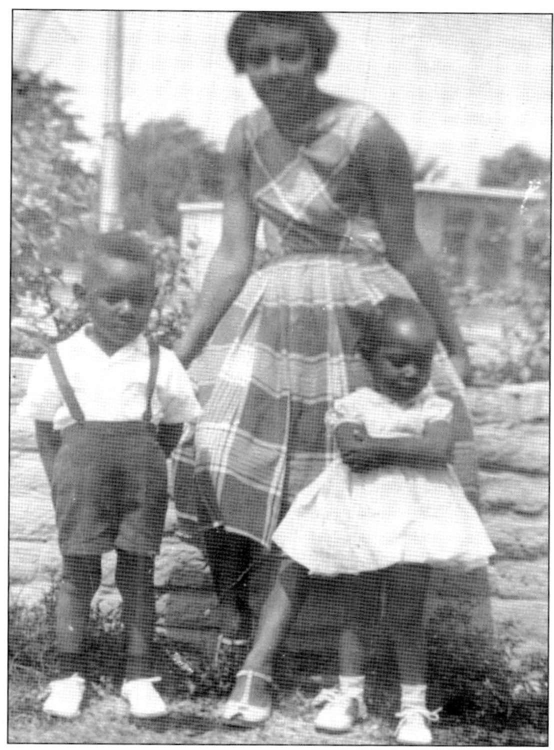

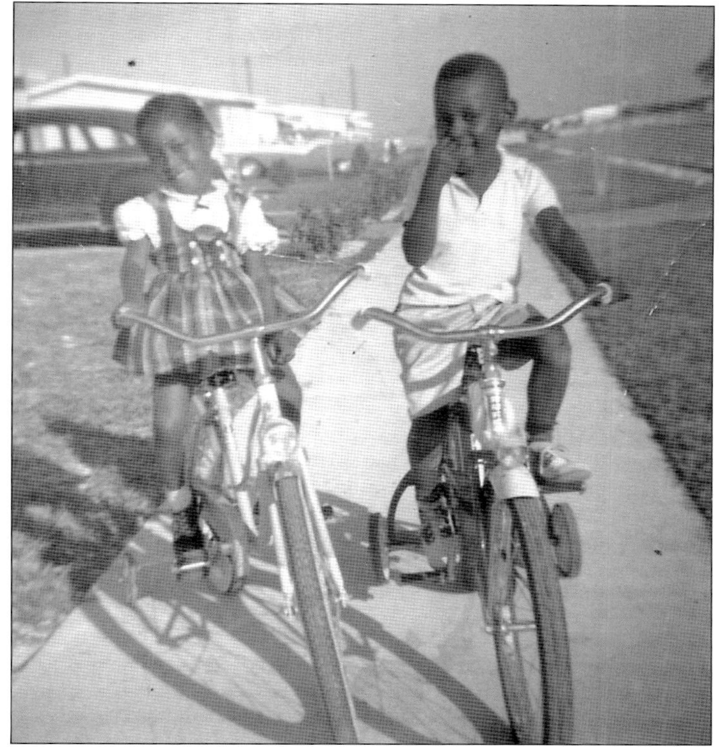

Ronald Smith remembers Richmond Heights as a safe community. He was the first of his siblings, Marilyn Smith and Reginald Williams, to attend school in the community at Frank C. Martin Elementary. In this photograph are Marilyn Smith (left) and Ronald Smith (right). The sister-brother duo are posing in front of their 149th Terrace home. (Courtesy of the Smith family.)

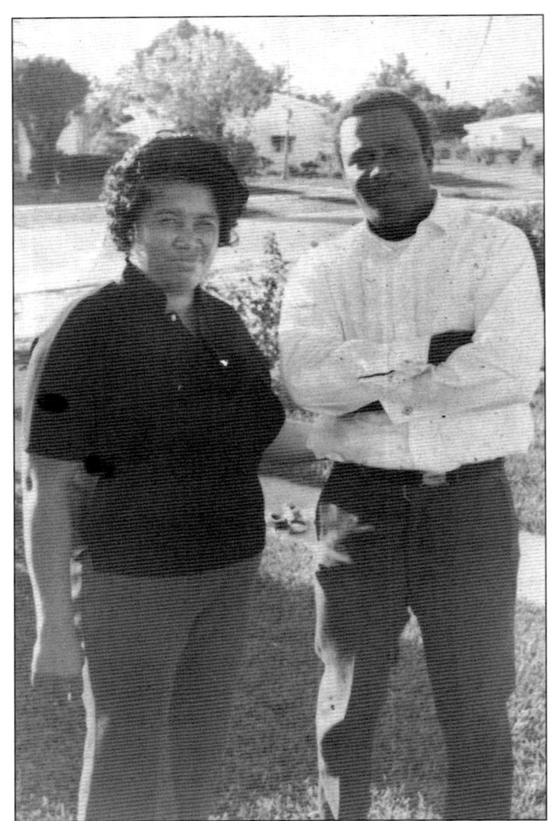

Neather and George Mathis met in Monticello, Florida, and later married in 1951. Five children, Helen, Barbara, Linda, Geraldine, and Gerald, joined this union. After moving in the apartments near Bethel Baptist Church in 1960, the family decided in 1962 to permanently reside at 14841 Polk Street. Helen, Barbara, and Linda had to be bused out of the neighborhood to attend school, but when twins Geraldine and Gerald were able to attend school, they went to Frank C. Martin Elementary and Richmond Junior High School.

Geraldine Mathis enjoyed most of her childhood on Polk Street, playing four-square and dodge ball until the street light came on. That was her cue that play time was over. On Sundays she would walk to Bethel Baptist Church for Sunday school and then walk to Second Baptist Church for worship service. From left to right in this picture are (first row) Geraldine Mathis and Melissa Mathis; (second row) Helen Mathis and Barbara Mathis holding Jessica Garrett.

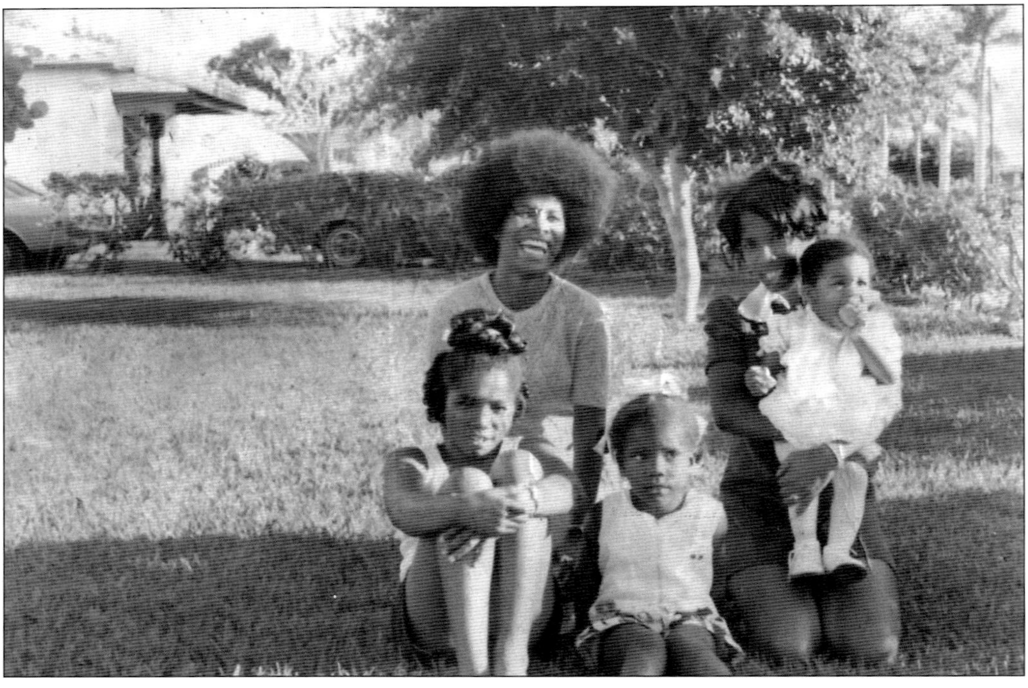

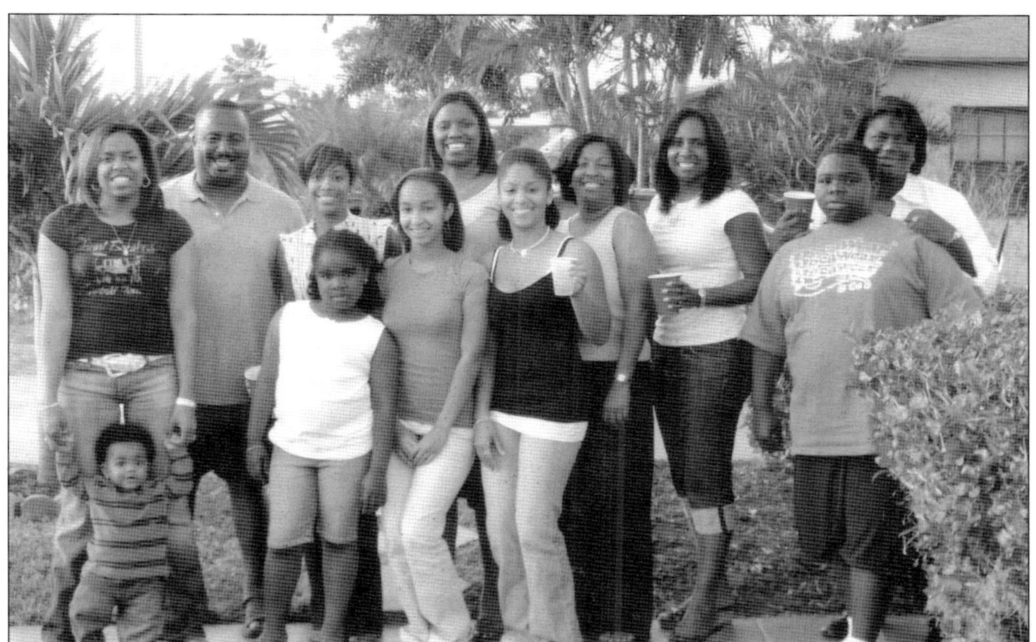

This spring photograph captures family life on Polk Street. The Mathis family and the Garrett family share memories together on this Saturday afternoon. Photographed are, from left to right, (first row) Jaden Gilliam, Tia Belle, LaTrice Stirrup, LaTasha Stirrup, and Terrance Belle; (second row) April Garrett, Gerald Mathis, LaToya Stirrup, Melissa Mathis-Christian, Barbara Stirrup, Ruth Edwards, and Lenora Mathis.

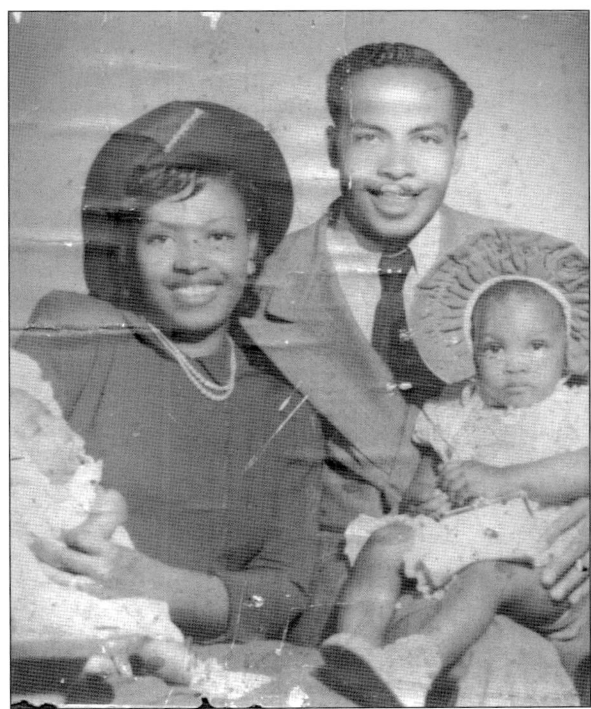

In 1950, the Palmores decided to move from Overtown into their new two-bedroom home on Jackson Street. Anthony Palmore became the first black postmaster for the State of Florida. He and his wife, Laura Ann, ran the first post office in Richmond Heights, located at the dead end of Pinkston Drive and Polk Street. This late-1940s photograph is of the couple and their first two children.

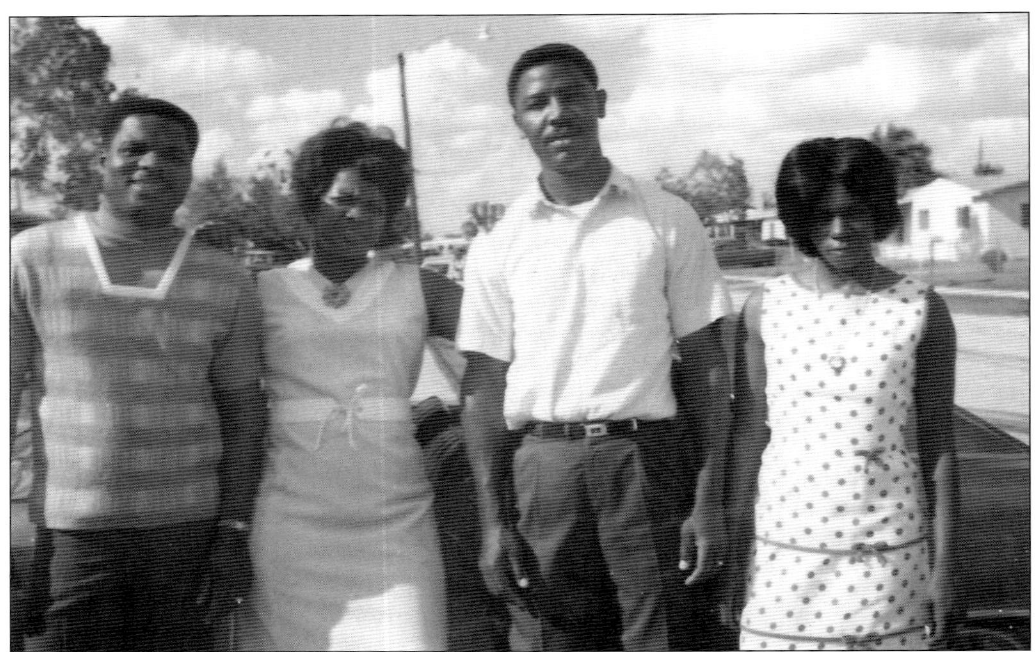

The Andrews moved to Monroe Street in 1959 to lot 24, block 24. Haman met his wife, Jessie, in Perrine. Haman is a contractor, and Jessie worked as a cook for various Catholic schools. Leroy Lightbourne and his wife, Geraldine, lived on Jackson Street, and both worked for the Catholic schools as well. This 1960s photograph shows, from left to right, Haman R. Andrews Sr., Jessie Andrews, Leroy Lightbourne, and Geraldine Lightbourne standing on Monroe Street.

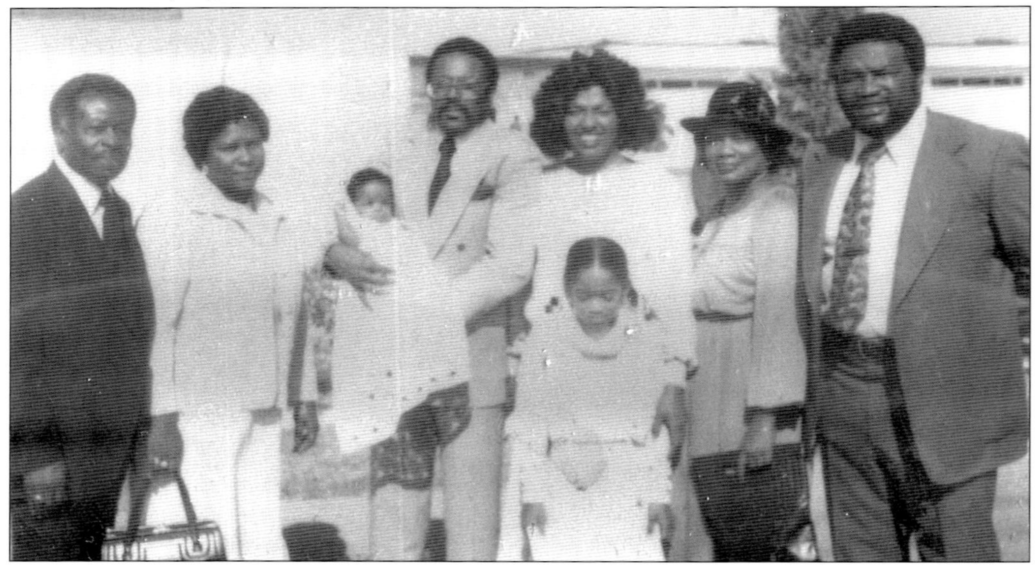

A great deal of socializing went on at church. It was a time for neighbors and friends to catch up about their week. Here is a 1978 picture of the Garrett family at Second Baptist Church joined by friends to celebrate the christening of their daughter April Garrett. Pictured are, from left to right, Burk Jones, Josie Jones, April Garrett, Willie Garrett, Patricia Garrett, Lessie Canada, Otis Collier, and Jessica Garrett (in front).

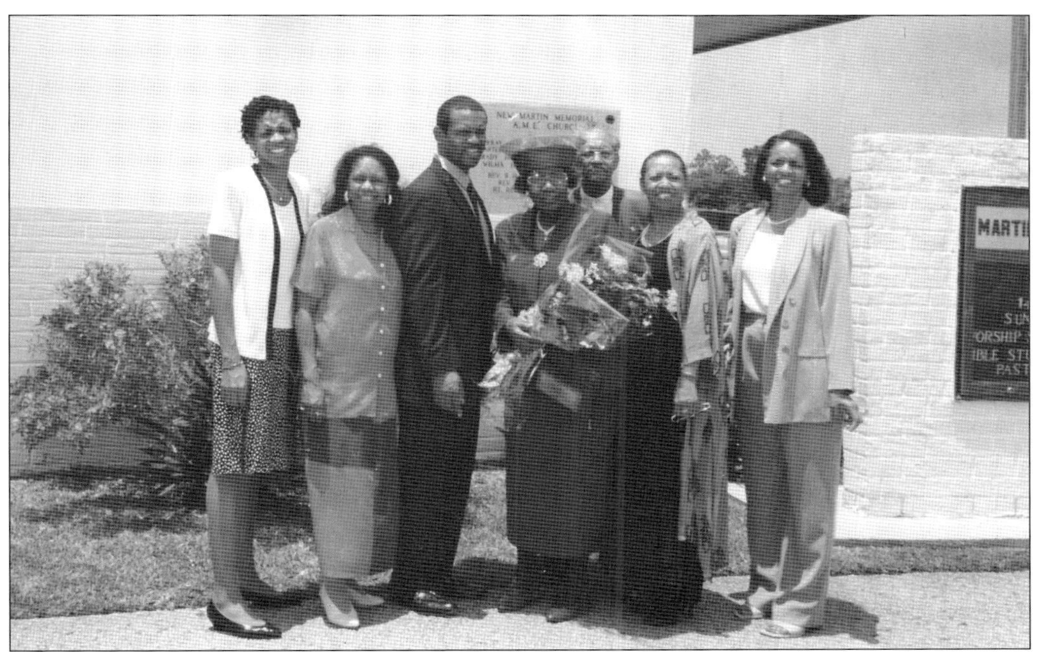

The Armstrong family came home for Queen Armstrong's 80th birthday and attended church together at Martin Memorial AME Church, one of the first churches in Richmond Heights. Pictured from left to right are Apryl Armstrong, Jewel Player, Samuel Armstrong Jr., Queen Armstrong, Samuel Armstrong, Arlie Holiday, and Gwen Johnson

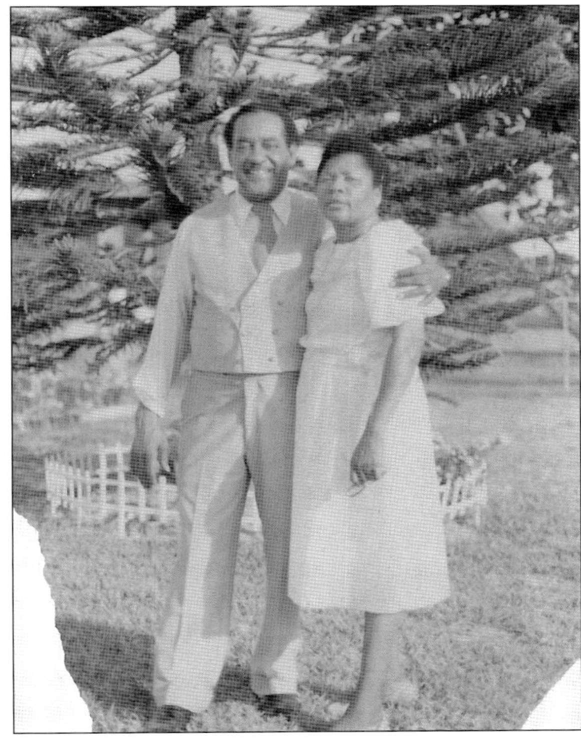

The Andersons moved to Richmond Heights in 1952. They decided the better housing community was the perfect alternative to their home in Liberty City. Charlie and Gloria Anderson had five children, Charles, Dora, Herbert, Verbert, and Starr Anderson. (Courtesy of the Anderson family.)

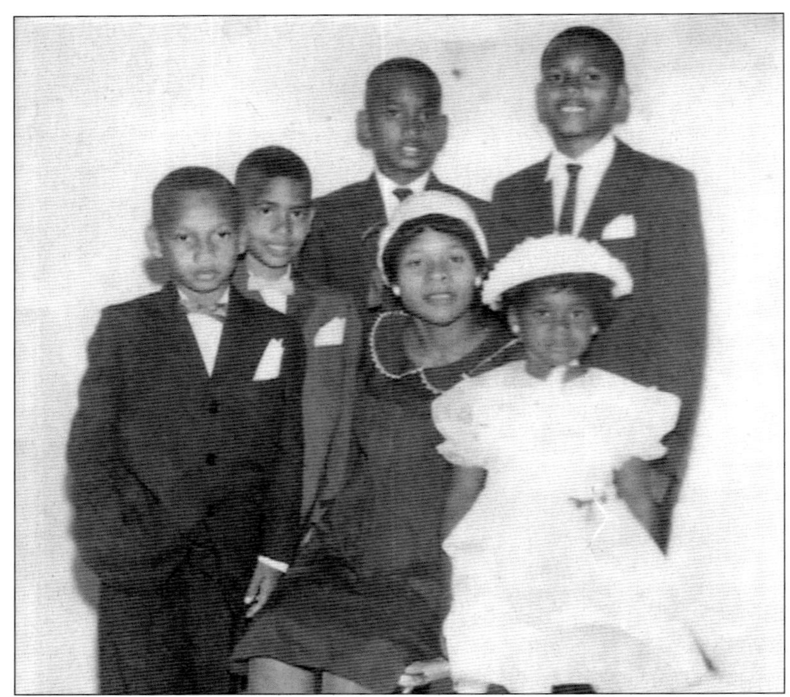

The Anderson family is dressed in their Easter clothes and is set for a day of worship at Martin Memorial AME Church in 1962. They are the descendants of the Richmond Heights' Anderson Fairdeal Grocery store owner, Charles Anderson. Pictured are, from left to right, (first row) Clifton, mother Dora, and Dora; (second row) Herbert, Verbert, and Charles. (Courtesy of the Anderson family.)

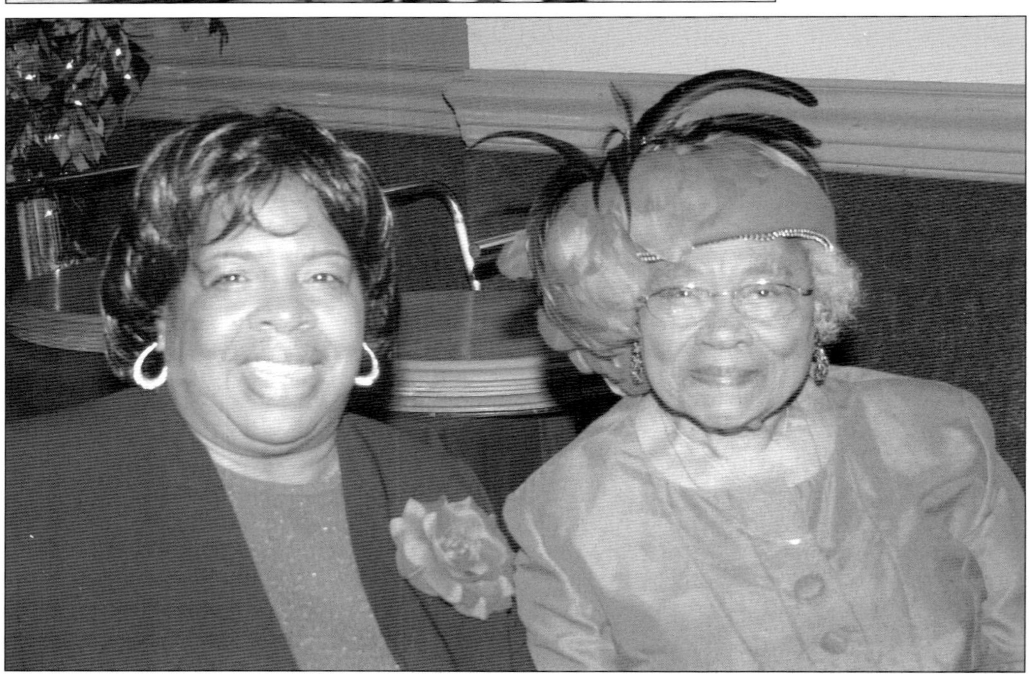

Pictured are, from left to right, Sylvia Stevens and Ella Thompson at the Richmond Heights 60th anniversary gala at Signature Gardens. Robert and Ella Thompson moved to Richmond Heights by way of Camden County, Georgia. They had four children, Shirley, Robert, Kenneth, and Gail. Ella has been a faithful member of Martin Memorial AME Church since 1953 and the Richmond Heights Woman's Club.

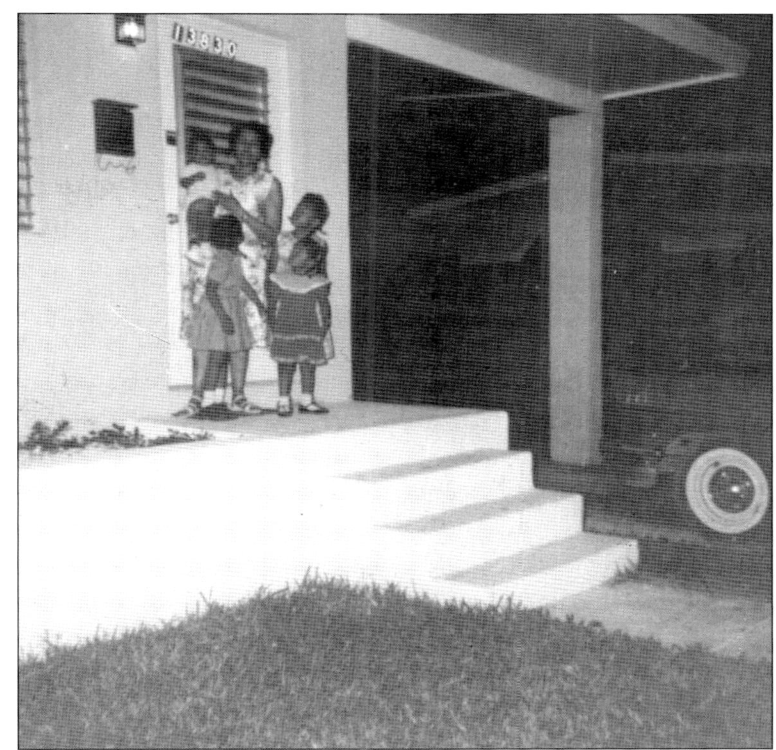

The Gaines family is enjoying time together on the porch of their home. The picture was taken in the late 1950s on Van Buren Street. Pictured are, from left to right, (first row) Veronica and Alicia; (second row) aunt Rosa Lee Taylor holding toddler Rose and Jacqueline. (Courtesy of the Gaines family.)

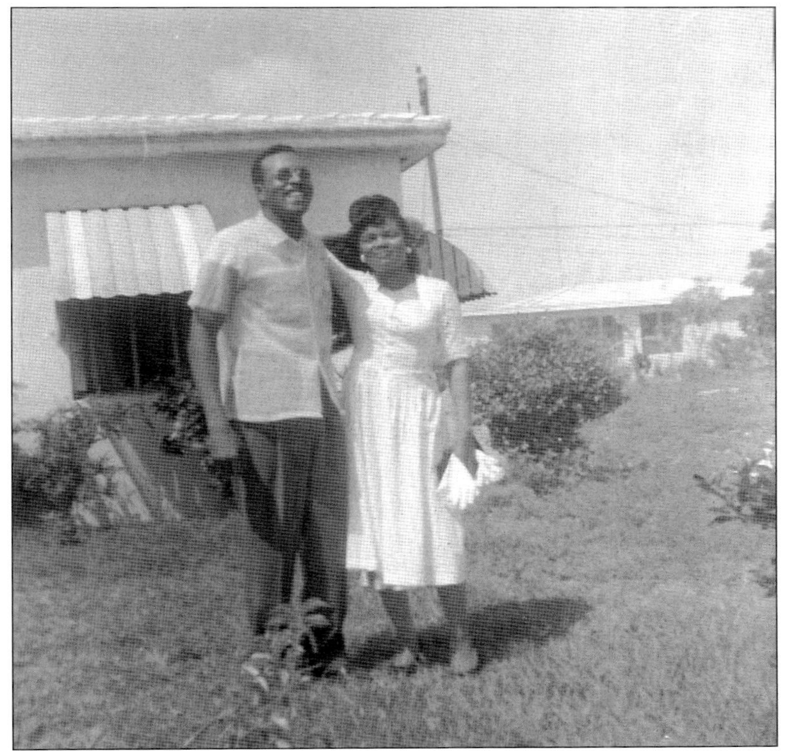

George and Alice Gaines are pictured in front of their Jackson Street home in the 1960s. George served the United States in the Army during World War II as a sergeant stationed in Japan. The couple had seven children, Charles Green, Darryl, Jacqueline, Veronica, Alicia, Rosa, and Cecilia. (Courtesy of the Gaines family.)

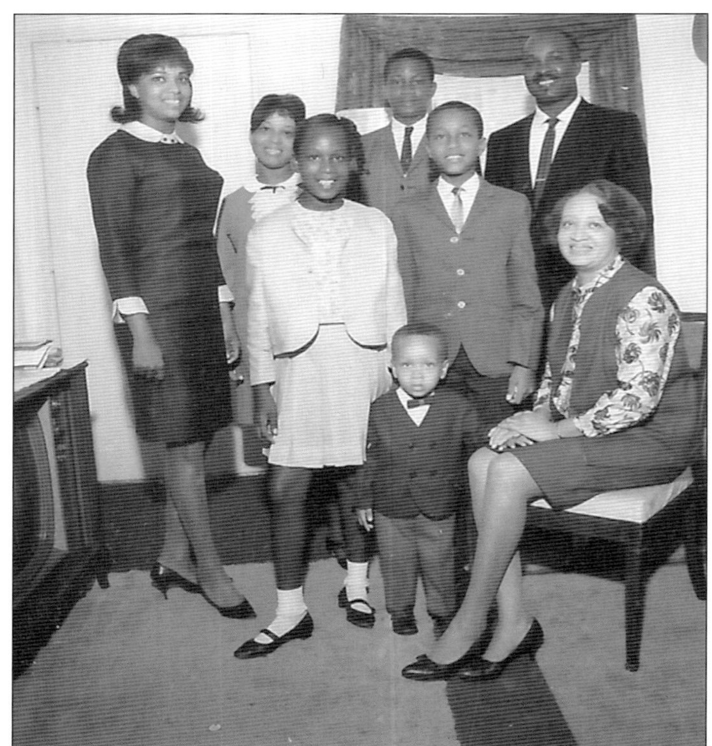

Taken in a living room portrait studio on Tyler Street, this photograph is of the Stringer family in 1968. Pictured are, from left to right, (first row) 2-year-old Leroy and mother Rosemary; (second row) 10-year-old Valorie and 12-year-old Ronald; (third row) 18-year-old Sandra, 17-year-old Shelia, 15-year-old Leronardo, and father Leroy Stringer Sr. (Courtesy of the Stringer family.)

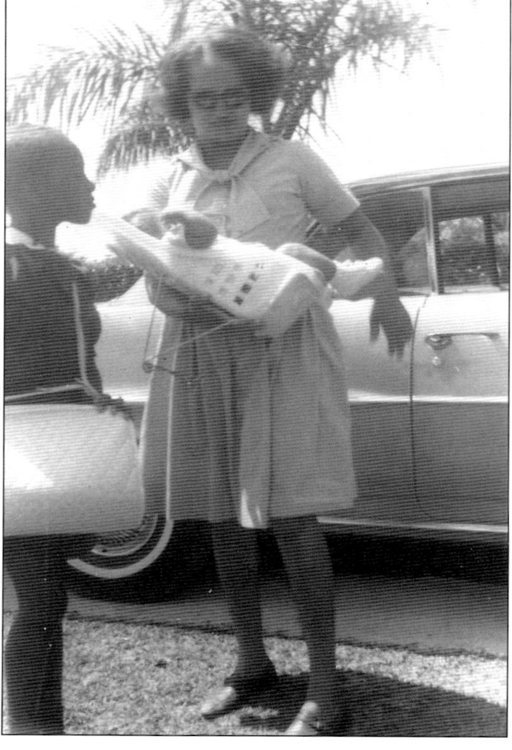

The Stringer family is seen returning to their 14681 Jackson Street home from an outing in October 1958. Pictured are, from left to right, Sandra Stringer, Valorie Stringer (in infant car seat), and Rosemary Stringer. Sandra is helping her mother by holding her handbag. (Courtesy of the Stringer family.)

Bibliography

Bethel, Alison, Sandra Dibble, Larry Josephs, and Deb Kollars. "In Their Own Words." *Miami Herald*. February 19, 1984.

Campbell, Geneva, Vernetta Erwin, Kennedy Mumford, Eddie Redding, and Jessie Tribble, *Dedicatory Program Frank C. Martin Elementary School*. Miami, FL: Frank C. Martin Elementary School, Board of Instruction of Dade County, 1957.

Forbes, Charles. "Richmond Heights Challenge to Negro Community Builders." *Miami Daily News*. May 20, 1951.

Messner, Marcus. "Richmond Heights Strives to Regain Glory Days." *Miami Herald*. September 23, 1999.

Miami-Dade County Department of Planning and Zoning. "Community Planning Section." *Richmond Heights Charrette Area Plan Report*. 2010.

Narine, Dalton. "Barber of the Ville." *Miami Herald*. July 7, 2000.

The Story of Richmond Heights, Miami, FL: Richmond Middle School, Dade County Public Schools, 1996.

Consistent with our mission to preserve history on a local level, this book was printed in South Carolina on American-made paper and manufactured entirely in the United States. Products carrying the accredited Forest Stewardship Council (FSC) label are printed on 100 percent FSC-certified paper.

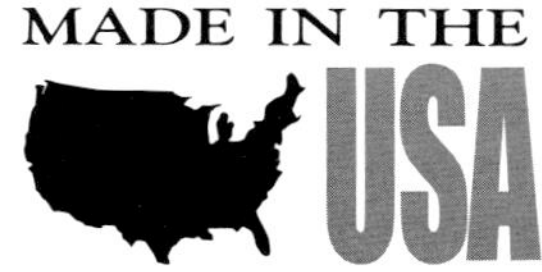